IMAGES OF BLACK MODERNISM

IMAGES OF BLACK MODERNISM

Verbal and Visual Strategies of the Harlem Renaissance

Miriam Thaggert

University of Massachusetts Press ■ Amherst and Boston

LC 2010018923
ISBN 978-1-55849-831-0 (paper); 830-3 (library cloth)

Designed by Dennis Anderson
Set in Garamond Premier Pro by Westchester Book
Printed and bound by Thomson-Shore, Inc.

Library of Congress Cataloging-in-Publication Data

Thaggert, Miriam.
Images of Black modernism : verbal and visual strategies of the Harlem Renaissance /
Miriam Thaggert.
    p. cm.
Includes bibliographical references and index.
ISBN 978-1-55849-830-3 (library cloth : alk. paper) —
ISBN 978-1-55849-831-0 (pbk. : alk. paper)
1. American literature—African American authors—History and criticism.
2. African Americans in literature.   3. African Americans in art.
4. Visual perception in literature.   5. Art in literature.   6. African American art—20th
century.   7. Harlem Renaissance.   8. African Americans—Intellectual life—20th century.
9. Modernism (Literature)—United States.   I. Title.
PS153.N5T455   2010
810.9'896073—dc22
                        2010018923

British Library Cataloguing in Publication data are available.

for Mom

Contents

Illustrations

Acknowledgments

THERE ARE a number of people who helped me bring this book to fruition. First, I thank Elizabeth Abel for being such a gracious and generous adviser. She has provided a model of mentorship and scholarship which I was very privileged to observe and learn from. I also received support and guidance from Maryemma Graham, Stephen Best, Valerie Smith, Abdul JanMohamed, Waldo Martin, Tyler Stovall, Saidiya Hartman, Ula Taylor, and Richard Hutson.

Several of my former colleagues at the University of Tennessee, Knoxville, read drafts of the manuscript. In particular, I thank Matthew Abraham, Olaf Berwald, Alexis Boylan, Allen Carroll, Allen Dunn, Amy Elias, Stan Garner, Tom Haddox, Heather Hirschfeld, Chuck Maland, and Alan Rutenberg. A very special thanks goes to Mary E. Papke for reading the full manuscript and providing engaging, constructive criticism and collegial support. While at the University of Tennessee I received grants and support from the John C. Hodges Fund and the university's Humanities Initiative. I am also grateful to my colleagues at the University of Iowa who read this book in manuscript and offered other forms of support. In addition to my colleagues in African American Studies, these include Bluford Adams, Linda Bolton, Florence Boos,

Aimee Carlos-Rowe, Mike Chesar, Corey Creekmur, Mary Lou Emery, Ed Folsom, Claire Fox, Miriam Gilbert, Loren Glass, Kevin Koppleson, Ruedi Kuenzli, Priya Kumar, Teresa Magnum, Dee Morris, Kevin Mumford, Lauren Rabinovitz, John Raeburn, Harry Stecopoulos, Richard Turner, Deborah Whaley, and Doris Witt. I reserve very special thanks for my colleagues Horace Porter and Fred Woodard, who read the complete manuscript and shared their insights on African American literature. Thanks also to Hsuan Hsu for reading and commenting on several chapters, even while he was teaching and writing his own work; Carter Mathes for sharing his insights on black sound and music; and Jackie Fulmer. Sara Blair provided valuable knowledge about various photographic repositories and artists' representatives.

The staff at the Beinecke Rare Book and Manuscript Library at Yale University was extremely helpful and tremendously patient in explaining the intricacies of the James Weldon Johnson Collection. In particular I thank Alice Prochaska, University Librarian, and Patricia Willis, Curator of the American Division, and the staff librarians, especially Susan Klein and Leigh Golden. Thanks as well to Laura Wexler for letting me attend the Photography and Memory Group while at Yale.

I am grateful to my editor at the University of Massachusetts Press, Bruce Wilcox, and to Myriam Chancy of *Meridians*. Allon Schoener graciously provided me with an image from the "Harlem on My Mind" exhibition. Bruce Kellner offered information about Carl Van Vechten and his relationship with the *Crisis* symposium, as well as some of Van Vechten's photographic props.

I completed this book while on a Ford Foundation Postdoctoral Fellowship, and I also received support from the University of Iowa's Obermann Center for Advanced Studies. Sections of the book were discussed in workshops sponsored by the University of Iowa's Center for Ethnic Studies and the Arts. I would also like to thank the University of Iowa Office of the Vice President for Research for its assistance with the cost of the illustrations.

I thank my friends Shaden Tageldin and Jeff Walshire for providing perspective while I was writing the book.

Finally, and most important, I thank my wonderful family for their sacrifices, for their plan As and Bs, and for making the year-long Ford postdoctoral experience possible for me. This book is especially dedicated to my first teacher, also known as Mom.

* * *

MATERIALS BY James Weldon Johnson, including lines from "The Creation," "The Reverend Jasper Jones," "Let My People Go," and the "working titles" for *God's Trombones*, are reprinted here by permission of Sondra Kathryn Wilson, Executor for the Estate of Grace and James Weldon Johnson.

Photographs by Carl Van Vechten are reproduced by permission of the Carl Van Vechten Trust. Yale Collection of American Literature, Beinecke Rare Book and Manuscript Library, Yale University.

The caricature by Miguel Covarrubias is copyrighted by Maria Elena Rico Covarrubias and is reproduced with permission of the National Portrait Gallery, Smithsonian Institution/Art Resource, NY.

Photographs by Man Ray are copyrighted by the Man Ray Trust/Artist Rights Society (ARS), NY/ADAGP, Paris; copyrighted by The Museum of Modern Art/Licensed by SCALA/Art Resource, NY; CNAC/MNAN/Dist. Réunion des Musées Nationaux/Art Resource, NY.

Photographs from the Aaron Siskind Collection of Photography are reproduced courtesy of the George Eastman House, International Museum of Photography and Film and The Aaron Siskind Foundation.

Photographs by James Van Der Zee are reproduced by permission of Donna Mussenden Van Der Zee. The installation photograph of "Harlem on My Mind" is courtesy of Allon Schoener and reproduced by permission of Donna Mussenden Van Der Zee and the Metropolitan Museum of Art. Image © The Metropolitan Museum of Art.

Thanks also to the Beinecke Rare Book and Manuscript Library, which holds the letter from Jessie Fauset to Langston Hughes.

An earlier version of chapter 2 appeared in *Meridians*, published by Indiana University Press, and I thank the press for republication here. Billie Holiday™ is a trademark of the Estate of Louis McKay, licensed by CMG Worldwide.

IMAGES OF BLACK MODERNISM

There has long been controversy within and without the Negro race as to just how the Negro should be treated in art—how he should be pictured by writers and portrayed by artists. Most writers have said naturally that any portrayal of any kind of Negro was permissible so long as the work was pleasing and the artists sincere. But the Negro has objected vehemently . . . that while the individual portrait may be true and artistic, the net result to American literature to date is to picture twelve million Americans as prostitutes, thieves and fools and that such "freedom" in art is miserably unfair.

Crisis, February 1926

The kind of work I have always wanted to do requires me to learn how to maneuver ways to free up language from its sometimes sinister, frequently lazy, almost always predictable employment of racially informed and determined chains.

Toni Morrison, *Playing in the Dark*

Introduction

A *Crisis* in Black Art and Literature

THE YEAR 1926 was a challenging one for the magazine *Crisis: A Record of the Darker Races.* The official publication of the NAACP, it competed that year with another African American magazine, *Opportunity,* for literary pre-eminence; and the editor of *Crisis,* W. E. B. Du Bois, sought to counteract the magazine's declining influence on the participants of the Harlem Renaissance.[1] Despite these challenges, the *Crisis* continued to argue for the civil rights of African Americans and attempted to shape Americans' perception of blackness by focusing on the written word, art, and other forms of cultural expression during a remarkably productive moment for African America. The literary reviews that appeared in the first and last issues of 1926 reflect the range of books published by or about African Americans that year. In the January number there was a review of *The New Negro,* the optimistic collection that would help shape African American writing and artistic production over the next few years, and the December issue included a review of *Nigger Heaven,* a book that would have an impact on the movement as well, but for entirely different, less optimistic reasons. This was also the year in which the *Crisis* sponsored a symposium, a series of discussions of seven questions regarding the representation of African Americans in literature and art and the evaluation of aesthetic quality as African Americans achieved racial uplift. In the February issue the magazine posed the question "The Negro in Art: How Shall He Be Portrayed?" Specifically the editors asked their readers and several well-known authors, poets, and publishers, both African American and white:

1. When the artist, black or white, portrays Negro characters is he under any obligation or limitations as to the sort of character he will portray?
2. Can any author be criticized for painting the worst or the best characters of a group?
3. Can publishers be criticized for refusing to handle novels that portray Negroes of education and accomplishment, on the ground that these characters are no different from white folk and therefore not interesting?
4. What are Negroes to do when they are continually painted at their worst and judged by the public as they are painted?
5. Does the situation of the educated Negro in America with its pathos, humiliation and tragedy call for artistic treatment at least as sincere and sympathetic as "Porgy" received?
6. Is not the continual portrayal of the sordid, foolish and criminal among Negroes convincing the world that this and this alone is really and essentially Negroid, and preventing white artists from knowing any other types and preventing black artists from daring to paint them?
7. Is there not a real danger that young colored writers will be tempted to follow the popular trend in portraying Negro characters in the underworld rather than seeking to paint the truth about themselves and their own social class?[2]

These questions and others like them which were asked throughout the course of the New Negro Movement and beyond were meant to promote idealized, aspirational depictions of African Americans. They presented, in concise form, the concerns about representation that African American writers faced then and have faced for decades: the role of loyalty and obligation to "the race" versus the author's duty to aesthetics or beauty. Though focused on literature, the queries exposed the presence of the visual embedded in the literary, with their frequent ekphrastic allusion to "painting" to suggest, figuratively, the literary imaging of blackness.

Despite the familiarity of the questions, there is something limiting and unsatisfying about them. The symposium assumed a racial particularity; that is, the "right" answers appear to be already formulated and embedded in the queries. The questions were not just rhetorical but confirmatory. For Du Bois the danger of "the continual portrayal of the sordid, foolish and criminal" was precisely that it would "convince[e] the world that this [characterization] and this alone is really and essentially Negroid." The inquiries revealed Du Bois's preference for what Madhu Dubey appropriately calls "a crisis-free literary representation," an uncomplicated equivalence between language and referent in which "positive images" confirm for an American public "positive African Americans," in other words, the assumption that language reflects a literal reality.[3] But there were several writers, intellectuals, and artists during the Harlem Renaissance, or the New Negro Movement, who recognized much more experimental and productive possibilities in the interaction between language and referent, language and image.[4] The way in which these figures experimented with the visual resonances in language, and the resulting images of blackness they created, is the story I seek to tell. By studying how the visual imbricates with language, we find that a complex narrative emerges about the images of blackness prevalent in the 1920s and 1930s, revealing a black modernism that is both experimental and progressive.

This book examines questions such as those asked by the *Crisis* and the literary and visual responses to them. I examine how multiple forms of the image (visual, verbal, mental) organize and structure the valuations of race and how the visual constructions of blackness are articulated, reproduced, and guaranteed through the written word. Because of the era's conscious and contentious reconstruction of black representations, the Harlem Renaissance is an ideal period in which to explore the link between word and image, as well as the influence of this dynamic within black literary and visual culture. The book examines literary and visual attempts to rupture, rethink, and realign the entanglement of word and image. It revisits a well-examined moment in black cultural history by focusing on the visual in black culture and analyzing how the visual is represented narratively in poems, novels, and photography.

I argue that there is a dynamic present within early black American modernism that is characterized by a heightened attention to and experimentation with visual and verbal techniques for narrating and representing blackness. This form of the black modern emerges from the contradictions between the material and the evanescent—between the materiality of the body evoked by stereotypical representations of blackness, such as "Negro" dialect, and the intangibility of other forms of black expression, such as the spirituals. The creative tension that results from such materiality and elusiveness, embodiment and abstraction, marks some of the most experimental writings and images associated specifically with the Harlem Renaissance and, more expansively, with African American modernism. Throughout this book I explore the distinctions and similarities between language and the image, particularly in the way literary and photographic artists of the 1920s and 1930s used both the verbal and the visual to undermine the assumptions and stereotypes of coherent racial and sexual identities.

I concentrate on a specific timeframe, from 1922 to 1938, with a particular focus on the years 1926 to 1932. This temporal focus was determined not so much by the publication dates of the books I discuss as by the debates and deliberations that were then taking place concerning black representation in literature and other forms of art. By the end of the 1920s a critical tone had entered into discussions about the art and aesthetics of the Renaissance; and essays and book reviews by and the personal correspondence among major figures of the movement reflect these critical perspectives. The writings and photography of James Weldon Johnson, Nella Larsen, George Schuyler, Carl Van Vechten, Wallace Thurman, James Van Der Zee, and Aaron Siskind provide an engagement with narrative and black images, a dynamic that contributes to a particular aesthetic of the black modern; through this constellation of sources I investigate how images and language work together to shape the production of racial knowledge. What fascinates me about the writings and images created by these figures is the different ways in which the artists' portrayals of the body clarify elusive and unacknowledged connections between the verbal and the visual and their relevance to black representation, and, further, how concerns about language and representation complicate the period's assumptions about an embodied, visually apprehended blackness.

PERHAPS ALL writers are concerned with how language "courts" certain images and enables and shapes visualization. I would argue, however, that African American writers of the 1920s were explicitly engaged with the process of transforming language into images and were deeply invested in altering the way certain words conjured particular black images. Indeed this literary and visual investment is one of the reasons why the Harlem Renaissance has been judged a "failure." In the two classic analyses of the period, Nathan Huggins's 1971 *Harlem Renaissance* and David Levering Lewis's 1981 *When Harlem Was in Vogue*, the movement is cast as a failed quest to achieve an authentic and more "positive" literary or artistic representation of black Americans. According to Huggins, writers' "naïve assumptions about the centrality of culture" led to a dependence on art to challenge American racism.[5] More recent evaluations of the period have interrogated this declaration of failure. Houston A. Baker Jr. develops a theory of black vernacular performance in order to argue that European "high" modernism was aesthetically and motivationally distinct ("optically white") from the modernism of the Harlem Renaissance.[6] In contrast to Baker, other scholars have detailed the collaboration between writers and artists across the racial and geographical spectrum in order to elucidate the remarkable convergence of racial, political, and aesthetic interests during the 1910s and 1920s. Works in this vein, such as those authored by George Hutchinson, Michael North, and Brent Hayes Edwards, examine the interconnections between white and black modernism.[7] This book recognizes that even the most oral elements of African American culture are infused with a visual dynamic, and black modernism takes such abstract elements and shapes them into concrete textual forms. A reading of this period attuned to the visual would address not only the dichotomy between text and image but also the narrative portrayal of the visual construction of "race" and the form or function of the verbal in shaping the images of blackness.[8]

How, during a moment of increasingly sophisticated awareness and use of the visual, were new possibilities for African American representation expressed in the literary and visual arts? How in the depiction of a New Negro was the "old Negro" visually and narratively left behind? And what relation do these conceptions authored during the New Negro Movement bear to the period of aesthetic risk-taking which occurred contemporaneously and throughout the twentieth century? These questions expand the discourse about racial representations beyond the usual terms in which the Harlem Renaissance has been cast and fracture the familiar binaries that have traditionally structured discussions of the period, such as folk versus urban, lower class versus middle class, or North versus South.[9] The period known as the Harlem Renaissance was not only a moment characterized by a call for more virtuous black images and more depictions of the middle- and upper-class black elite. It was also a period when black writers and artists experimented and took narrative risks in the representations of African Americans. Focusing on these narrative and visual strategies sheds new light on a much-discussed era, provides information about artists of the period who have been overlooked in more conventional analyses of the New Negro Movement, and clarifies the attributes of black writing that would follow later in the twentieth century. While the dominant concern with fashioning positive images raised by writers such as W. E. B. Du Bois and Alain Locke no doubt contributed to the judgment of "failure" by historians of the Harlem Renaissance, there were other artists, both writers and photographers, who created more experimental images. This book examines the work of seven such artists and the contexts in which that work was imagined and inscribed.

Vision and the Body: The Material and The Abstract

If we were to focus only on the cognitive transformation of image into concept, on the methods by which visible blackness is forced into the historically assigned role of the negative and devalued, our objectives and aims would be much easier. There now exists a rich and productive history of optics and sight which addresses how the sense of vision has been either privileged or "denigrated," along with accounts of the scientists and philosophers whose writings contributed to this body of work.[10] I am interested, however, not only in the ways in which the physiological facts of visible difference have been transformed into moral, intellectual, or social hierarchies but also, and for me more significantly, in the impact this transformation has had on our language and the ways we talk about race in the context of American modernism. Although the late nineteenth and early twentieth centuries questioned the epistemological certainty of the gaze and witnessed the development of technologies of the visual, such doubts about the knowledge obtained from sight failed to register in regard to nonwhite subjects. As suggested by Shawn Michelle Smith and Daylanne English, at the same time that scopically derived knowledge encountered these philosophical and technological challenges, intellectuals as diverse as Du Bois and T. S. Eliot relied on visual images or experiences to characterize or depict the African and the African American. As Karen Jacobs reminds us, "the diverse constructions of modernist observers are imbricated in the production of Others."[11]

In *Images of Black Modernism* I analyze the construction of those "Other" observers, specifically the portrayal of their bodies. Because of earlier histories of the visual, we are now more critically attuned to the erroneous belief that the visual sense is divorced from the body, as well as more aware of the institutional and social power of those who claim such a division. Jonathan Crary in *Techniques of the Observer,* for example, studies early optical instruments, such as the camera obscura and the stereoscope, and argues that such devices helped to construct an observer (distinct from a spectator) whose body helped to register both the capabilities and the limitations of the eye. Crary's work charts the awareness of the fallibility of vision and, relatedly, the situatedness of vision in the body. In opposition to the familiar belief in a Cartesian disembodiedness, Crary argues that by the mid-nineteenth century "it rapidly became obvious that efficiency and rationalization in many areas of human activity depended on information about the capacities of the human eye."[12] Crary's formulations, however, do not account for race or for the subject who is racially marked as nonwhite, and this leads one to wonder where, who, and what is the "black" observer?[13] In discussions of blackness, the visual and the body are inevitably intertwined, whether the discussion involves the literal anatomical body or, more metaphorically, the negative assumptions about subjects who are not associated with the qualities of the mind, who are not, that is, figuratively disembodied.

The book engages this polarity—the difference between the tangible and the abstract, between the literal and the figurative conceptions of corporeality, and the ways in which these divisions shape the representation of the black or mixed-race body. In the too familiar mind/body, white/black dichotomies, the implicit assumption of white disembodiedness or abstraction and black hyper-visibility, or a materiality of the body, has had significant implications for language, black representation, and American and African American narrative. Lindon Barrett, for instance, has traced the significance of language and literacy to challenge, if not erase, the concept of embodied, devalued blackness, the belief that the "corporeal particularity" of black skin places the nonwhite body "outside signification." Whereas blackness readily connotes bodiliness, whiteness assumes the values of rationality and intellect, for unlike black bodies, "white bodies never signify foremost their own materiality."[14] Robyn Wiegman and Karen Sánchez-Eppler further reveal that these qualities of bodily abstraction are pivotal not only in terms of evaluating a group's ability to define and describe itself but also in the ability to receive and exercise the rights granted to individuals in a representative democracy.[15] A subtle notion of bodily abstraction permeates the work of all three scholars as they discuss how blackness and language, blackness and text, and blackness and American political representation have often been perceived as oppositional.

More immediately relevant for this study is how these various binaries calcified in the period known as "modern." The conventional valuations of Anglo-American modernism and black modernism are revealed in the designations of "high" and "low," with high modernism's reverential embrace of obscurity contrasted to the primitivity associated with black modernism. Despite attempts to explore more fully the complex network of relationships and contributions between white and black American modernism, the divisions in the study of modernism continue along these lines of cultural highs and lows. Because of these enduring oppositions, perhaps one cannot fault too harshly the Harlem Renaissance writers who placed too much faith in the transformative potential of literature, since, as Wiegman notes, "the written ... displaces the text of black inferiority."[16]

Writing and the Body: The Material and the Abstract

And yet, as I hope to make clear throughout this book, writing itself generates the dynamic of abstraction and materiality, the marks or poles by which the image of the body may be perceived. Just as vision divides conceptions about the body into the literal and the figurative, writing may be separated into the material and the abstract, the physical writing on the page and the imagined object signified by that writing.[17] For African American writers in the early twentieth century, the act of writing challenged the assumption that blackness was, literally and figuratively, consigned brutally to type, to stasis, becoming "a signifier that has no movement in the field of signification."[18] In this book I critique the marks of writing, specifically black dialect, as both material and conceptual, the physical writing on the page and the abstract (immaterial) images inferred from the writing. The Harlem Renaissance writers I investigate were aware of the dual qualities of this writing and negotiated with this doubleness in order to break the chain of both stereotypical portrayals and mimetic, transparently "positive" or literal representations. By literal representation I mean to suggest the one-dimensional portrayal of black life so frequently criticized by both Harlem Renaissance participants and later scholars of the period. Nathan Huggins provides apt examples of such writings: novels peopled with characters who "merely stand for points of view, or styles of life"; novels "filled with set speeches by characters, which have no other purpose than to place in the record a particular fact or nuance of Negro life."[19] The use of such deliberate didactic and moralizing methods to convey black life reflects faith in an equivalence between language and referent, a correlation that some New Negro writers, though they complained of it in white American literature, sometimes practiced themselves. One goal of this book is to delineate the paradox that two distinct groups share this literary transgression, a similarity recognized, articulated, and sometimes parodied by the figures I discuss, particularly Carl Van Vechten and George Schuyler.[20]

Several works on images and representation offer useful points of departure for a foundational discussion of black literary modernism and help us critique the evanescence privileged by high modernism as well as the exaggerated "thereness" often assumed of the black body. W. J. T. Mitchell and Henry Louis Gates Jr., in two different yet related venues, foreground the ways in which the literal and figurative elements of writing correspond to the materiality and the abstraction of the body and bodily images and the ramifications of these dualities for black representation. Mitchell analyzes various interpretations of the term "image" and questions the "compulsion to conceive of the relation between words and images in political terms, as a struggle for territory, a contest of rival ideologies."[21] In *Iconology: Image, Text, Ideology,* he examines the theoretical link between the word and verbal and mental images, all of which are as vital as the "image proper," or what we generally refer to as "real" material images. Verbal images capture the dual imperatives of the sign as both a lexical element or linguistic unit and a perceptible mark or representation. As Mitchell argues, "the idea of a 'speaking picture' . . . is not merely a figure for certain special effects in the arts, but lies at the common origin of writing and painting."[22] Although he does not specifically refer to African American visual culture, several of his insights bear significant pertinence to black representation. There is first, of course, the materiality of the form of black dialect writing, the literal ramifications of Negro dialect as a "speaking picture," the voice of an assumed nonvalue or absence. More significant is the manner in which images determine what we say or think about the person or group represented, how they have "a way of shaping the things that can be said," how a mental image translates into a "real" image, and the use of language as the recording of such a movement. It is this sort of movement that Harlem Renaissance leaders attempted to influence.[23]

While Mitchell interrogates the hierarchy of word and image, Gates analyzes anthologies concerned with redressing the black image and demonstrates how, historically, image and text have been alternately aligned and ruptured, always at the disadvantage of represented blackness. Gates discusses the reproduction of the likenesses of seven "representative" black men in *A New Negro for a New Century,* a 1900 anthology and a precursor to Alain Locke's edited collection of 1925, *The New Negro,* and examines the belief that there was "a correlation between the specific *characteristics* of the individuals depicted and the larger *character* of the race." The portrayal of a few proper, dignified black men and women could, according to the anthology's editors and contributors, transmit such images to both black and white readers and, eventually, to the American public at large. Gates illustrates how such metonymic representation—the usual method of describing and defining African Americans—proceeds through a subtle dance of the literal and figurative possibilities of language. This metonymic representation moves from the physical features of the individuals presented to the "mental image" of the race collectively.[24] The metonym works not just physically, visually, but also narratively. In the most optimistic reading of what the anthology could achieve, the literal writings of black writers would affect the "mental picture" other Americans have of them as well as promote and make a space for black writers who, ideally, would create more "positive" or "proper" images of blacks in their own writings.[25] What becomes apparent is that the editors of and contributors to both of these *New Negro* anthologies believed that better literature *by* blacks and better images *of* blacks in literature would positively affect the general, national perception of African Americans. What obtains in Gates's essay and Mitchell's work is an understanding of the literal and figurative possibilities of language and the way such language anchors the images of blackness. Both Mitchell's and Gates's arguments pivot on a distinction between and an affinity for the "image proper" and the "proper image." Gates shows how abstract images, the perception of black "representative-ness," feeds into the material "image proper," not only in Mitchell's sense of this phrase but also as conceptualized in the pages and illustrations of the two black anthologies.

The Proper Image and the Image Proper

I want to keep in play this chiasmus of image proper and proper image, as it reflects a central issue that reverberates within this book and is a pivotal concern of the figures I examine. The image proper and the proper image of blackness are not always one and the same. Black representation negotiates the tension between literal and metaphorical language and, as Mitchell states, of word and image; and as has been frequently true in discussions of black representation, the two types of language and representations have often been conceived of as a "contest of rival ideologies."[26]

One of the best-known formulations of the question of black representation highlighted the dilemma of the literal and the figurative—the query with which this introduction began. *Crisis* magazine's 1926 symposium "The Negro in Art: How Shall He Be Portrayed?" proffered a series of questions and answers that defined the crucial concerns of the Harlem Renaissance. The most interesting—and problematic—aspect of the symposium, what the poet and novelist Arna Bontemps remembered as an "agonizing debate," was the respondents' struggle with the certain value of literal language, that is, unambiguous, "positive" images on the one hand and the effect of more figurative representational possibilities of blackness on the other.

So that we might appreciate fully the significance of the symposium and comprehend the intense divisiveness of the debate, I first briefly detail this episode in the context of the magazine's history.[27] The questions themselves conveyed a certainty and a directness (one could almost say a literalness) and assumed a one-to-one relation between writings about blacks and the images of blacks. The most compelling answers to the symposium's questions, however, were those that argued not for or against the realism of New Negro representation but instead settled the matter as a question of craft, by acknowledging the presence and burdensome history of metonymic representation but then exploding such narrative constraints. The challenge then in 1926, as it would be for Toni Morrison in 1992, was "to free up language from . . . racially informed and determined chains."[28] The *Crisis* symposium, rather than breaking such chains, may indeed have shackled blackness to type and unintentionally served as a marketing platform for one of the most controversial writers of the time, a writer who, not ironically, straddles the image-text divide.

The *Crisis* Symposium

Awkward questions inaugurated the symposium on producing better black art. As David Levering Lewis notes: "There was something slapdash and repetitive about [the symposium]. . . . Clearly, [managing editor Jessie] Fauset hadn't been asked to give the document the benefit of her punctilious scrutiny."[29] The blunt, transparent questions left no room for equivocation. Instead they demanded certainty and assumed that literary depictions could be measured in absolutes ("really and essentially Negroid"). Or as Fauset herself stated in a letter asking Langston Hughes for his opinion, the "questionnaire speaks for itself" (figure I.1).

Despite the seemingly obvious responses the questions were designed to provoke, the editors and writers who commented on them expressed wide-ranging

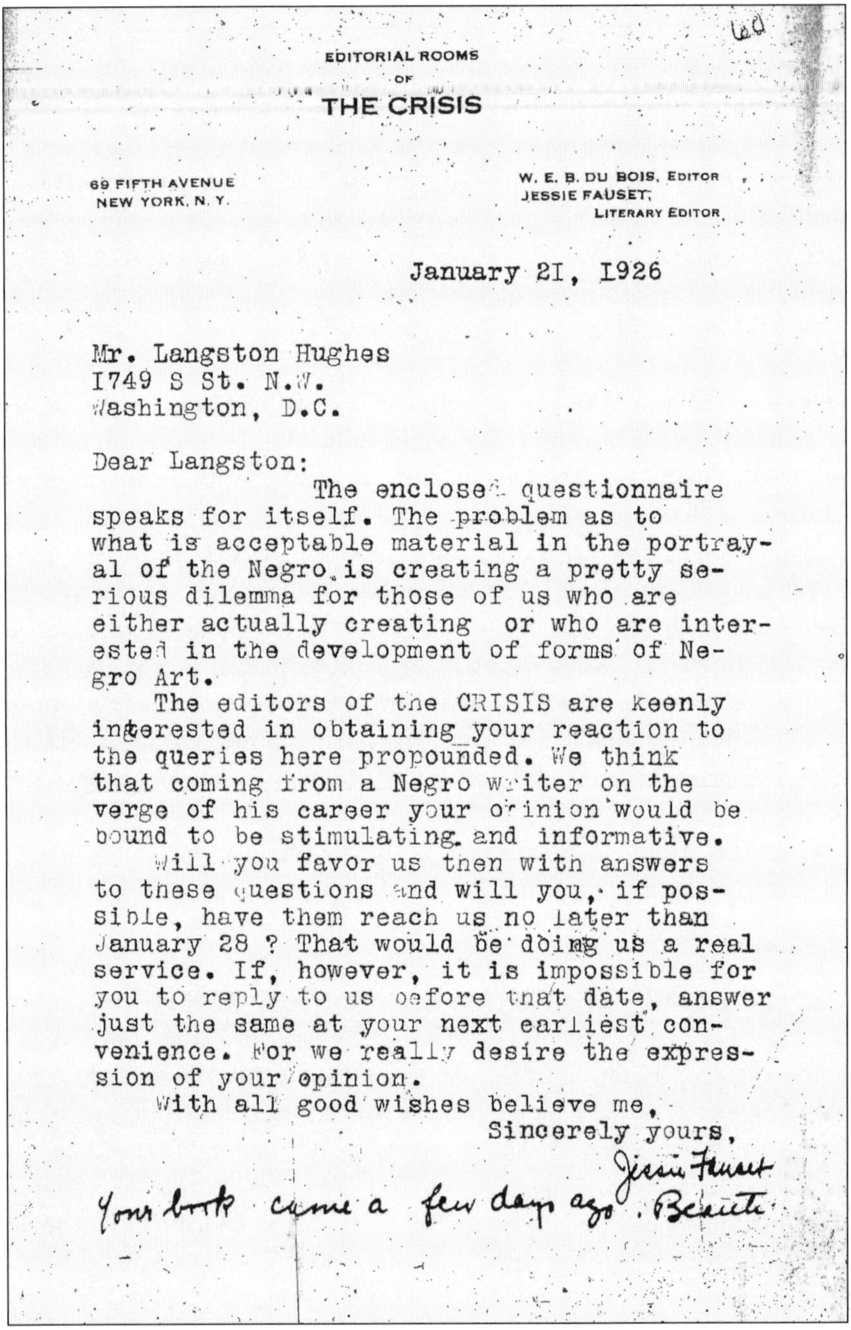

EDITORIAL ROOMS
OF
THE CRISIS

69 FIFTH AVENUE
NEW YORK, N.Y.

W. E. B. DU BOIS, EDITOR
JESSIE FAUSET,
LITERARY EDITOR

January 21, 1926

Mr. Langston Hughes
1749 S St. N.W.
Washington, D.C.

Dear Langston:
The enclosed questionnaire
speaks for itself. The problem as to
what is acceptable material in the portrayal of the Negro is creating a pretty serious dilemma for those of us who are
either actually creating or who are interested in the development of forms of Negro Art.
The editors of the CRISIS are keenly
interested in obtaining your reaction to
the queries here propounded. We think
that coming from a Negro writer on the
verge of his career your opinion would be
bound to be stimulating and informative.
Will you favor us then with answers
to these questions and will you, if possible, have them reach us no later than
January 28 ? That would be doing us a real
service. If, however, it is impossible for
you to reply to us before that date, answer
just the same at your next earliest convenience. For we really desire the expression of your opinion.
With all good wishes believe me,
Sincerely yours,

Jessie Fauset

Your book came a few days ago. Beaut.

Figure I.1. Jessie Fauset to Langston Hughes. Courtesy of the Yale Collection of American Literature, Beinecke Rare Book and Manuscript Library, Yale University.

viewpoints. The first printed response, one of four by white authors on black themes, appeared in the March issue and was written by Carl Van Vechten, author of the scandalous, soon-to-be-published *Nigger Heaven*. Van Vechten's answer gave license to anyone to use wholeheartedly the risqué elements of black life: "The squalor of Negro life, the vice of Negro life, offer a wealth of novel, exotic picturesque material to the artist. . . . Are Negro writers going to write this exotic material while it is still fresh or will they continue to make a free gift of it to white authors who will exploit it until not a drop of vitality remains?" (219). Van Vechten raised questions not just for black writers but also for white ones, who were assumed to have better access to publishers and editors yet lacked knowledge of certain aspects of black life. His explicit encouragement to capitalize on the underside of black culture served as the opening salvo in the nearly yearlong debate on black representation and white access, black aesthetic competency and white authority, in a manner that almost dared respondents to challenge him.

Different solutions were offered by the respondents, from developing and promoting black publishing houses to erecting a national monument honoring the "Black Negro Mammy" (September, 238–39). While white author Mary White Ovington noted that "publishers will take books dealing with the educated Negro if he can be written of without our continually seeing his diploma sticking out of his pocket" (March, 220), poet Countee Cullen rejoined that creators of black images should realize that "the Negro has not yet built up a large enough body of sound, healthy race literature to permit him to speculate in abortions and aberrations which other people are all too prone to accept as truly legitimate" (August, 193). The African American author and NAACP official Walter White disagreed with Van Vechten's position that the "squalor of Negro life" provided the best material for the black artist. White considered it "unfortunate . . . that at the very time when Negro writers are beginning to be heard there should arise a division of opinion as to what or what not he should write about" (April, 279). Between the extremes of these positions were those of writers such as Langston Hughes, Vachel Lindsay, Sherwood Anderson, and to a lesser extent H. L. Mencken. Black representation for this group was a matter of craft and the writer's individual interests. Anderson urged: "Why not quit thinking of Negro art? If the individual creating the art happens to be a Negro and someone wants to call it Negro Art, let them" (May, 36). Langston Hughes concurred, though his almost dispassionate response for the symposium—"What's the use of saying anything—the true literary artist is going to write about what he chooses anyway regardless of outside opinion" (April, 278)—was in contrast to the spirited argument in his essay "The Negro Artist and the Racial Mountain."[30]

Although there was no consensus from the symposium, some voices carried more weight than others. In a move that was arguably designed to give some finality to the debate, Du Bois published his well-known essay "Criteria of Negro Art" in the October issue. It was one of the final, though indirect, statements on the symposium.[31] Originally written for the national NAACP convention of 1926 and in honor of the historian Carter G. Woodson, the winner of that year's prestigious Spingarn Medal, Du Bois's speech was the highlight of the convention, an event that emphasized the importance of art in achieving the organization's goals.[32] The speech was published in the *Crisis* with pictures of young children on opposing pages. As Daylanne English has noted, this combination of image and text, of photographs alluding to the future of the race and Du Bois's words, links his dual projects of the "aesthetic and reproductive" to challenge the visual grotesqueries produced by racial stereotypes.[33] Du Bois's essay works by appealing to the reader's sense of fairness and justice, but it also rehearses the dichotomy between high and low modernism. He evoked the binaries of abstract and concrete, evanescent art versus the day-to-day reality of black life, primarily to parody the assumptions embedded in such binaries: "How is it that an organization like this, a group of radicals trying to bring new things into the world, a fighting organization which has come up out of the blood and dust of battle . . . how is it that an organization of this kind can turn aside to talk about Art? After all, what have we who are slaves and black to do with Art?" (290) The elegiac essay is most famous for proposing the two extremes possible for black aesthetics: "All Art is propaganda and ever must be despite the wailing of the purists. I stand in utter shamelessness and say that whatever art I have for writing has been used always for propaganda, for gaining the right of black folk to love and to enjoy. I do not care a damn for any art that is not used for propaganda. But I do care when propaganda is confined to one side while the other is stripped and silent" (October, 296). To be fair to Du Bois, the author posits a more complicated view of "propaganda" than is usually assumed. Du Bois's definition of the term reads as an injunction to black artists to express a necessary correction to the propaganda of white "infallibility." Du Bois notes in some white authors such as Octavius Roy Cohen "racial prejudgment which deliberately distorts Truth and Justice" (297). The question remains, however, what exactly is "Truth and Justice," and who fashions those definitions?

"Criteria of Negro Art" is an odd piece. One notes, for instance, Du Bois's proclivity toward abstraction in the essay, though ideal concepts such as "Beauty," "Truth," and "Freedom" were, according to him, quite specific, material objectives which he sought in his writings and the works of other black authors. Du Bois contradicts himself, however, just a few paragraphs later in this essay as well as in his other writings. The man who advises readers to drop Van Vechten's *Nigger Heaven* "gently in the grate" in the December issue is the same adjudicator who complains in October that "the black public" is "ashamed of sex and we lower our eyes when people will talk of it."[34]

The *Crisis* symposium can be credited with raising the issue of black representation in a public and accessible forum and with disseminating the terms and positions that would shape future discussions of the Harlem Renaissance.[35] Du Bois's vocabulary of "art and propaganda" was picked up and used by other writers during the period, usually those resisting the unforgiving binary; and the repetition of the questions month after month, with no introductory statements in the later issues to provide context, created a textual insistence and operated almost as injunctions by the time Du Bois published his essay. The most experimental writers of the period rejected such specificity as it was articulated by the symposium's questions. For such artists, rather than opening up a forum, the questions assumed a one-dimensional blackness that was always evident and recognizable. Jean Toomer, to cite one well-known example, refused to call himself a "Negro" for Boni and Liveright's publicity department and resisted the type of racial definitiveness implied by the questions proposed in the symposium.[36] Although the publication of *Cane* (1923) preceded the symposium by three years, its mixture of poetry, short stories, and drama, its lyrical presentation of the South, and its sometimes cryptic portrayals of African Americans refuse to be contained by or analyzed profitably through such questions as "Can any author be criticized for painting the worst or the best characters of a group?" The terms used by the *Crisis* symposium were, so to speak, so black and white, so cut and dried, that nuances of various positions necessarily got lost in the debate.

Du Bois's symposium questions may have had an enduring, unintended effect. They work not to deflect but to heighten, or at least to provide a forum for, the publicity and attention generated by the author Du Bois perceived as most guilty of harmful black imaging. Through his response, Carl Van Vechten not only answers the symposium questions but also prepares a reading public for the "squalid" aspects of *Nigger Heaven,* which would be published in August of that year. More important, Van Vechten's answers have the effect of emphasizing the hypersensitivity of some African Americans to the low material. The *Crisis* questions and answers, particularly Van Vechten's, introduce one reason for the narrative of failure so familiar to contemporary scholars and students of the Harlem Renaissance: the fact that black leaders of the New Negro Movement had inflexible ideas about how the younger group should portray African Americans. According to this reading, the attempt to limit and predetermine the subject matter of Negro Art derived not from white editors and white dilettantes fascinated by the sensational, as was frequently claimed, but by African American writers such as Du Bois and Walter White, who expected positive mimetic representation and, implicitly, literal, static images. When the questions are read in this light, their earnestness encourages the belief that certain aspects of black life should be off-limits for both whites and blacks, immuring the discussion of the proper image of blackness within restrictive, literal terms. It is perhaps, then, the height of irony that the *Crisis* symposium on proper black representation may have helped advertise the one author who appears to have best exploited black hesitancy about and white fascination with this material—Van Vechten, who, as I discuss later, created problematic narrative and celebrated photographic images of blackness.[37]

After the Symposium

Understanding the impact and implications of questions such as the symposium's during a period when the African American image was being rigorously debated provides a new awareness of the metonymic imperatives that some New Negro exponents attempted to satisfy, and it can promote a greater appreciation for those overlooked writers who do not fit into the well-worn Harlem Renaissance or New Negro paradigms. Although it is impossible to measure the impact of the symposium on individual black writers, it is intriguing to note that a number of innovative or disaffected Harlem Renaissance writings were published at the end of the 1920s and later, once the idealization of the New Negro had reached its peak, during and after the yearlong symposium.[38] Indeed, in this book I use the term "black modernism" to refer to a period later than what is commonly known as the Harlem Renaissance, and which was more experimental than that suggested by the ideology inherent in the *Crisis* symposium questions. Though temporal markers of modernism in general and the Harlem Renaissance in particular have been difficult if not impossible and reductive to determine, I understand black modernism to register in American culture as early as the late 1920s and as late as the mid-1950s, a time when some of the most critical assessments of the New Negro Movement were made. In this sense I disagree with the claim that "after 1926 the range of [black literary] subjects was, to all intents and purposes, compelled by mercenary considerations . . . to be limited to those aspects of Negro life which had proved financially successful."³⁹ As this discussion indicates, I believe that the late 1920s were a crucial moment for those artists whose conceptions of black life and culture competed with traditional assumptions about black representation as voiced in some of the responses in the symposium.

Toward the end of the 1920s more frequent vocal and public exhortations for quality, not quantity, in black writing surfaced in the African American press. What Nathan Huggins perceives as a more depressing turn in the Harlem Renaissance I read as a challenge to the earlier tepid, predictable writing, a posture perhaps best illustrated by the always critical Wallace Thurman. Thurman's letters to friends and collaborators offer perceptive appraisals of the period's writing and track the agreement of some other Harlem Renaissance participants. In 1926 Thurman argued that although propagandists had previously used the literary stage to proclaim the worthiness of the Negro, it was "about time for the next step, about time for the ballyhooing to cease and for the genuine performance to begin." Notably, those early black novels of the 1920s, such as Walter White's *Fire in the Flint* (1924) and *Flight* (1926), and Jessie Fauset's *There Is Confusion* (1924), do indeed display the proper lives of the black elite and strive self-consciously toward a literal, Du Boisian Truth. But as Thurman states in a review of *Flight,* "all art no doubt is propaganda, but all propaganda is most certainly not art."⁴⁰ Calling the journals that promoted Negro writing and art contests "foster agencies," Alain Locke in 1928 similarly complained that in order for art from African American hands to flourish, artists needed space for "a sustained vehicle of free and purely artistic expression." Parodying "Criteria of Negro Art," Locke advised, "After Beauty, let Truth come into the Renaissance picture."⁴¹ Romare Bearden in 1934 also articulated his regret that endowments devoted to helping black artists, such as the Harmon Foundation, cultivated a "coddling and patronizing" attitude toward them.⁴² *Harlem,* the journal edited by Thurman in 1928, was one attempt to showcase the more ambitious talent. Designed to be "a journal of free discussion, open to all sides of the problem and to all camps of belief," *Harlem* unfortunately, like another Thurman-edited journal, *Fire!!!,* was short-lived and published only one issue.[43] My point in mentioning Thurman, Locke, and Bearden here is to suggest that the claim that black writing suffered from a decreasing level of quality by the end of the 1920s is just another paradigmatic cliché that has marked the discussion of the Harlem Renaissance. What was read as the end of the Renaissance was in fact a growing awareness, a growing maturity. In yet another irony in the field of Harlem Renaissance studies, those most "modern" black writers of the period were published outside the temporal framework designated as the Renaissance, writers such as Sterling Brown, who wrote the groundbreaking *Southern Road;* Rudolph Fisher, who wrote the mystery novel *The Conjure Man Dies;* and Thurman, author of *Infants of the Spring.* All three books were published in 1932. Just at this moment's "end," more critical appraisals and expectations of black writing appeared.[44] This desire for more nuanced depictions of black life and dissatisfaction with simplistic characters and tropes can be considered one of the significant achievements of the Harlem Renaissance. Indeed the struggle for more complex literary portrayals in the late 1920s would provide a basis for the later contributions of Richard Wright, Ann Petry, and Melvin Tolson in the 1930s and 1940s.[45]

THIS BOOK expands the frame within which the Harlem Renaissance and its legacy have been conceived by examining artists and writers whose work did not respond to the problem of representation within the conventional terms of the period. It pays special attention to the contributions of visual artists such as photographers who have been neglected by previous scholars of black modernism. I attend closely to the ways in which artists working in the 1920s and 1930s experimented with narrative and image to develop different solutions to the problem of black representation and played purposefully with the narrative assumptions about and perceptions of blackness. Through strategies such as the revision of "Negro" dialect, satire, narrative and visual ambiguity, and experimental photographic perspective, these writers and photographers interrogated either the visual production of racial knowledge or an idea of "blackness" that was scopically derived. The chapters that follow examine the tension between the written and the visual arts, demonstrate the visual imperatives of black representation, and clarify the relationship between the activities of the 1920s and later forms of black writing and art usually included within the category of "black modernism." I perceive "visual culture" as a field that recognizes the importance of language in conditioning what and how we see. Visual culture, as I use the term, includes the various forms of images identified by W. J. T. Mitchell—material, verbal, mental—with an emphasis on the spectacle as well as the spectator and the culturally and socially determined relation between them.[46]

Some remarks are necessary on why photography occupies a privileged space in this discussion of black visual culture. Both photography and racial stereotypes suffer from easy readings. In the perusal of race, it is often thought that there is no "reading," in fact, to be done, since a stereotype is immediately and evidently "there." But as Roland Barthes demonstrates, a photograph is more than the sum of its parts. One of the attractions for scholars of *Camera Lucida,* Barthes's reflections on photography, is its expansiveness, the way it circulates, eliding the "reprimand" of the literal referent and forcing the reader to travel with Barthes to various discoveries about photography. This second instinct—to question what appears to be explicitly evident and not take things at "face value"—is one shared by the figures in this book; and the similarities between the assumptions about the transparency of photography and the assumptions about the transparency of race make photography a particularly useful model for more fully complicating discussions of the representation of blackness.

I begin by illustrating the connections between the literary and the visual in early-twentieth-century African American literature. In his prefaces to *The Book of American Negro Poetry* (1922) and *The Book of American Negro Spirituals* (1925), James Weldon Johnson critiqued a mode of expression explicitly identified with African Americans: American "Negro" dialect. I read Johnson's prefaces as two of the earliest and clearest articulations of a black artist's desire to complicate the dynamic between image and language. Johnson criticizes the use of dialect in literature because it conjures an anachronistic blackness and functions as a linguistic version of the racial stereotypes dramatized in minstrel shows. Dialect reveals the pernicious link between the verbal and the visual in African American representation because expressions are rendered with aural deformations and represented on the printed page through "mutilations" of the English language.[47] "Visual" in this context encompasses more than the ways in which the words are disfigured on the page: Johnson argues that the deformed voice of black dialect contributes to the stereotyped image of the African American. His early black literary criticism cautions against the perceived dependence of the African American artist solely on physical, bodily qualities and calls instead for intellectual activities actions that will construct new black images and "disembodied" texts.

Dialect was the literary conceit that embodied the yoke of the visual and the verbal for African American authors of the late-nineteenth and early-twentieth centuries. Gavin Jones, reading black writers such as Paul Laurence Dunbar more ironically than previous scholars, argues that dialect was a "subversive medium of double meaning." For Michael North, dialect was also subversive— not for black authors but for the "high" moderns, who found in dialect a private, coded language with which "to mock the literary establishment" as well as to adopt indecorous personas in personal letters.[48] My analysis differs from Jones's and North's by focusing on the bodily and performative aspects of dialect's elusive nexus of word and image, the way in which dialect summons the visual image of the black American. In the first chapter I examine the limitations of the visual as revealed in specific forms of dialect: the spirituals and black sermons. The writing and textual compilation of spirituals foreground the difficulty of accurately transcribing black sound. Spirituals were impossible to write down and notate accurately. Any act that caters to the gaze in the notation of spirituals is inadequate. In fact, volumes of compiled spirituals indicate the frailty of the visual, for the spirituals and the sermons replicate a problem those early writers of black dialect also encountered: the qualities that made the Southern sermon and spirituals so dynamic were also the qualities that made them so hard to put into print. *God's Trombones* (1927), Johnson's poetic "experiment" in a non-dialect language, indicates the difficulty of placing black speech into a visual medium, as well as the difficulty of preserving the spirituals.

Johnson's concept of an identifiable and proper black literature that would refute a "picturesque," stereotypical African American literature guides the remainder of the book. The second and third chapters discuss two novels that offer competing narrative interpretations of the difficulties and limitations of Johnson's injunction. Nella Larsen's *Passing* (1929) is the subtle tale of light-skinned African American women who "pass" for white; and George Schuyler's *Black No More* (1931) is a satirical story about African Americans who, through a skin-lightening procedure, are turned white. The body informs these two experiments in narrative, one of which privileges ambiguity while the other exaggerates through parody. *Passing* calls into question how the spectator or observer categorizes the black body, while *Black No More* suggests that any "racial" category, white or black, is fraudulent or suspect. The novels, through opposing methods, challenge the concept of either an essential form of or an ideal figure for black literature, a concept foregrounded by the *Crisis* symposium's questions and by some respondents' answers.

The two novels highlight the difficulties of "reading" any body, whether black or white, but do so through competing means. Whereas *Passing* denies a representative blackness through the use of ambiguity—of the characters, of their race and class, of the story itself—*Black No More* rejects an authentic blackness through exaggeration. The differences between *Passing* and *Black No More* are differences of narrative and of the body: Larsen's narrative works through an elusive representation of the fashionable mixed-race body and an enigmatic storyline; Schuyler's functions through an over-the-top portrayal of black Americans who become too "white" in an embellished, at times unbelievable story. Both texts offer further considerations of women, the act of storytelling, and nation. The concern with nationality in *Passing* is briefly evident when the central character, Irene, realizes that she cannot leave the United States to live in another country: "She would not go to Brazil. She belonged in this land of rising towers. She was an American. She grew from this soil, and she would not be uprooted."[49] Lauren Berlant notes of these lines that "Irene's embrace of the nation seems a pathetic misrecognition."[50] Indeed it is just one in a series of misreadings. *Passing* and *Black No More* both demonstrate the extent to which race depends on readings and politics, but *Black No More* deliberately exposes how nationality is tied to race and vice versa. The character Max Fisher's embrace and eventual exploitation of nationalistic rhetoric reflects a clear-eyed awareness of how national and racial mythologies work together to form narratives of white and black masculinity. Schuyler actively pushes the genre of ironic narrative to its limits, first by exaggerating national discourses in hyperbolic stories about the American political system, and second by questioning anyone's ability to correctly "read" or see race and by extension, in the context of the novel, nationality.

Chapter 4 more explicitly considers the tensions between image and text by focusing on Carl Van Vechten's *Nigger Heaven* (1926) and his private photographic collection of African Americans. A white author accused of exploiting his black friendships in his novel, Van Vechten created literary images (and collected photographic ones) that celebrated an embodied, "authentic" blackness rooted in the most salacious and stereotypical aspects of black life. And yet the other writers I study—Johnson, Larsen, Schuyler, and Thurman—were among the black writers who publicly supported his novel. In this chapter I examine this apparent contradiction. *Nigger Heaven* was less successful as a primer on black representation than as an experiment in narrative that affected the period and its participants in fundamental ways, providing recognizable codes that black writers would ironically cite in their own novels just a few years later. My discussion is neither an apology for Van Vechten nor a castigation of his overwhelming influence on and his problematic appropriation of black culture. Rather, I attempt a nuanced, reasoned appraisal, informed by the statements of Johnson, Larsen, Schuyler, and Thurman. I also read the novel in connection with Van Vechten's photography collection in order to examine his use of ironic and sardonic sensibilities, which defined his conception of the modern. The self-referential, avant-garde style of the novel extends to the photos in Van Vechten's collection, which pose the black body in self-conscious, satirical ways. By examining both his novel and his photography, I hope to turn the gaze back on the period's most influential and controversial promoter, the critical, well-placed spectator who often thrust himself onto Harlem's stage. Van Vechten's novel privileges black men and women who contrast with the New Negro ideal: the most interesting characters in the novel are a street hustler and an exotic, impetuous lover of men. These bodies on the border of the story are arguably Van Vechten's true interest and his ideal of black embodiment, the representatives of an uninhibited sexuality.

Sterling Brown quite aptly characterized Van Vechten as a too inquisitive spectator. Reminiscing about the Harlem Renaissance, the poet chastised those black writers who "trooped off to join Van Vechten's band and share in the discovery of Harlem as a new African colony."[51] According to Brown, Van Vechten "was a voyeur. He was looking at these Negroes and they were acting fools for him."[52] The two cultural forms Van Vechten used to celebrate Harlem, the collection and the photograph, do in fact privilege the visual. Like *Nigger Heaven,* Van Vechten's photographs depend on the reader's ability and desire to recognize irony, a willingness contingent on several factors, not the least of which is the reader's or spectator's social and historical positioning. Van Vechten's irony is more prevalent and, I believe, more successful in his photographic collection precisely because assumptions about the referentiality of blackness are foregrounded and exposed. This helps to register the paradox of Van Vechten's two collections: the photographs resist the reduction to (stereo)type, to the body, while the novel *Nigger Heaven* does not.

I continue my analysis of photographic images in chapter 5 by analyzing the work of two figures central to a visual understanding of the Harlem Renaissance and by examining the discussion of blackness in what may appear to be a surprising source, Roland Barthes's last book, *Camera Lucida* (1981). The photographers, James Van Der Zee in the 1920s and 1930s and Aaron Siskind in the 1930s and 1940s, present through their photography the profound expressiveness and distinct visual moments of black modernism and so help to define the often conflicting character of this moment and style. The photographers' images both complicate and literalize James Weldon Johnson's imperative for a "less picturesque blackness," but Van Der Zee's determined optimism offers an unsettling counterpoint to the hard clarity of Siskind's photographs. Their temporally and aesthetically distinct representations of black life and bodies undermine assumptions about the black body as "non-art." Rather than offering an exhaustive history of the Harlem Renaissance in photography, the chapter explores the body as it is reflected in the psychic dissonance of Siskind's images of African Americans in *Harlem Document: Photographs, 1932–1940* (1981) and in the aggressively middle-class, patriotic portraits by Van Der Zee. Both men challenge the spectator to "see" the black body in new ways and refute the concept of and the need for a definitive blackness, as suggested by the *Crisis* symposium. Van Der Zee worked within the photographic conventions of the time and fostered new ones, such as his "death pictures," techniques that we now read as emphasizing artifice. Siskind's images of Harlem's gritty exterior serve as a documentary indictment of the American ideals so heavily ridiculed by George Schuyler and photographically embraced by Van Der Zee. The progression from the interior of Van Der Zee's Harlem studio with its fabricated backgrounds to Siskind's depictions of Harlem's overpopulated streets and buildings, from Van Der Zee's reification of a past, "proper" time to Siskind's emphasis on details and objects in Harlem's contemporary urban spaces, suggests the visual movement away from stereotypes of blackness and the body. This chapter is also about the relation between photographic images of blackness and the writing *about* such images. I look at Barthes's discussion of a well-known Van Der Zee image, "The Family Portrait," as well as other fleeting images of blackness in *Camera Lucida*. While most analyses of *Camera Lucida* focus on the absent image of the Winter Garden Photograph, another physically absent but visually present photograph is the one depicting slavery which Barthes saw and preserved as a young boy. My reading of this second absent image questions how blackness is both reified and abstracted in *Camera Lucida*.

The Harlem Renaissance is a privileged moment of postmodern intellectual inquiry. For the postmodern scholar of African American literature, a "return to the scene of the modern" is often a return to the Harlem Renaissance, an occasion of turning back that Jonathan Culler calls a "mirror stage moment," in which scholars examine an earlier literary era and "see" themselves.[53] One other motivation for my study is to examine how the periodization of the Harlem Renaissance as a romanticized time in African American cultural history has been appropriated as a precursor to a later, postmodern "renaissance" in African American culture, endowing the images associated with the Harlem Renaissance with cultural capital. The concluding portion of the book thus engages with a concept of temporality briefly hinted at in the beginning: the retrospective, comprehensive look which is necessary in order to conceive of a collection, to see the whole from individual parts, that is, the backwards glance contemporary scholars give to the Harlem Renaissance. In the conclusion I look at two specific moments, one that is contemporaneous with the supposed end of the Harlem Renaissance and the other a cultural moment that extends beyond what is usually associated with the "modern." First, I analyze Wallace Thurman's novel *Infants of the Spring* and show how the novel's ambivalence about the Harlem Renaissance is reflected in Thurman's own ambivalence about one character's sexuality, a character who cannot complete a novel that might rescue him from unproductive decadence. Thurman's novel and essays he wrote in 1927 align him with Alain Locke's more vocal criticisms of the New Negro Movement throughout the 1930s. Although Thurman acknowledges the common criticism of the period (that black authors catered to white interest), it is important to note that he does not stop there. Thurman criticizes as well those who cannot capitalize on a moment of promise and who fail to translate the elusiveness of black modernism into something concrete. Second, I examine the representation of Harlem and the Harlem Renaissance as they were reimagined and reinvented in late-twentieth-century American culture by focusing on the controversial art exhibition "Harlem on My Mind: The Cultural Capital of Black América, 1900–1968," held at the Metropolitan Museum of Art in New York in 1969. Except for the work of black photographers such as James Van Der Zee and Gordon Parks, the exhibition displayed no work by black visual artists. It was criticized as discriminatory and paternalistic because it relied primarily on enlarged reprints of newspaper texts and sought few suggestions from African American art historians or curators. I suggest that we look at this exhibit as an event that, in an effort to celebrate the city's past, could not be divorced from the aesthetic debates of the earlier period. Indeed the Met's portrayal of the Harlem Renaissance demonstrates the difficulties of representing this fundamental cultural moment, which was itself mired in representational "crises." The alternating influence of time becomes apparent in any study of the Harlem Renaissance: How does one negotiate the past in light of the inevitable pull of nostalgia? How does one navigate through the fog of history to see the period "as it really was" and as it shapes our own? By studying the various narratives and images of the collective story known as "Harlem," by questioning how it has been received and why some images have left an indelible impression, we also gain valuable insights into our own cultural moment which is so heavily invested with the visual.

Images of Black Modernism draws on fields as diverse as American studies, visual culture, and black literary theory, but the primary work of the book remains the close analysis of literary and photographic texts. The key word here is "close." I keep the interpretive focus on narrative about and images of the black body in order to investigate how blackness, assumed to be outside signification, is shaped by language and contests this assumption. As Joseph Boone notes in *Libidinal Currents,* there is a tendency to reject close reading as an artifact from New Criticism, a dangerous dinosaur that ignores the interpretive advances that have been achieved through more contemporary fields such as cultural studies.[54] But my inquiry into the way black writers used language to shape perception and the way photographers used images to tell their own stories about Harlem and its residents demands a sustained engagement with the details that make up the whole. "To free ourselves from the often invisible grip of power or ideology," writes Boone, "we need first to see—which is to say *read,* and read closely and well—the discursive strategies that imprison us within their prescribed meanings. Only then can we begin to unravel the regulatory logic by which more visibly oppressive social institutions keep us in 'our place'— which is to say, the place that has been discursively assigned to or textually inscribed upon us."[55] His eloquent "defense of close reading" puts before the contemporary reader the same demands that some of the most experimental writers would ask of their readers. Indeed one could argue that the practice of close reading in itself serves to challenge the sociological reading of black fiction so prevalent in early interpretations of African American literature. Black modernist fiction, like its white counterpart, invites sustained engagement with word, sentence, narrative. The keen attention paid to the portrayal of the African American in the 1920s and later requires us to read carefully in order to sense the texture of the text. The readings made available by such steady, rigorous practice do not attempt to uphold the "unity" of the text, which is a central feature of New Criticism. Except for perhaps Johnson in *God's Trombones,* none of the authors examined in this book reflects the New Critical desire for wholeness; and even Johnson's *Autobiography of an Ex-Colored Man* (1912) demonstrates the pleasure of strategic nondisclosure and fractured identities. Rather, the intimate interpretations of blackness in this book compel the questioning of a racial (il)logic and an understanding of how a system of racial difference affects images and the way they operate in our culture.

One goal of this book is to understand how the look or the gaze functioned during this early-twentieth-century period of black writing and how concepts of visuality mediate depictions of the New Negro. It attempts, in other words, to bring the visual to bear on narrative in African American literature. Michele Wallace, for one, articulates the undervaluation of the visual in comparison to other arts such as music and writing in the field of African American studies. She argues that "Afro-Americans have not produced (because they have been prevented from doing so by intra-racial pain and outside intervention) a tradition in the visual arts as vital and compelling to other Americans as the Afro-American tradition in music. Moreover, the necessity . . . for drawing parallels or alignments between Afro-American music and everything else cultural amongst Afro-Americans stifles and represses most of the potential for understanding the visual in Afro-American culture."[56] While I agree with her that black visual culture has not received the same amount of attention as have black musical traditions, I am less convinced that it is "intra-racial pain" that has restricted the development and study of the visual. Perhaps what we need to do is examine how the visual has impacted these other forms of artistic expression. Rather than pitting the visual against the aural/oral, writing, or music, for example, perhaps a more expansive understanding of black visual culture will help us recognize how the visual and language inflect each other, affecting African American modernity. By reconfiguring this link in new ways, we can begin to understand and to provide a base for a larger study of black visual culture.

Reflexive studies of the Harlem Renaissance register in some fashion, in some form, the questions of black authenticity that are prevalent today. Though voiced in different words and raised in more diverse and public "symposiums," the quest for ideal representations of blackness still occurs, but now with even more pressing implications. In a 2006 opinion piece in the *New York Times,* the African American author Nick Chiles bemoaned the apparent publishing successes of "street lit" and "ghetto fiction," contemporary fiction with mostly

African American characters who experience decidedly "urban" adventures. Walking into the African American literature section of a Borders bookstore was for Chiles like "walking into a pornography shop," in which he was accosted by "lurid book jackets displaying all forms of brown flesh, usually half-naked and in some erotic pose, often accompanied by guns and other symbols of criminal life."[57] Throughout Chiles's article one hears echoes of Du Bois's disgust with Van Vechten's *Nigger Heaven*. Chiles writes, "It's depressing that this noble profession . . . has been reduced by the greed of the publishing industry and the ways of the American marketplace to a tasteless collection of pornography." Although he raises significant questions about how literature is marketed to black readers, one cannot ignore a certain elitism, a bias against a form of literature that may appeal to the urban masses. How, indeed, do we distinguish the iconic cover images which Chiles dismisses from those on books located in other sections of the store, such as the detective and suspense aisle or the romance shelves? How do the book jackets of current "ghetto fiction" differ, if at all, from the paperback covers of some of the books written during the New Negro Movement, such as Claude McKay's *Home to Harlem* or, later, Chester Himes's novels? Admittedly Chiles seems to be more concerned with the content of what he calls "this new black erotica" than with the images on the covers, and he takes exception to having canonical works such as *Invisible Man* (1952) and *Beloved* (1987) categorized generically under "African American Literature" along with, one imagines, a contemporary mass market novel such as the urban-based *Dime Piece* (2004).[58] Yet the impulse to make distinctions (*this* is black literature, *that* is not) seems eerily similar to some of the responses that appeared in *Crisis* circa 1926.

This book aims to comprehend the visual imperative of narrative that underlies such questions and recriminations so as to help us understand more broadly American modernism, the dynamics of racial representation in the twentieth century, and the status of visual culture in the United States. I hope also to complicate the concept of black modernism through dedicated attention to the intersection between the visual and the literary, a relationship that adds greatly to our understanding of the aesthetic pressures on black representation and of the experiments that shaped African American modernism.

If we are to believe the majority of writers of Negro dialect and the burnt-cork artists, Negro speech is a weird thing, full of "ams" and "Ises." Fortunately we don't have to believe them. We may go directly to the Negro and let him speak for himself.

Zora Neale Hurston, "Characteristics of Negro Expression"

To *speak* properly was to *be* proper.

Henry Louis Gates Jr., "The Trope of the Negro and the Reconstruction of the Image of the Black"

Tone Pictures

James Weldon Johnson's Experiment in Dialect

IN A 1929 letter to James Weldon Johnson, the black film producer and actor William "Bill" Foster asserted a claim about the African American voice and a rising form of entertainment, the talking picture. According to Foster, the new medium offered unprecedented opportunities for the African American performer: apparently the smooth, tonally low voice of the African American recorded better than white voices. Once film studios realized that the black voice was an exceptional addition to the new cinematic technology, large numbers of black actors and singers would be hired, and steady work would be possible. It was a simple matter of numbers: "Nine out of ten Negroes who take the [screen] test pass—no training. Seven out of ten cultured white[s] fail. It's the Negroe's [*sic*] natural and mellow voice that reproduces even, the white voice is high pitched and reproduces sharp."[1] Johnson, well versed in music and sound himself, agreed: "What you say about the recording of Negro voices in the talkies is very important, and I do not see how they are going to keep the Negro from achieving a permanent place in the movie world. . . . I myself have noticed that their voices record much better than white voices."[2] The sound film would be

29

an important vehicle to change the negative perception of the black voice, for, as Johnson stated repeatedly in his writings, "Negro" dialect maligned black representation. The new technology would help introduce more complex portrayals of African Americans and "dub over" a pre-technological minstrel past. The talkies, in short, would help black artists translate black sound into a better—more modern—image of the African American.

The exchange between Johnson and Foster captures an early black modernist idealism, an understandable "cultural innocence" and faith in technology. Unfortunately for the two men as well as the black talent of the time, editing out black images and dubbing black sound to white face would become just as popular in movie studios as the talking picture itself. According to Michael North, "the arrival of the talkies" brought "an unmasking" for white actors and singers such as Al Jolson but not for those black actors who were limited to performing stereotypes. Although "the new voice" that appeared in the 1920s via film, music, and literature "was very largely a black one," it was not the type of black voice Foster and Johnson had in mind, the voice they had hoped would resound throughout America through the new visual and aural technologies.[3]

If this exchange on the significance of sound seems a somewhat surprising way to begin a discussion of black literary and visual representations, my purpose is to emphasize the role of black dialect in early-twentieth-century American culture, particularly in the construction and reproduction of black images. Improving the perception of the black voice was one of Johnson's many goals in publishing his poetry collection *God's Trombones* (1927); and though not conceived on as massive a scale as a Hollywood film, the slim volume of poems did provide a needed vehicle for demonstrating the creativity of the black vernacular and, as Johnson hoped, changing the literary and cultural image of the African American.

My aim in this chapter is to rethink the question of African American representation as situated in the 1926 *Crisis* symposium, not as a rivalry between "art or propaganda," a division, it seems, in which neither term wins, but through a creative tension which reappears in black modernism, that between word and image, the verbal and the visual. That early-twentieth-century black writers sought to distance themselves from the stereotypes suggested by dialect is not a new claim. I am interested, however, in the imagistic quality of Negro dialect, the status of dialect as a visual and verbal sign which troubled black writers of the period and challenged the portrayal of a new type of African American. The Negro dialect popular in nineteenth- and early-twentieth-century

American fiction functions as a unique literary paradigm; it is both a visual misconstruction and, when spoken, a mis-hearing, a textual and aural maladjustment. I am less concerned with what Gavin Jones calls the "politics of dialect" than with the aesthetic and conceptual effects of dialect—that is, dialect as a textual metaphor for the challenges confronted by black writers because of the literary and visual stereotypes it reflected and enabled.[4] This chapter questions the fundamental premise of the role of dialect (both as sound and as a literary convention represented textually in print), its status as a means for "reading" race, and the efforts to change the use of dialect in the hopes of altering images of blackness.

In what follows I examine James Weldon Johnson's attempt to (re)present language and the black body through an engagement with this literary convention. Johnson's prefaces to *The Book of American Negro Poetry* (1922) and *The Book of American Negro Spirituals* (1925), pivotal anthologies of the New Negro Movement, demonstrate how image and text are troublingly linked in Negro dialect, a relationship that Johnson would seek to rupture and then realign. Johnson's prefaces to the two collections delineate his ideas on dialect, language, and music, particularly ragtime and the spirituals. The two essays illustrate what may be called the textualization of the black image, that is, the process by which the evanescent elements associated with blackness, such as black dialect, the spirituals, and certain forms of the black sermon, are rendered into the material form of print.[5] As the prefaces point out and as *God's Trombones* demonstrates, this transformation of abstract oral expression into concrete textual form is not an uncomplicated process. Johnson's efforts to change Negro dialect raise fundamental questions about orality, literacy, and language itself. How does one make the Southern sermon and the spirituals, two of the elements that, in the early twentieth century, were strongly identified with "blackness," "readable"? How to capture an art form that was slowly disappearing, such as the spirituals, an art form whose very poignancy rested upon its ineffable qualities? How to capture accurately the notes of a sermonic performance which hauntingly escaped the usual methods of recording or textual representation? Johnson tries to transcribe essentially oral material into a non-denigrated form of print, but *God's Trombones* and the prefaces raise larger questions about how a visual conception of blackness mediates between black oral and aural culture and a "higher" print culture in which black aesthetic expressions are preserved. Often when Johnson criticizes Negro dialect, he is indirectly criticizing black performance and its confinement to outdated and particular

modes of embodiment and temporality. Johnson would like to limit the significance of the devalued body in evaluations of black writing and music, but he
depends on the corporeal in order to conceptualize subtle distinctions among
African American aesthetic practices.

Before I look into the two prefaces in detail, some initial remarks are necessary on why the textual representation of the spirituals and, relatedly, dialect is
so significant, both to James Weldon Johnson and to a discussion of early-
twentieth-century African American literature and culture. As with other discussions of blackness and print culture, the preservation of the spirituals in the
form of readable text invokes long-held stereotypes about visuality and the
black body. The challenge was first to record the strange sounds and then to
make such sounds (and the bodies that produced them) familiar and accessible,
less strange to white Americans, and as "readable" as other types of music. As
illustrated by the exchange between Foster and Johnson on black voice, black
sound contributed to black textual, and relatedly, visual representation.

A PROFOUND sense of loss marks African American spirituals, a loss felt not
only in the subject matter of the slave songs but also in the manner in which
they were recorded and compiled. Thomas Wentworth Higginson offered one
of the earliest written accounts of the songs, which foreshadowed the recording
difficulties later compilers of the spirituals would face. In an 1867 article in the
Atlantic Monthly, and in his account of his experiences as a Union Army officer
during the Civil War, Higginson published the lyrics to thirty-six spirituals,
songs he had heard his African American troops sing as they relaxed during
their moments off the battlefield.[6] Throughout Higginson's article, the need
for preservation confronts the encroachments of memory loss and time. Long
enchanted by the spirituals, Higginson delighted in the fact that he "could now
gather on their own soil these strange plants, which [he] had before seen as in
museums alone." But we learn that hearing the spirituals being performed,
even under concealment, does not lead to easily repeatable transmission of their
lyrics. Higginson, in fact, describes his method of recording as if he were an
infiltrator in his own camp:

> Writing down in the darkness, as I best could,—perhaps with my hand in the
> safe covert of my pocket,—the words of the song, I have afterwards carried it to
> my tent, like some captured bird or insect, and then, after examination, put it by.
> Or, summoning one of the men at some period of leisure,—Corporal Robert
> Sutton, for instance, whose iron memory held all the details of a song as if it were

a ford or a forest,—I have completed the new specimen by supplying the absent parts. The music I could only retain by ear, and though the more common strains were repeated often enough to fix their impression, there were others that occurred only once or twice.

Higginson's romantic account of recording the words ("Often in the starlit evening I have returned from some lonely ride by the swift river") sets the stage for the haunting ephemerality of the songs. There is an element quite intangible and evasive about the spirituals. With no textual referent, the songs are as swiftly fleeting as a bird or an insect, for despite Higginson's simile, the lyrics to the songs are only haphazardly and gradually "captured" and often must be corrected and revised through the memory of another.[7] Lacking a textual or fixed origin, they seem changeable and deliquescent, a delicate art one would like to place for posterity in a museum if only one could gently and correctly secure the "real thing." Higginson's article encodes the concerns of collectors of the spirituals. Even those compilers skilled in writing music had difficulty determining the exact notes they heard when the spirituals were sung. Because so many of the notes of the spirituals escaped the usual methods of transcription, collectors of the songs were sometimes forced to approximate the notes, an approximation that did not fully capture the notation and contributed to a lack of uniformity in the appearance of the spirituals in different anthologies.

In order to preserve the spirituals for posterity, two important elements were required: the notes had to be arrested, and the notes had to be accurately placed in print. In this way a readable referent could be established. The transformation of the spirituals from unique sounds to readable notation involved both the auditory and the visual senses. It called upon an aspect of visuality with regard to language that has appeared in studies of "high" literary modernism but has sometimes escaped attention in discussions of African American modernism: the appearance of the word on the space of the page and the effect of this appearance on signification and meaning. The poet Nathaniel Mackey discusses some of the key points involving this visual element of writing. Concerned about "the placement of words on the page," Mackey takes into account such issues as "the use of variable margins, intralinear spacing, [and] page breaks," all in order to "advance a now swept, now swung, sculpted look, a visual dance down the page and from page to page." He explains this attention to visuality as a mode of "speaking, by way of the eye, to a mind's ear that hears every line break as a caesura, every break between sections or pages as an amendment or an addendum or even a new beginning, [and] additional space between words as a pause."[8] The visual appearance of the poem is, then, another way to create and affect poetic meaning and works in concert with other methods of poetic invention.

But Mackey's awareness of the fluid "graphic amenities" available to the poet also raises the specter of its opposite: textual rigidity. Contrary to Mackey's suggestion of movement, the effect of print on the spirituals amounted to a sterilization of the otherwise emotive songs. For as Walter Ong notes, "print locks words" onto the space of the page. Unlike handwritten manuscripts, whose appearance can be "ornate" and which can vary even if the same text is written twice by the same manuscript writer, the printed text "typically impress[es] more by its tidiness and inevitability: the lines perfectly regular, all justified on the right side, everything coming out even visually, and without the aid of the guidelines or ruled borders that often occur in manuscripts." The regularization of the printed words, however, creates the feeling that the text is finite and "closed." As Ong puts it, the world of print is "an insistent world of cold, nonhuman, facts."[9]

This "tidiness" contributed to the refinement, and as James Weldon Johnson and Zora Neale Hurston would argue the weakening, of the reprinted and reproducible spiritual. Histories of the spirituals reveal two levels of containment: of the slaves' bodies as they sang the songs and of the songs themselves as they were reified into print. Early white listeners were "bothered" by the slaves' movement of their bodies as they sang the spirituals, which contrasted to the accepted manner of worship.[10] Observers of the slaves' singing were particularly struck by what has now come to be known as the "shout," which usually followed the slaves' religious program and which stood out to the observers because of the extreme bodily movements of the participants. The nineteenth-century African American teacher Charlotte Forten in her "Life on the Sea Islands" offers a classic description of the shout and the role the body plays in the performance: "The children form a ring, and move around in a kind of shuffling dance, singing all the time. Four or five stand apart, and sing very energetically, clapping their hands, stamping their feet, and rocking their bodies to and fro. These are the musicians, to whose performance the shouters keep perfect time.... [I]t is probable that [the shouts] are the barbarous expression of religion, handed down to them from their African ancestors, and destined to pass away under the influence of Christian teachings."[11] Perhaps influenced by her New England upbringing, Forten offers a familiar disparagement of the activity and of the participant's body. "Under the influence of Christian teachings," not only would the shouts disappear, but also bodily movement would become more sedate and "civilized."

The appearance of the spirituals in the collections also required containment. In his detailed history and analysis of the nineteenth-century collection and notation of the spirituals, Ronald Radano notes that collectors "disciplined" the sounds of the spirituals within conventional musical notation, a containment that Radano recognizes as a kind of violence. Faced with trying to represent unusual and unique sounds, "transcribers altered staff notations to obey a new logic that exceeded the confines of common time and well-tempered scales. The disciplining effects of notation accordingly engendered a kind of counterviolence that related directly to the impossibility of transcription."[12] To physically represent inexpressible black sounds such as those heard by Higginson, early collectors such as William James Allen used the discourses of standard musical systems. In this way black sounds were made accessible and legible to white Americans who had only recent contact with the spirituals. Though admittedly not as authentic as the untranscribed slave sounds, the transcribed spirituals implied a sense of progress, a sense of improvement. Zora Neale Hurston, however, called these transcribed spirituals "neo-spirituals" and mocked how refinement made them alien even to those to whom the spirituals were most familiar: "I have noticed that whenever an untampered-with congregation attempts the renovated spirituals, the people grow self-conscious. . . . Perhaps they feel on strange ground. Like the unlettered parent before his child just home from college."[13] Refurbished spirituals are recognizable but not quite the same as before.

If the notes were difficult to capture, so too was it difficult to duplicate the environment that generated the songs. Absent conditions as harsh as slavery, could the songs be repeated with as much emotion? How would the different experience of the non-slave African American in the late nineteenth century be expressed in song, a difference the black composer Nathaniel Dett alluded to as "the principle of ease"? He writes:

> One must remember that the young Negro student of today is not quite the slave of yesterday; a different outlook on life, the influence of the white man's education, of the concert-hall, the phonograph, and the radio, all in conjunction with the adventurous spirit characteristic of all youth, makes one hesitate to accept present-day arrangements as authentic, even though done by natives. Furthermore it has already been pointed out that it was a religious "urge" born of a great experience which gave rise to these songs; not having this experience it is impossible to get, and unreasonable to expect, a duplication of the primary effect.

This also explains why much of the present-day singing by colored people lacks something of the depth, sincerity, and pathos which marked that of other days and of which lack, many, remembering, justly complain.[14]

The repeated aim of collections of the songs was to "get back" to that "urge," a backward-focused temporality that was part and parcel of the forward-looking impulse of this new generation of African Americans. The goal was to achieve progress by preserving the past, a contradictory formula made smooth by a series of black authors, including Johnson and Hurston. Inevitably, as the poetry and beauty of the spirituals became recognized, charges appeared that the songs were derivative of white Christian hymns, which the slaves had adapted for their own purposes.[15] In response, writers as diverse as Johnson, Dett, Allen, and H. E. Krehbiel argued for the songs' originality to black and American culture.[16]

Perhaps, then, the most difficult aspect of collecting spirituals consisted of the apparently contradictory demands of the African Americans who had created the songs and those who wanted them preserved. Printed versions of the spirituals documented evidence of the Negro's artistic abilities and ensured that the songs could be handed down from one generation to the next. But that next generation was also the problem: ex-slaves sought to distance themselves from a form of expression so intimately attached to their former lives even as the remarkable poetry of the spirituals demanded that they be preserved before they completely disappeared. For Johnson, the imperative was even more significant in the 1920s: by illuminating the artistic beauty of the spirituals, as well as the other black creations developed on American soil, he could demonstrate the aesthetic sensibilities of African Americans—the one way, according to Johnson, for a group of people to be looked upon favorably by a nation.

Johnson's Aesthetics

Although it is sometimes easy to lump the elder statesmen of the 1920s together, Johnson's aesthetics help to distinguish him from the other "old guard" architects of the New Negro Movement. Johnson's wide and surprising range of interests placed him in the musical, literary, and cultural worlds as well as in politics and the law. He was one of the few elder African American intellectuals and leaders of the time to garner respect from a diverse group of black and white, young and established writers.[17] Well known for his 1912 novel *The Autobiography of an Ex-Colored Man,* Johnson has not received as much critical notice for his nonfiction writings on topics such as music and the spirituals.[18]

Before the *Opportunity* magazine awards dinner that announced the arrival of several young black writers, even before the publication in 1925 of *The New Negro,* the anthology edited by Alain Locke which collected the historical, literary, and visual strains of the Harlem Renaissance, the poet and scholar Johnson identified in several essays an emerging artistic element in the group of African Americans centered in New York. These essays are notable not only because they prefigure Locke's but also because Johnson pinpoints the need for literary, textual excellence to challenge visual images of blackness. Providing both a historical framework for past black poetic accomplishments and a guideline for future black poets, the introductory essays to *The Book of American Negro Poetry* and *The Book of American Negro Spirituals* present Johnson's ideas on how to change the social and cultural perception of the African American and the appraisal of African American art. In the process of providing this historical and creative frame, Johnson urges the elimination of a style of writing that has long been associated with the African American, and which he claims had reached its peak—American "Negro" dialect, the sounds traditionally captured on the printed page by means of misspelled words, malapropisms, and grammatical errors. Two elements of dialect, according to Johnson, make it inadequate for a writer desiring to evoke what Sterling Brown termed "complete, complex humanity."[19] First, as a form of black writing, dialect is simply unintelligible, too clunky on the printed page to be raised to the level of art. Second, dialect problematically calls forth or "conjures" a bodily permanence. The effect of dialect is to create the image of the African American as rooted to the past, that is, as unable to progress aesthetically from the slave tradition. By formulating sustained discussions about dialect and spirituals and the way they are presented to an American public, the prefaces situate the central concerns of representation and authenticity, black aesthetics and embodiment, language and the depiction of a "New Negro." *The Book of American Negro Poetry* and *The Book of American Negro Spirituals,* then, were more than compilations. They were concerted attempts to change and improve the regard for African American literature and music in the early twentieth century.

Dialect and *The Book of American Negro Poetry*

Dialect has been intimately linked with modernism on both sides of the Atlantic. According to Michael North in *The Dialect of Modernism,* Anglo-American modernism depended on the dialect rejected by Afro-American modernism, so

much so that "it is impossible to understand either modernism without reference to the other, without reference to the language they so uncomfortably
shared." Black dialect offered endless creative opportunities for white writers
such as Ezra Pound and T. S. Eliot, who appropriated black cultural expressions
in order to experiment with language and, to use the well-known modernist
injunction, "make it new." According to North's discussion of dialect, white
modernists seem to have had easy access to black dialect with no consequences,
since black dialect appears to function as an empty signifier by which to construct challenges to inherited European literary traditions. For Eliot, in the
poetic drama *Sweeney Agonistes,* for example, "blackness is both freedom and
servitude, opportunity and obstruction, variety and a blank absence." For
North, dialect appears as the white modern's creative muse and abject, rejected
other. But it is important to ask if the "freedom" appropriated by Pound and
Eliot was also available for the African American writer, if he or she vacillated
between linguistic extremes through dialect; or, in the words of the *Crisis* questionnaire, if instead "such 'freedom' in art [was] miserably unfair."[20] While
dialect offered a strategy for writers such as Eliot and Gertrude Stein to
challenge tradition and to reflect their outsider status, for others such as James
Weldon Johnson, dialect—what Johnson called the means of "delectation" for
"an outside group"—was the instrument of unflattering black representations and
perceived as a tool of racist propaganda by prominent writers of the plantation
tradition such as Thomas Nelson Page, author of *In Ole Virginia,* and Thomas
Dixon, author of *The Clansman.*[21]

Johnson's prefaces lay out a subtle case for the problem with dialect for the
early-twentieth-century African American writer, dialect's relationship of word
and image to mind and body, and the possible "corrections" to the appearance
and use of dialect. In the preface to *The Book of American Negro Poetry,* Johnson argues that a reconsideration of black people's talent will come about only
through advances in poetic and artistic expression. His early black literary criticism reveals the consequences of a perceived dependence on physical, bodily
qualities rather than mental activities to depict African Americans:

> A people may become great through many means, but there is only one measure
> by which its greatness is recognized and acknowledged. . . . No people that has
> produced great literature and art has ever been looked upon by the world as
> distinctly inferior.
>
> The status of the Negro in the United States is more a question of national
> mental attitude toward the race than of actual conditions. And nothing will do

more to change that mental attitude and raise his status than a demonstration of intellectual parity by the Negro through the production of literature and art.[22]

Written six decades after the Emancipation Proclamation, Johnson's statement recognizes the enduring problems African Americans faced in obtaining full rights as citizens despite their legal emancipation from slavery. Whatever the arguments for restricting opportunities for African Americans, the perception of a lack of culture, an absence of an aesthetic sense and sensibility, sustains majority belief in their inferior position.

Johnson notes, for instance, that whenever the black man is thought of artistically, that image almost always associates the artist with his body and an assumed instinctual rhythm. One way to challenge that perception is to stop using dialect or to alter the form dialect takes. In a rich paragraph, and in imagery similar to that which Alain Locke would employ three years later, Johnson laments the anachronistic permanence of dialect and calls for a new form of writing that better represents the progress of the race:

> When [the Negro] is thought of artistically, it is as a happy-go-lucky, singing, shuffling, banjo-picking being or as a more or less pathetic figure. The picture of him is in a log cabin amid fields of cotton or along the levees. Negro dialect is naturally and by long association the exact instrument for voicing this phase of Negro life. . . . [T]he Aframerican poet realizes that there are phases of Negro life in the United States which cannot be treated in the dialect either adequately or artistically. Take, for example, the phases rising out of life in Harlem, that most wonderful Negro city in the world. I do not deny that a Negro in a log cabin is more picturesque than a Negro in a Harlem flat, but the Negro in the Harlem flat is here, and he is but part of a group growing everywhere in the country, a group whose ideals are becoming increasingly more vital than those of the traditionally artistic group, even if its members are less picturesque. (*NP*, xl)

Johnson's ideas about dialect trace how African American oral expressions turn into visual images, into embodied stereotypes. Dialect calls forth the body, literally giving "voice" to an old image, and conjures up the "more pathetic figure." Rather than presenting the black artist in his own home or flat, reading, if not writing, his own poetry, dialect suggests the image of that older Negro sitting satisfied before his own, if not his master's, cabin. As the "exact instrument for voicing this phase of life," dialect mimics a way of life and compels an image of the black artist as slack body, a "happy-go-lucky, shuffling, banjo-picking being." Though characters by Charles Chesnutt and Paul Laurence Dunbar, and figures recounted by Joel Chandler Harris, do use dialect perceptively and deceptively, as a tool in a trickster's bag, such opportunities made available by wearing and speaking through a mask of dialect no longer appeal to Johnson, who, as he notes elsewhere in his preface, used such dialect in theatrical songs he composed in his earlier years with his brother. The trickery available through this form of writing confers a fairly individual and localized success that contrasts here with Johnson's pointed emphasis on the group.[23] Dialect writing transmits a stagnant picture of the black American, creating an anachronistic, rigid effect Johnson calls the "picturesque." In moving from the more to the less picturesque, Johnson performs a spatial move from the South to the North, from "fields of cotton" to a "Harlem flat," enacting a metaphorical version of the Great Migration and a linguistic version of what Robert Stepto terms the "ascent" in African American literature.[24]

But what exactly is this "picturesque"? And why does Johnson find it untenable? The "picturesque," an art-historical term, functions here as a racialized word denoting visual pleasure, an aesthetically pleasing reference to diversity. Reading turn-of-the-century descriptions of travels into the exotic but "charming" parts of New York, Carrie Tirado Bramen illustrates how the "picturesque" has been racialized in American contexts, particularly in cities with large immigrant populations. The "picturesque" is pleasing but safe; it refers to immigrants from eastern European countries who display an acceptable form of whiteness. Though Bramen alerts us to the different valences of the picturesque, a key term in the "rhetoric of [American] variety," she argues that the urban picturesque does not include New York's black inhabitants, for "blackness signaled the representational limit of the picturesque" in that blackness was assumed to be incapable of conveying the various shades of difference that would attract native-born white Americans without scaring them.[25] And yet in the 1920s, scenes of a picturesque blackness filled American novels and magazines—not as pleasing but as *pleasure*, as the space for sexual and artistic experimentation. Harlem in particular appeared to be outside the bounds of convention.[26] Bramen unintentionally highlights the paradox of the term "picturesque" as it would repetitively appear in white descriptions of the Negro mecca and its inhabitants: blackness operates as the "banished" picturesque, a departure from accepted standards.[27] More detailed possibilities of the term "picturesque" are revealed in *The Autobiography of an Ex-Colored Man*. Even Southern whites are, in the words of Johnson's unnamed narrator, "picturesque": "The Southern whites are in many respects a great people. Looked at from a certain point of view, they are picturesque. If one will put himself in a romantic frame of mind, he can admire their notions of chivalry and bravery and justice." But like the stereotype of the "banjo-playing uncle," picturesque whites are rooted to a past time that ignores the progress of (Northern) civilization, for the ex-colored man continues in his thinking, "The southern whites are not yet living quite in the present age; many of their general ideas hark back to a former century, some of them to the Dark Ages."[28]

In *The Book of American Negro Poetry* Johnson evinces a hierarchal dichotomy between images and some other, non-dialect mode of textual representation. He suggests that it is now time for the advancement of members of a group who are "less picturesque": taken literally, less pleasing to the eye; taken figuratively, less associated with the embodied debasement (that is, the pathos) of the shuffling old Negro. The cumulative effect of the passage, coupled with Johnson's earlier call for "great literature and art," implies a privileging of word over (minstrel-like) image.[29]

Johnson criticizes dialect because the unintellectual "remnant[s]" of dialect never dissolve.[30] Dialect as critiqued by Johnson remains positioned in a historical moment rooted in the plantation and the cabin; it denies the temporal progression implied in the term "New Negro." This sense of stagnation is further developed in Johnson's *Book of American Negro Spirituals,* published in 1925. As a special use of dialect, the song lyrics to the printed spirituals, as well as the printed spirituals themselves, are a more concrete example of textual maladjustments, and as such they demonstrate more markedly—more physically and visually—the problems inherent in this type of writing as it has been produced by others.

Dialect and *The Book of American Negro Spirituals*

Johnson's ambivalence about the body becomes more noticeable in the preface to *The Book of American Negro Spirituals.* In this collection, which he coauthored with his brother Rosamond, Johnson makes a distinction between spirituals as they are printed on a page and spirituals as they are "felt." The written, physical notation of the spirituals can never adequately represent the elusiveness of this genre of song. Johnson, like later critics, observes that in order to notate the spirituals and present dialect on the page, writers often relied on "mutilations of English spelling and pronunciation" (*NP,* xli), "the absurd practice of devising a clumsy, outlandish, so-called phonetic spelling for words . . . when the regular English spelling represents the very same sound" (*NP,* 44).[31] As suggested earlier, the duplication of the spirituals on the page renders them less true to their form: "I doubt that it is possible with our present system of notation to make a fixed transcription of these peculiarities that would be absolutely true; for in their very nature they are not susceptible to fixation" (*NS*, 30). Furthermore, rather than offering a factual recording of a song, the written language of the spirituals belies the subtlety of the spoken words and is "far from [their] true manner and spirit" (*NS*, 30). The written copies of spirituals are inauthentic versions, then, and the further away one gets from the source, the less original the song becomes. Johnson demonstrates the dilemma for anyone who wants to preserve the spirituals for future generations: it is only by being written down that the spirituals will continue to survive, but written dialect has the potential to bastardize these songs, as Johnson himself realizes when he collects and prints the spirituals (*NS*, 46).[32]

In addition, the written form of the spirituals may be read and performed too literally. Commenting on the trouble Europeans have in playing black music, the "difficulty of getting the 'swing' of it" (*NS*, 28), Johnson writes that their main problem is that they read the music too exactly; "they play the notes too correctly; and do not play what is not written down" (*NS*, 28). Confining oneself to the fixed notes on the page limits the musician. There are no possibilities for experimentation or play, no potential for improvisation. The threat of written notations is that they stabilize an old image: they present the language of the spirituals within the realm of minstrelsy, far removed from the felt experience of the songs.

We may be cautious about Johnson's ideas, for his theories about dialect appear to invoke an essentialist relationship to black language and black music—the belief that only African Americans can translate such expression to paper and, furthermore, that only African Americans can give voice to the artistic emotion behind the spirituals. But Johnson does argue persuasively that dialect in the hands of any writer and spirituals from any singer's mouth can turn into slapstick. There are "two extremes" in singing spirituals: "to attempt to render a Spiritual as though it were a Brahms song, or to assume a 'Negro unctuousness' that is obviously false, and painfully so." Johnson then continues to refine his antiessentialist stance: "I think white singers, concert singers, can sing Spirituals—if they *feel* them. But to feel them it is necessary to know the truth about their origin and history, to get in touch with the association of ideas that surround them, and to realize something of what they have meant in the experiences of the people who created them. In a word, the capacity to *feel* these songs while singing them is more important than any amount of mere artistic technique" (*NS*, 29). It is a distinction that should make not just white singers, but also black singers, wary: "I have seen more than one colored singer floundering either in the 'art' or the 'exhibition' pit. The truth is, these songs . . . are not concert material for the mediocre soloist" (*NS*, 29). What at first appears to be Johnson's insistence on an authentic relation to the spirituals above all else is in actuality a call to research and study the history of these songs and to refuse the easy solution offered by either the caricatures of dialect or the showy display of "mere artistic technique." Johnson's terms for this dichotomy of possible extremes, between "art" and "exhibition," illustrate the division the singer of the spirituals must overcome: that space between pretentious "serious" art and superficial visual display.

Intriguingly, Johnson refers to the body in order to delineate a better, higher form of black musical expression. Dividing African American music into two categories, the religious and the secular, he distinguishes between them by noting the bodily movements each musical genre compels: the swaying and swinging identified with the eloquent spirituals and the patting of the hands and feet identified with secular songs. He first delineates the spirituals:

> We were discussing the "swing" of the Spirituals, and were saying how subtle and elusive a thing it was. It is the more subtle and elusive because there is still further intricacy in the rhythms. The swaying of the body marks the regular beat or, better, surge, for it is something stronger than a beat, and is more or less, not precisely, strict in time; but the Negro loves nothing better in his music than to play with the fundamental beat and pound it out with his left hand, almost monotonously; while with his right hand he juggles it. (*NS*, 29–30)

Johnson describes the spirituals by observing the movements of the musician, playing the "fundamental beat" with the left hand and "worrying the line" with the right.[33] The sway and swing of the spiritual is in contrast to the performance of secular music, in which "the fundamental beat is chiefly maintained by the patting of one foot, while the hands clap out intricate and varying rhythmic patterns. It should be understood that the foot is not marking straight time, but what Negroes call 'stop time,' or what the books have no better definition for than 'syncopation.' The strong accent or down beat is never lost, but is playfully bandied from hand to foot and from foot to hand" (*NS*, 31).

But how is Johnson's reliance on the body here different from the earlier problematic invocations of the body in Negro dialect? How is the sway, the swing, or the clap different from what someone such as Charlotte Forten objects to, the uncontained body involved in the "shout"? What, and who, defines the "proper" use of the body in discussing black expression? Johnson's allusion to the body in his prefaces is ambivalent; although he attempts to move beyond the body by advocating "less picturesque" representations of blackness, he depends on the body in order to delineate the elusive elements of black expression.

Johnson's attempt to raise black expressions into higher art forms curiously entails a *dematerialization* of the body, a figuration of the body that is, to use Johnson's words, "more or less, not precisely," present. In a reading of Johnson's prefaces, Brent Hayes Edwards locates "the espousal of what eludes" in black expression within the body, whether the expression is in the form of music, poetry, or a hybrid type of the lyric.[34] The body "manifests," "holds," or "realizes" the elusive elements of black expression, so that "vernacular musical form is transcribed through a figure of the black body." Edwards attaches importance to an effect he calls a "realization." In his argument, blues poetry functions precisely because the band is not present, and the reader must instead imagine this construction: "Perhaps the power of the blues as a form is intimately linked to the fact that we are not offered a realization; the performance setting and musical backdrop are absent or unavailable."[35] In other words, blues poems such as those by Langston Hughes work because they are "less picturesque"; they force the reader to conjure them herself, and the band escapes physical materialization in the genre of blues poems.[36]

Similarly, in Johnson's formulations the black body does not have to be present to model these elusive moments. In perhaps an extreme form of less picturesque blackness, it can be "realized." It is through the body—whether the individual's body or the collective body of the congregation—that the "swing" of black music "manifests" itself. Johnson's descriptions of both religious and secular music evoke the mental image of the black body marking time. In embodied formulations of the spirituals and secular music, the body not only defines the music but also models the unusual temporality inherent in both musical forms. Each additional attempt to concretize the ineffable elements of musical blackness—"a minute fraction of a beat," the "playfully bandied beat," "what the books have no better definition for than syncopation"—leads to further emanations of an indescribable element. Only with the inclusion of the "realized" body does some semblance of stasis appear. The black body becomes the referent that stabilizes the fluidity of the spirituals. Johnson relies on the body at the moment when black expression resists "conventional" expression. Body parts mark not only the "fundamental beats" but those *other* beats as well, those that are juggled, bandied, syncopated—music and moments that resist the certitude of the stereotype, or the "exact" voice of Negro dialect.

Johnson's reliance on the body reflects the larger problem of trying to quantify the black modern, of trying to capture, like Thomas Wentworth Higginson, elements of black expression that are resistant to stable or literal referents. The otherwise inexpressible distinction among black musical styles is thus an embodied—and visual—difference, the disparity between a sway and a pat; and Johnson's calculated distinctions among physical movements offer a careful reading of the body that contradicts the perception of an uncontrolled black bodily mass, primitively moving to music. Johnson, then, rejects not the category of the body but the conceptualization of the body either as "fixed" in one place, set and unchanging, with no ability to move, rise, or advance, or as wildly "shuffling," so familiar to the minstrel stereotype.

THE TWO characteristics of dialect identified by Johnson in *The Book of American Negro Poetry* and *The Book of American Negro Spirituals*—temporal inaccuracy and developmental stagnation—thus situate it within both a visual and a linguistic system. This "picturesque" literary and visual art form contains the qualities of language and the characteristics attributed to the black body. There are other dualities of language and the body that Johnson presents in his prefaces (for example, juggling versus pounding, terseness versus diffuseness). The effect and potential of dialect concern Johnson to such an extent that he returns to the subject repeatedly in his writings, always to highlight the previous ineffectiveness of the device of dialect, which evokes an overembodied black image consisting of "exaggerated geniality, childish optimism, forced comicality, and mawkish sentiment."[37] What is significant about the prefaces, then, is the way in which Johnson associates attributes of language with the negative representation of the black body: dialect deformed becomes a linguistic version of the minstrel tradition. In order for dialect to remain viable, the black writer must use it without recourse to "humor or pathos" and must learn how to call up not the black body of the past but the artistic feeling of an as yet (in 1922) undefined period.

Other Approaches to a "Living Language"

It is important to note that Johnson is not against dialect itself; rather he is opposed to the way dialect has been represented and used. He notes, for instance, that "it would be a distinct loss if the American Negro poets threw away this quaint and musical folk-speech as a medium of expression" (*NP*, xl). The problem is that too few writers are able to infuse diversity into the one-dimensionality of it. This form of writing is "not capable of giving expression to the varied conditions of Negro life in America, and much less is it capable of giving the fullest interpretation of Negro character and psychology" (*NP*, xli). Dialect fails as an artistic method because of its inability to represent a progressive image of the African American as one who has taken advantage of the limited opportunities available in the early twentieth century; instead dialect conjures up an "old Negro," one who seems, in this moment of newness and change, distinctly rooted in an anachronistic past. Moreover, dialect implicitly does not participate in what Johnson calls "a living language." Commenting on the refusal of the *New York Times* to capitalize the word "Negro," an issue George Schuyler and H. L. Mencken also discuss, Johnson noted that "words in a living language have no fixed value or meaning. Many words are born and go through various changes in meaning; often they absolutely die; and sometimes they are reborn with still a different shade of meaning."[38] According to this definition, black dialect, rooted to an embodied stereotype on the page and in the American imagination, was *not* a living language.

These criticisms of dialect were expressed by other writers such as Sterling Brown, Langston Hughes, and Zora Neale Hurston, yet not all of them were as convinced as Johnson that dialect had reached its full potential. In a fascinating exchange of letters, for instance, Brown explained to Johnson how folk expressions animated his dialect poetry and provided a way to reshape black sound. Discussing Johnson's draft of the introduction to Brown's *Southern Road* (1932), Brown is at pains to demonstrate that his poetic sources derived from folk life and folk experience rather than the already assembled folk ballads:

> What I am most desirous of being known is that I have zealously attempted to understand and interpret folk life—in a manner as you have clearly and ably indicated, different from the minstrel, plantation tradition. That folk life is my unfailing source. The folk ballads (John Henry, etc.) stem from the same source.
>
> This isn't to deny my overwhelming interest in these ballads; I treasure them—but generally as indices to folk life, never as ultimate sources. Who wouldn't want to do a John Henry? But it's done. And as you have indicated mere reportorial photography of it would never mean real poetry.[39]

Brown rejects a one-to-one replication of the ballads, a simple transcription, which he equates with photography and which would not make "real poetry" possible. Clearly Brown's anxiety is that his work may be perceived as merely derivative. Unlike the dialect writers who were more concerned with "echo[ing] the minstrel or plantation traditions of dialect usage rather than its vital origins," and for whom creative inspiration occurred several steps removed from the actual source, Brown engaged with folk life rather than the songs and ballads based on that life; and he was apprehensive that this engagement would not be recognized by the reader of his poems.[40] In the published version of the introduction, Johnson acknowledges the imaginative originality of Brown's poems, praising the way Brown "absorbed the spirit of his material, [and] made it his own."[41] Brown's close experience with Southern black dialect also enabled him to appreciate Zora Neale Hurston's black vernacular in *Their Eyes Were Watching God* (1937). Like Brown, Hurston disagreed with Johnson regarding the future of dialect. In his review of her novel, Brown acknowledged Hurston's skill in "the recording and the creation of folk speech" and praised the novel's "earthy and touching poetry."[42] For Brown, *Their Eyes* demonstrated the powerful effect black dialect can achieve when handled by an informed writer.[43]

Hurston's theories of black language are intriguing because, like Johnson's, they incorporate a visual paradigm; but whereas Johnson advocates abandoning black dialect, at least as it had been used by white writers, Hurston revises our understanding of both stereotypical dialect and standard English. The language she describes in fact clarifies the sometimes vague descriptor "standard English" and more adequately represents the black vernacular that, she claims, white writers have failed to render into print. In her essay "Characteristics of Negro Expression," Hurston articulates a process of "dressing up" stereotypical dialect and staid standard language so that they function more concretely, a manner of revision she calls "adornment." Appearing in *Negro* (1934), Nancy Cunard's eclectic tribute to African and African American culture, "Characteristics" posits a theory of modern black expression, a manifesto proclaiming the relation of the black modern to language, style, and dance.[44] In Hurston's wide-ranging analysis of black vernacular patterns, verbal expressions are consistently clarified by the visual. That is, actions influence phrases so that verbal and physical expressions reveal similar attributes. A quality such as "asymmetry," for instance, not only defines the "quick changes" in black dances and the "frequent change of key and time" in black music, such as the blues, but also captures the juxtapositions of ideas in Langston Hughes's poetry (CNE, 26). Hurston's analysis demonstrates how closely African American language is to the aural and the visual, dependent on sound and rhythm as well as performance.

"Characteristics of Negro Expression" functions as a key text for a discussion on early African American modernism, not just because of Hurston's explicit ideas about the body and language but because of her concept of the body *in* language as well. In trying to describe black expression, Hurston consistently turns to the body to exemplify her ideas. Consider, for example, the young boy who, through his pose, "exults 'Ah, female, I am the eternal male, the giver of life. Behold in my hot flesh all the delights of this world.'" Or the young girl who knows she is attractive and reveals her self-confidence not with words but through the body. Hurston refers to both instances as "little plays by strolling players . . . acted out daily" (CNE, 24). Her treatise on black expression complicates any theory of language that confines blackness or the black body to stable signifiers of meaning, that would render the black body into what Lindon Barrett has called an "obdurate materiality."[45] She details a system of communication that works in a different fashion from one significantly invested in blackness as the absence of meaning: "Action. Everything illustrated. So we can say the white man thinks in a written language and the Negro thinks in hieroglyphics" (CNE, 39). Her distinction recognizes pictures as a language, as "hieroglyphs," the visual as an expressive system in and of itself. "Characteristics of Negro Expression" is a model of negotiating the abstract and the concrete elements of black language, and though her discussion of black language is at times romantic, Hurston's essay challenges the stereotypes of dialect.[46]

Though not explicitly mentioned in "Characteristics of Negro Expression," imagism would appear to be a close cousin to the verbal nouns that appear in Hurston's essay. Hurston's black modernist manifesto reinvents Ezra Pound's essay "A Stray Document" (1934). Pound's injunction to "go in fear of abstractions" privileges specificity. He writes that "an 'Image' is that which presents an intellectual and emotional complex in an instant of time." Pound's aphorisms suggest the immediacy of the imagist poem.[47] For Hurston, intangible expressions, what she calls "detached language," must be rendered concrete with pictures. In her formulation, the use of a word to describe an idea or an object should be "close-fitting," as exact as possible (CNE, 39). And yet Hurston's close-fittingness is not quite the same as Pound's "Precision." When Hurston describes, for example, a black family's style, those elements of close-fittingness and angularity appear in the decorations of the family abode, which is anything but "precise." The living room reveals an appreciation for art that is visual but also cumulative and collective. Hurston's description of the black home is worth quoting at length in order for us to appreciate the elaborate setting and design of the room:

> On the walls of the homes of the average Negro one always finds a glut of gaudy calendars, wall pockets, and advertising lithographs. I saw in Mobile a room in which there was an over-stuffed mohair living-room suite, an imitation mahogany bed and chifferobe, a console victrola. The walls were gaily papered with Sunday supplements of the *Mobile Register.* There were seven calendars and three wall pockets. One of them was decorated with a lace doily. The mantelshelf was covered with a scarf of deep home-made lace, looped up with a huge bow of pink crepe paper. Over the door was a huge lithograph showing the Treaty of Versailles being signed with a Waterman fountain pen.
>
> It was grotesque, yes. But it indicated the desire for beauty. And decorating a decoration, as in the case of the doily on the gaudy wall pocket, did not seem out of place to the hostess. The feeling back of such an act is that there can never be enough of beauty, let alone too much. (CNE, 40)

Whereas Pound would advocate a minimalist yet keen standard for language, adornment functions here according to an aesthetic principle of the surplus. "Decorating a decoration" conveys an impulse to possess and personalize commodities, but through measured additions. The surfeit of possessions also exemplifies the distinctions between Hurston's black dialect and the kind critiqued by Johnson. Unlike the Northern, urban Harlem flat Johnson describes in *The Book of American Negro Poetry,* Hurston's room in Alabama is packed with various commodities to convey beauty. The "Negro in the Harlem flat" does not animate as pleasurable a mental image as the banjo-playing uncle in the plantation cabin; Johnson's almost nondescript living space is "less picturesque." The difference between Hurston's dialect and the dialect that Johnson criticizes, in short, is one of visual degrees.

Hurston, then, presents alternative possibilities of black dialect, and her delineations thus help to clarify further Johnson's position on the genre and refine Johnson's ambiguous, and ambivalent, use of the body in his theories. Offering one of the few discussions that examine Johnson's and Hurston's theories of dialect, spirituals, and the sermons together, Eric Sundquist identifies the subtle differences between Hurston and Johnson as having to do with the degree to which white expectations about the spirituals saturated the songs: "The question was not at what point the spirituals or their derivatives became white, but at what point they ceased to be black."[48] His discussion raises a number of questions in the context of a visually inflected representation of the black vernacular. Sundquist suggests that Hurston's dialect is better than "standard" Negro dialect and better than the revised dialect Johnson attempts in *God's Trombones*. But in what way is Hurston's an improvement?

Like Johnson, Hurston perceived written spirituals as derivative. But unlike him, she was able to effect a change by inserting movement into the written text through her idea of "adornment" and "verbal nouns." Johnson's "picturesque" and Hurston's "decorating a decoration" are visual paradigms that measure the degree of black performance. The body appears in both Johnson's and Hurston's formulations of dialect but with quite different effects. There is a definite sense of freedom of the body in Hurston's analyses. Johnson's prescriptions for elevating dialect into a higher art form called for an understated adornment of language and a controlled "sway" and "pat" of the body that contrasted with Hurston's exuberant "decorating a decoration." What determines that subtle but "decided aesthetic gulf between Johnson and Hurston" regarding the spirituals is the body.[49] Johnson and Hurston present different conceptions of the body and, as a consequence, of the image/text duality in black fiction. Hurston's writings exhibit a recourse to embodiment that, I would argue, James Weldon Johnson did not see as possible or productive for his own literary projects and that he fails to recognize in his discussion of dialect and the spirituals.[50] The difference between Hurston and Johnson, in other words, appears to be that between the body and the valuation of text. In contrast to Johnson, who seems to privilege word *over* image,[51] as suggested in the movement from the more to the less visually inflected, Hurston's essay erases the boundary between word and image; these two elements of black expression are "close-fitting," necessary, and dependent on each other for producing the best meaning.[52]

Johnson argues, in contrast, that a different kind of writing by black authors, a different kind of inscription, must be used if the "true spirit" of the African American is to be demonstrated successfully. These new forms may not create such a nostalgic picture for the white reader—that is, they may be "less picturesque" than dialect—but they will more adequately reflect the sense of newness infecting a young group of writers, particularly a group located in the urban space of Harlem. It is not that Johnson does not want to call forth the body; it is that he wants to call forth a different image of the black body, one distinguishable from the familiar physical stereotypes: "What the coloured poet in the United States needs to do is something like what Synge did for the Irish; he needs to find a form that will express the racial spirit by symbols from within, rather than by symbols from without."[53] Challenging the image and theory of the racialized "more" picturesque, of the African American as "all body" and little mind, Johnson attempts to alter the ontology of black art, which is itself assumed to be in and of the body. For Johnson, the new type of black writing he wanted to develop would alter how the black body itself is perceived, thus challenging the simplistic rigidity of the black body in the existing sign system.

Johnson's own experiment with dialect, the poems of *God's Trombones*, would help him give voice to an image, specifically, to use W. J. T. Mitchell's term, a "verbal image."[54] More than just refuting the oversimplification of the African American image, Johnson's optimistic argument would ideally energize the black arts as well.

Johnson's Experiment

Designed to put into practice the ideas articulated in the two prefaces, *God's Trombones* adjusted the picture created by the tradition of black dialect and challenged conventional ideas of black language. Instead of using the unreadable marks associated with Negro dialect, Johnson represented the black vernacular without the distorting visual components. His experiment with a new vernacular in *God's Trombones* was thus an attempt to erase the visual deformation of the black body that is contained within the representation of Negro dialect. *God's Trombones* illustrates as well the difficulty of challenging linguistic conventions and "freeing the language." His sermon-poems are not spontaneous but scripted recitations that belie the extemporaneity of the preachers. As I will show, the eventual legacy of the poems highlights one of its paradoxes: the verses of *God's Trombones* have been retranslated into various vehicles of performance that, notably, call upon the characteristics of the body and the visual.[55]

The poems in *God's Trombones* were Johnson's attempt to find and to form the "symbols from within." A collection of seven poems evocative of the sermon, *God's Trombones* revised dialect by using the words of common speech and by rejecting the faulty spelling of traditional Negro dialect. Early drafts of the sermons, Johnson's correspondence with friends, as well as the final version of the collection itself demonstrate the textualization of the black image. Three elements were essential to this experiment: the title of the poetic collection, the figure of the speaker, and the language of the speaker. And once again, Johnson's preface would play an important role.

The revisioning of sonic and vernacular possibilities begins with the title it-self. The difficulty Johnson had in selecting a name for his volume of poems throws into relief the challenge of finding the best medium for representing black speech. As with his other works, Johnson sought the help of friends to assist him in titling the sermons.[56] In a letter to Joel E. Spingarn, for instance, Johnson admitted to being "absolutely at a loss" in choosing a name. He pre-sented "a list of eight or ten titles" to his NAACP colleague and asked him to rank his choices (figure 1.1). Noting that some of Johnson's selections sounded "too Zane-Greyish," including, notably, the eventual title, Spingarn ranked "That Old Time Religion" as number one, possibly, as he tells Johnson, because of a "fondness for the spiritual."[57] But perhaps in an effort to guide his friend toward selecting "God's Trombones," Johnson includes in his letter a brief explanation for this phrase. Although Johnson was certain that he wanted to use a musical instrument to represent the constellation of music and voice, which instrument should it be: the trombone, the saxophone, or the trumpet? Significantly he chose the trombone, a brass instrument, because it is the one that best approximates the ranges possible in the human voice. The trombone "has its modern Negro connotations in its connection with the modern jazz band. It is the wind instrument that is nearest to the Negro's heart and colored perform-ers have done much to develop its modern use."[58] The image of the trombone, then, metonymically represented the tonality of black sound. The trombone, not the trumpet or saxophone, evoked the sound of the human voice. Johnson also exploits the intimate association of the instrument with black musicians. Although there was "a slight touch of the fantastic" about the title, the trom-bone quite literally helped Johnson answer the question of how to represent and "speak for" black America.[59] As he states in his autobiography *Along This Way,* "I had found it, the instrument and the word, of just the tone and timbre to represent the old-time Negro preacher's voice."[60]

Johnson further challenged the image created by dialect, the too familiar image of the "banjo-playing uncle," by selecting a new representative for his experiment, a figure who, like the uncle, was susceptible to satire yet, when his skills were highlighted, offered a bridge to black respectability. There was something almost old-fashioned about the spokesman Johnson used to recon-ceive the creativity of the black vernacular in the late 1920s. Johnson's poetic hero was not the African American professional or the young black writer of the North but another model of dexterity with language, the African Ameri-can Southern minister. The black preacher was an artist experienced in both

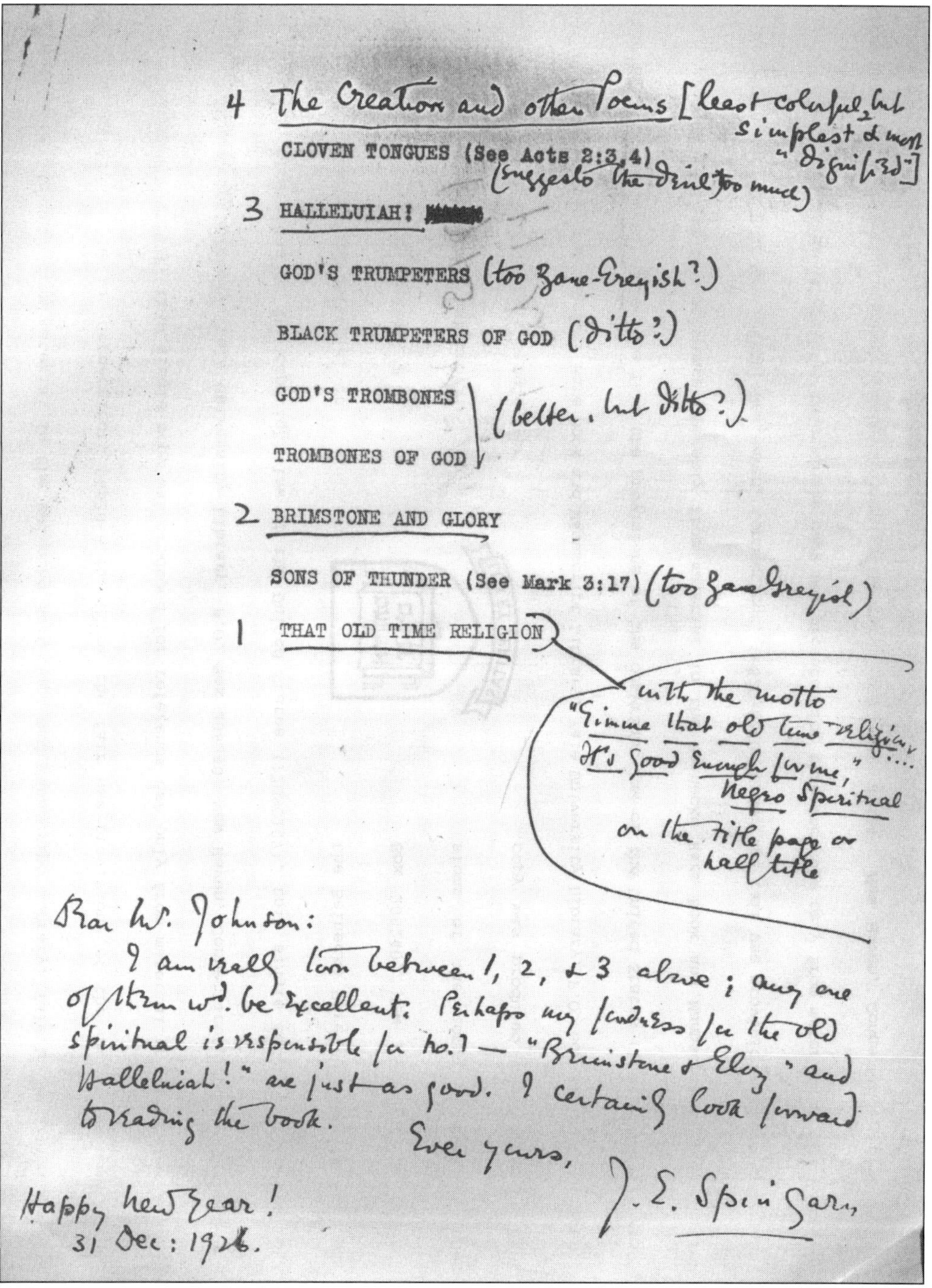

4 The Creation and other Poems [least colorful, but
                                      simplest & most
                                      "dignified"]

CLOVEN TONGUES (See Acts 2:3,4)
                    (suggests the devil too much)

3 HALLELUIAH!

GOD'S TRUMPETERS (too Zane-Greyish?)

BLACK TRUMPETERS OF GOD (ditto?)

GOD'S TROMBONES ⎫
                 ⎬ (better, but ditto?)
TROMBONES OF GOD ⎭

2 BRIMSTONE AND GLORY

SONS OF THUNDER (See Mark 3:17) (too Zane-Greyish)

1 THAT OLD TIME RELIGION

                        "with the motto
                        "Gimme that old time religion
                        It's good enough for me,"
                                    Negro Spiritual
                        on the title page or
                        half title

Dear Mr. Johnson:
    I am really torn between 1, 2, & 3 above; any one
of them wd. be excellent. Perhaps my fondness for the old
spiritual is responsible for no. 1 — "Brimstone & Glory" and
Halleluiah!" are just as good. I certainly look forward
to reading the book.
                        Ever yours,
                                    J. E. Spingarn
Happy New Year!
31 Dec: 1926.

Figure 1.1. Working titles, *God's Trombones*. Materials by James Weldon Johnson are reprinted by permission of Dr. Sondra Kathryn Wilson, Executor for the Estate of Grace and James Weldon Johnson. The James Weldon Johnson and Grace Nail Johnson Papers, Yale Collection of American Literature, Beinecke Rare Book and Manuscript Library, Yale University.

rhetoric and performance, but, as Hurston also claimed, his skill was neither fully appreciated by other African Americans nor known to those outside the group. In a letter to Johnson, Hurston criticizes a review of her book *Jonah's Gourd Vine* (1934), whose main character, John Pearson, is a preacher.[61] While the reviewer failed to note the oratorical power of the preacher, Hurston identifies in Johnson someone who recognizes the verbal influence of the black man of the cloth.

> It just seems that he [the reviewer] is unwilling to believe that a Negro preacher could have so much poetry in him. When you and I (who seem to be the only ones even among Negroes who recognize the barbaric poetry in their sermons) know that there are hundreds of preachers who are equaling that sermon weekly. He does not know that merely being a good man is not enough to hold a Negro preacher in an important charge. He must also be an artist. He must be both a poet and an actor of a very high order, and then he must have the voice of the figure. [62]

Without doubt, African American religious men suffered from negative perceptions among the American public. Even Booker T. Washington's reminiscences, for example, cast aspersions against them. In an incident Washington first wrote about in the *Christian Union* and then repeated in *Up from Slavery,* he relates a humorous version of the "call" that compels preachers to seek the life of the church: "The character of many of these preachers can be judged by one, of whom it is said that, while he was at work in a cotton field in the middle of July, he suddenly stopped, looked upward, and said, 'O Lord, de work is so hard, de cotton is so grassy, and de sun am so hot, I bleave dis darkey am called to preach.'"[63] Johnson sought to elevate the black preacher from an object of ridicule, as in this account by Washington of a figure "saved" from hard labor, to the place of honor that he held in black communities, as Hurston suggests in her letter.[64]

Johnson spotlights the verbal feats of the black Southern preacher in *The Autobiography of an Ex-Colored Man,* when, near the end of the novel, the unnamed narrator observes in silent wonder preacher John Brown's performance: "He knew all the arts and tricks of oratory, the modulation of the voice to almost a whisper, the pause for effect, the rise through light, rapid-fire sentences to the terrific, thundering outburst of an electrifying climax. In addition, he had the intuition of a born theatrical manager. Night after night this man held me fascinated. He convinced me that, after all, eloquence consists more in the manner of saying than in what is said. It is largely a matter of tone pictures."[65] Johnson's term for the effect of Brown's verbal skills reflects the distinctly visual quality of the preacher's language and performance. "Tone pictures" suggests the union of sound and sight, the tonal eloquence hoped for but not achieved with the talking picture. With "tone pictures," Johnson captures the polarities of abstract and concrete expressions which mark black representation and Negro dialect itself. The Ex-Colored Man's comment betrays a privileging of style over substance, a subtle tension between orality, the manner in which something is said, and sermonic content, or the substance of what is said. Walter Ong examines this tension in his discussion of the transformation of oral culture into print culture, noting that the "spoken word is always an event, a movement in time, completely lacking in the thing-like repose of the written or printed word."[66] For Johnson the question becomes: How does one capture "the event" in print? How can he make the orality of the preacher as seductive textually as it was in person?

In light of the regard Johnson had for the black preacher, it is perhaps surprising that the poem that was to begin *God's Trombones* actually recapitulated a picture of the preacher that, while not exactly negative, did reflect the sense of comedy which had attached itself to that figure. Johnson originally composed an introductory poem to the sermons, "The Reverend Jasper Jones," written in rhymed couplets. More lighthearted than the others, the poem describes the preacher-speaker of the sermons. It notably focuses on Jones's body, from his head to his feet, and pays particular attention to the relation of his body to his oratorical powers:

I see him now, the Reverend Jasper Jones,
A man of medium height but massive bones.

A ponderous head, a brow both wide and full,
A neck like that of Bashan's famous bull.

His shoulders broad and thick and slightly humped,
A chest which held a pair of lungs that pumped

Of air to larynx such a monstrous deal
As gave his voice the sound of an organ peal.

Quickly to make this catalog complete,
Add on short arms, bow legs and ample feet.[67]

Jones's portly form seems to enable a deep, majestic sound, in Hurston's words, "the voice of the figure." Johnson ultimately eliminated the poem from the collection, perhaps because it contrasted too starkly with the dignity of the other sermons. "The Reverend Jasper Jones" would have been the only lyric in the

collection with a rhyme scheme.[68] Though it helped to establish the atmosphere and mirrored the actual event and speaker that sparked the sermons, the
poem itself would also not have worked in the collection because of its lighthearted description of the preacher's body. The poem offered in its place, "Listen Lord—A Prayer," does a better job of suggesting understated religious sup-
plication and illustrates yet another distinction between Johnson and Hurston.
In Hurston's analyses, God is as little revered as the devil, and both are "treated
no more reverently than Rockefeller and Ford" (CNE, 42). In contrast, in
"Listen Lord—A Prayer" there is a marked sense of veneration for both God
and His servants.

In his final, and riskiest, experiment with dialect, Johnson attempted to "fix
something" of this "rapidly passing figure" in language that had to accomplish
several tasks (GT, 11). The poet does not employ the traditional dialect of which
he had been so critical, not only because of its limitations, but also because
Johnson recognized the expansive oratorical performance of black preachers:
"The old-time Negro preachers, though they actually used dialect in their ordinary intercourse, stepped out from its narrow confines when they preached. . . .
[W]hen they preached and warmed to their work they spoke another language,
a language far removed from traditional Negro dialect" (GT, 9). In Johnson's
case, experiencing the preacher's oral and physical performance is so powerful
that it motivates his own writing experiment: the preacher's creative energy is
sublimated into the artistic production of God's Trombones. Johnson achieves
this transformation of black art even more precisely in yet another preface.

The preface to God's Trombones, like the other preludes Johnson wrote (he
dryly wondered in his autobiography Along This Way if he was "condemned
to do a preface for every book that [he] should write"), delivers a lesson, this
time on the preacher and his product, the sermon.[69] Providing a brief history of
the origin and status of the preacher in African American culture, the preface
also elevates certain sermons to canonical status, such as "The Valley of the
Dry Bones" and "The Train Sermon." Johnson also uses this opportunity to reevaluate the stereotypes of religious men and their language. Preachers welcomed
the challenge of biblical exegesis, and the ambiguous parables of the Bible
offered puzzles ripe for interpretation. Consider the example Johnson gives of
the preacher who reads "a rather cryptic passage" and then informs his congregation, "Brothers and sisters, this morning—I intend to explain the unexplainable—
find out the undefinable—ponder over the imponderable—and unscrew the
inscrutable." One objective of Johnson's preface is to gloss and then reject the

comedy of "gross exaggeration of big words," the frequently comedic portrayal of the preacher with his fondness for multisyllabic terms. Rather than touting the preacher's knowledge of language, Johnson notes his "highly developed sense of sound and rhythm" (*GT,* 9); and, Johnson points out, the elucidation of biblical passages by relying on a musical use of words is one outlet for this skill.

What is most interesting about this preface is the tension it stages between orality and literacy and Johnson's own role as a spectator in this drama. In the prefaces to *The Book of American Negro Poetry* and *The Book of American Negro Spirituals,* Johnson's learned demeanor paves the way for the reader's appreciation of the oral and the vernacular. Johnson's presentation of black oral culture conditions the reader's reception of it, shaping a favorable response. But in the preface to *God's Trombones,* although Johnson acknowledges the important role preachers have played in the African American's movement from slavery to freedom, one notes a slight cynicism regarding religion and the rhetoric of the preachers. This ambivalence toward both religion and rhetoric is evident as well in *Along This Way,* when Johnson recalls his experiences as a student at Atlanta University. Despite his eventual success as a debater, he admits that "for rhetorical oratory I have absolute distrust." Notably the discussion of the duplicity made possible by oratory is immediately followed by an account of Johnson's dislike of the prayer meetings at his school: "I doubt not that there were students who enjoyed these prayer meetings and were spiritually benefited, but I believe the main effect was to put a premium on hypocrisy or, almost as bad, to substitute for religion a lazy and stupid conformity."[70] In short, although Johnson appreciates the preacher's presence as a "vital factor" in the black person's development, there is also a subtle suspicion of the preacher's practice. In the other prefaces Johnson's admiration for the poetry found in dialect and the spirituals is unquestionable. But here his description of the preacher's oratory, which can sometimes consist of "the rhythmic intoning of sheer incoherencies," limits one's appreciation of its full power (*GT,* 5).

Moreover, Johnson pokes fun at himself and his skeptical view of religion in the preface to *God's Trombones,* becoming a character in the narrative he creates about the preacher's performance; as reluctant observer, he thus stands in for the potentially supercilious reader. Johnson initially finds some correspondence between himself and the preacher. He has, after all, just completed his own presentations and lectures to four separate black churches in one night; and if Johnson's talks were not "formal sermon[s] from a formal text," as the preacher's were, they were at least scripted to allow for multiple citations. In addition, Johnson appears reserved here when he attempts to excuse himself from attending yet another church service: "I demurred, making the quotation about the willingness of the spirit and the weakness of the flesh, for I was dead tired." But Johnson's reluctance becomes the preacher's test, for by the end of the night, the preacher and the preacher's performance have aroused the religious sentiment of even an agnostic such as Johnson: "I sat fascinated; and more, I was, perhaps against my will, deeply moved; the emotional effect upon me was irresistible. Before he had finished I took a slip of paper and somewhat surreptitiously jotted down some ideas for the first poem, 'The Creation'" (*GT*, 6–7) What more effective way to demonstrate the power of the preacher than by having Johnson, "the distinguished visitor," inspired "against [his] will" by the man of the cloth. It provides an apt example of the transfiguration Johnson hopes for: the physical, stimulating effect of the preacher is transformed into art. By offering this episode in detail, Johnson performs the type of movement from the more to the less "picturesque" which he advocates in the two other prefaces, and he models the distance and the disengagement needed to enact such transmissions.

The poem that resulted from Johnson's call to write, "The Creation," is an aptly titled challenge to the old form of dialect writing. Written in 1918 and published in 1920, it is one of Johnson's best-known verses. The body here is an especially complicated construct for Johnson within the terms he sets out for himself in *God's Trombones*. As drafts of the poems and Johnson's correspondence with the African American anthologist William Stanley Braithwaite indicate, it is ironically the precise moment of "creation," the actual moment when God creates man and man's body, that Johnson, as with those inexpressibly "black" moments in black music, had the most difficulty putting into words.[71]

The body makes its appearance throughout "The Creation." Johnson offers an "anthropomorphic" God, one who, through His physical movements, creates the earth and animals:

> And God stepped out on space,
> And he looked around and said:
> I'm lonely—
> I'll make me a world.
> .   .   .   .
>
> Then God smiled,
> And the light broke,
> And the darkness rolled up on one side,

And the light stood shining on the other,
And God said: That's good!
. . . .

And the earth was under his feet.
And God walked, and where he trod
His footsteps hollowed the valleys out
And bulged the mountains up. (*GT,* 17–18)

Although the poem asserts the desire for a self-sufficient body, a fantasy of one who can create within and from himself, without recourse to others, "The Creation" also functions as an intriguing microcosm of the problems of language, the visual, and the body. As with his discussion of spirituals, Johnson cannot advance his argument without reference to embodiment, for he must depend on the black female figure to emancipate the masculine form. Indeed he relies on the black woman's body even at the very moment when God embodies man:

... the great God Almighty
Who lit the sun and fixed it in the sky,
Who flung the stars to the most far corner of the night,
Who rounded the earth in the middle of his hand;
This Great God,
Like a mammy bending over her baby,
Kneeled down in the dust
Toiling over a lump of clay
Till he shaped it in his own image. (*GT,* 20)

Johnson's choice of words is odd, not only because "mammy" is the only reference to the female in the entire poem, but also because, as a pejorative name for the black maternal, "mammy" links the poem back to the minstrel language and space of which Johnson is so critical. His brief resort to the maternal in a poem about self-invention signals the unavoidability of the body as well as its culturally determined association with the feminine. And it is hard to escape the feeling that at this moment in a poem of procreation, the language dips into bathos, a descent in imagery. Johnson's poem erases the banjo-playing uncle, but the mammy has a persistent presence, regardless of how innovative his use of the vernacular becomes. Earlier drafts of the poem suggest the difficulty Johnson had writing this stanza, the actual moment of the "creation." This is confirmed by a marginal comment by Braithwaite, who marks this stanza with the command "Revise."[72]

Some of the poems that follow in *God's Trombones* are uneven, a problem that again demonstrates the importance of imagery. The best of the sermons create a picture even while retelling a familiar story. The poems that do not "move," as such, are those that merely narrate, that revise a well-known biblical episode. "The Prodigal Son," for example, parts of which read like a synopsis of *The Autobiography of an Ex-Colored Man,* is a didactic poem. Johnson literally tells us the meaning of the symbols: "Jesus spake in a parable, and he said: / A certain man had two sons. / Jesus didn't give this man a name, / But his name is God Almighty" (*GT,* 21). In contrast, "Noah Built the Ark," a conflation of the Garden of Eden narrative and the story of the Flood, uses a more colloquial tone for its characters. Drawing an image of the serpent and Eve together, the poem's speaker cynically notes, "I imagine I can see Old Satan now / A-sidling up to the woman / . . . Eve, you're surely good looking." Describing the ridicule Noah faced for building an ark when the weather was clear, the speaker states, "Some smart young fellow said: This old man's / Got water on the brain" (*GT,* 32, 35).

Some of the most memorable moments in *God's Trombones* are those representing beginnings and finality. Two of the more moving poems present a contrast with "The Creation." "Go Down Death" begins with simple solemnity; it paints the image of "Sister Caroline's" deathbed, surrounded by the surviving family. Sandwiched between two other poems which emphasize revelry, the stories of the Prodigal Son and the debasement that leads to the Flood, "Go Down Death" rewards Caroline, who "labored long in [a] vineyard," with final, domestic security. The figure of "Death" here is not of the familiar black-robed menace but of a liege on a "pale, white horse" (*GT,* 28, 29). "Let My People Go," in turn, displays visual energy near the close of the poem, when Johnson imagines the parting of the Red Sea. Short, declarative statements suggest the hurriedness of the pursuers and the pursued and contributes to the immediacy of the poem:

> And Pharaoh called his generals,
> And the generals called the captains,
> And the captains called the soldiers.
> And they hitched up all the chariots,
> Six hundred chosen chariots of war.
> . . . .
>
> And Pharaoh and his army
> Pursued the Hebrew Children
> To the edge of the Red Sea.
>
> Now, the Children of Israel, looking back
> Saw Pharaoh's army coming.

And the rumble of the chariots was like a thunder storm,
And the whirring of the wheels was like a rushing wind,
And the dust from the horses made a cloud that darked the day,
And the glittering of the spears was like lightnings in the night.

(*GT,* 50–51)

The alliteration in this last stanza ("whirring," "wheels," "rushing wind") suggests the frenzied energy and movement of Pharaoh's men and the Israelites. More than telling a story, the lines evoke the image of pursuit and escape. The gathering of Pharaoh's troops, a horde of men, horses, silver and gold: the language enlivens the description and paints a memorable picture. This literal and figurative movement in "Let My People Go" is all the more noteworthy because of the sometimes static quality of the collection as a whole. Although *God's Trombones* attempted to mirror a sermon improvised in black churches, the printed and fixed collection of poems diminishes the sense of improvisation and experimentation Johnson was trying to create; there is no sensation of a dynamic call and response in *God's Trombones.*

Ironically, then, as a new form of written dialect *God's Trombones* works better when performed or dramatically interpreted, when the poems are "intoned" rather than simply, silently read (*GT,* 10). Like the spirituals collected in anthologies, the poems leave much to be desired as mere text. They are "less picturesque," un-imagistic, to such an extent that performance and the theatrical have to be added.

"Echoes from *God's Trombones*"

Indeed the uniqueness of *God's Trombones* was in the sense of breathless performance that the reading of the poems achieved; and because of this, *God's Trombones* may have succeeded where the earlier compilations of the spirituals failed.

As Jacqueline Goldsby has argued, *God's Trombones* held a special significance for Johnson. Killed in a car accident in New York, he was buried in 1938 with a copy not of his first book, *The Autobiography of an Ex-Colored Man,* nor with his last book, published in 1934, *Negro Americans, What Now?,* but with *God's Trombones* placed on his breast.[73] One other fact that suggests the significance of the collection to Johnson is the second volume he created based on the responses generated by the poems. Titled "Echoes from *God's Trombones*: Appreciations and Comments," this second "book" consisted of letters from prominent friends and admirers. What is most intriguing about the collection is its rich appearance and the apparent effort it took to create the self-made, single volume. The book is covered in a rich green suede; Johnson's full name is written in gold lettering in the bottom right-hand corner; and the book itself is wrapped in gold leaf paper and further contained in a golden box. The individual letters are similar in appearance. All of them appear to have been typed on the same typewriter; and the watermark on the pages is the same, although the signatures on the letters are all unique. Apparently certain letters Johnson received from readers of *God's Trombones* were retyped, and then each letter writer was asked to sign the typed letter; there are no individualized letterheads; and the letters included in the volume appear in alphabetical order according to the writer's last name. Johnson thus creates another "book" testifying to the strength and power of the poems.

Read one after the other, the letters in "Echoes" become remarkable in the way they emphasize the vocal dimensions of the poems, that is, the poems' innovative way of evoking a performance. This "appreciation" from a reader from Georgia reveals the power of the spoken poems: "I find this peculiarity about 'God's Trombones,'—that the sermons lead one, not to read to oneself, but to *shout* to oneself. They have an exact and emotional cadence which, at their completion, leaves the reader as exhausted as if he had himself been delivering them.—And I shall never get done marveling at your ability to get the full flavor of the Negro preacher without a single use of dialect."[74] What is interesting, then, is the poems' effect via *performance,* an effect that replicates (in volume of sound, if not in bodily movements) the "shout," or the religious performance that earlier compilers tried to contain. By being enacted and "intoned," the poems have their greatest influence on the reader/hearer. This is made evident in the reaction of Helen Keller to the poems. In a letter written to a friend and then copied and mailed to Johnson, the well-known deaf and blind activist stated: "I feel the big, warm heart of the poet-preacher throbbing in 'Creation,' 'Go Down, Death' and 'The Crucifixion.' The tears running down my cheeks will speak for me more eloquently than words."[75] Whether intentionally or not, Keller's reactions mirror Frederick Douglass's sentiment when he recalls having heard spirituals as a slave and writes about that memory in *Narrative of a Life:* "The hearing of those wild notes always depressed my spirit, and filled me with ineffable sadness. I have frequently found myself in tears while hearing them. The mere recurrence to those songs, even now, afflicts me; and while I am writing these lines, an expression of feeling has already found its way down my cheek."[76] In both statements, language is insufficient to capture the raw emotion provoked by expressions which are themselves marked by an elusive black quality. In echoing this well-known evaluation of the spirituals, Keller's statement is perhaps the greatest compliment paid to Johnson's sermon-poems. But both remarks also signal an inability to escape from the body, as Douglass and Keller rely on bodily effects to measure the emotive impact of songs and poems. It is not through words but through the physical expression of sentiment that one validates the power of Johnson's poetry.

It is curious, then, that *God's Trombones* has not sustained the high evaluation and estimation reflected in "Echoes from *God's Trombones*." For example, Jean Wagner in 1962 called Johnson's experiment one of "limited" success and stated that the collection revealed Johnson's "outdated mentality." Wagner writes: "Like its author, the work set out to have a Negro soul, but one garbed in the distinction and respectability of whiteness. Despite appearances, its tendency was at odds with that total coming to awareness marked by the Negro Renaissance, and no more is needed to explain why *God's Trombones* remained an isolated venture."[77] More recently Eric Sundquist has remarked that "because *God's Trombones* is noticeably less interesting as sermonic language and as poetry, it raises pressing questions about idiom and about the context of publication by which we judge the value of cultural works."[78] Given the sense of fulfillment the collection instilled in him, Johnson would perhaps be disappointed to learn of its fall from aesthetic grace.[79]

Perhaps because of its reliance on intonation, the collection, as well as Johnson's other poems, became popular with schoolteachers as "speaking" or "enunciation poems," oratorical exercises for teaching students public speaking. As early as 1917 Alice Dunbar Nelson wrote to Johnson seeking permission to include his poems in her compilation *The Dunbar Nelson Speaker,* a sort of "greatest hits" anthology of poems, lectures, and essays by or about African Americans. The purpose of the *Speaker* was to teach more than just elocution. It was one of several manuals of oratory and etiquette created to encourage proper speaking, educate black youth, and shape students' morals and character.[80] Unpublished letters written to Johnson also recount numerous instances in which students recited the poems of *God's Trombones* in front of an admiring audience. They would practice breathing techniques to achieve an effect similar, one imagines, to the "arts and tricks of oratory" the ex-colored man admires in the preacher John Brown. The poems were more successful, then, as primers for public speaking than as textual poems.[81]

This discussion of intonation and enunciation returns us to the concern about the black voice which opened the chapter. We come full circle, from Higginson's attempt to capture black sounds in readable signs to the responses of Johnson's admirers, forced to rely on the body and the voice to convey the success of his written words. Johnson's critique of dialect is just one paradigm for understanding the challenges faced by early-twentieth-century black writers, a paradigm that took different forms during the Harlem Renaissance. Throughout the rest of this book I look at black writers' attempts to complicate the association between writing and embodiment, language and visual conceptions of blackness. For most of the figures I go on to discuss, the black body emerges as a site in which to posit unconventional ideas about the literary and visual representation of blackness. Extending Johnson's ideas about revisualizing blackness through language, Nella Larsen in *Passing* challenges the narrative act itself, particularly the act of "reading" the black or mixed-race body.

It is the spectator who manufactures the symptoms of a successful pass by engaging in the act of reading that constitutes the performance of the passing subject.

Amy Robinson, "It Takes One to Know One"

Reading the Body

Fashion, Etiquette, and Narrative in Nella Larsen's *Passing*

THERE IS a striking convergence of issues between James Weldon Johnson's *Autobiography of an Ex-Colored Man* and Nella Larsen's *Passing*. Not only do both novels of racial passing have narratives that revel in ambiguity, but also the frequently deceptive characters in the two novels are keenly attuned to bodies and to fashion. The ex-colored man's perceptive appraisal of others is rooted in the glance at their clothes. Even before he learns of his mixed racial background, for example, the unnamed narrator is aware that he is different from the other boys at his school because of his impeccable manner of dress; and, newly arrived in Atlanta, he determines the cleanliness of a woman's kitchen by assessing her clothes and appearance. Larsen's characters similarly evaluate others by their fashion tastes, by measuring how well women match their frocks to social occasions. The travel-weary Helga Crane in *Quicksand* reacts with both approval and relief to the personal appearance and the home of the appropriately clad Anne Grey. Like the body of the ex-colored man, the bodies of Larsen's heroines are never concretely fixed and solidified in their stories: after a searching look at himself in a mirror early in the text, Johnson's narrator does not focus again specifically on his body, and Larsen's characters know how to disguise the body in order to achieve specific social effects. Finally, both novels are filled with uncertainties: Johnson's book is a pseudo-autobiography that withholds the subject's name, while the ending of Larsen's novel can be interpreted in three different ways. How are we to understand these remarkable similarities between characters who are racially indeterminate and narratives that puzzle the reader or deny the reader full knowledge of their events? Novels that, however one interprets them, question the veracity of knowledge obtained through the gaze? Narratives whose literary and visual aesthetics have now come to be identified with an emergent black modernity?

These questions amplify an issue addressed throughout this book: How did early-twentieth-century African American artists creatively capture recognizable but elusive elements of blackness in material, visual, or textual forms that would be regarded as Art? How, in other words, can one codify evanescent feelings, reactions, or emotions into material form, a question present as well in the realm in which the ex-colored man and Larsen's heroines excel: the world and discourse of fashion. Their strategies for passing, racially as well as socially, involve transforming the subtle distinctions, equated in their world with an elite class of whiteness, into a material though still discrete quality, a strategy that is made possible by their awareness of fashion and appearance.

Fashion provides more clues to the elusiveness of black modernism, more opportunities to quantify a sometimes ephemeral quality. In what may appear to be a superficial topic, we find an important lesson, a model of how image and text, concrete object and abstract description, function within a system that is notoriously indefinite and vague—qualities that correspond with reading and representing blackness. Roland Barthes's interest in *The Fashion System,* for example, a quite dense and dry structuralist interpretation of fashion, is not so much with clothes but rather with the description of clothes, with the language that presents clothing to the reader of a magazine. By concentrating on the description of an outfit in a caption versus the picture of the garment, Barthes reveals the "transformation of an object into language."[1] As Jonathan Culler puts it, "language permits one to pass from the material objects to the units of a system of signification by bringing out, through the process of naming, meaning that was merely latent in the object."[2] Disclosing that latency, Barthes's writings transfigure the elements of fashion into a perceptible mood or style and articulate the relation between the physical representation of a garment and the textual caption, between the photographic image of a garment and a garment's description. One finds in *The Fashion System,* then, an alternate way of negotiating the "image proper" and the written text. Language is what makes the subjective meaning of fashion cohere, bringing the ineffable or immaterial to concrete status.

Significantly, fashion and passing draw upon the fleeting elements of "taste" or distinction, "the strategies aimed at transforming the basic dispositions of a life-style into a system of aesthetic principles"—strategies and principles that seem natural or arbitrary but are in fact conscious and deliberate choices and selections, as Pierre Bourdieu reveals.[3] Fashion, like racial or class passing, is a quality notoriously difficult to quantify and describe, a recondite quality that only those "in the know" can identify. Racial passing involves a simultaneous process of making the insignificant signify and concealing those qualities so immediately and evidently—so literally—identified with blackness. In what follows, I discuss the small elements, or details, of fashion and decorum, the performance of "etiquette," that have meaning when one is disguising one's race. Such elements highlight the ambiguity and obscurity that reside in the black body passing for white and the nuanced meanings attached to the visual cues which resonate in the black modern narrative. If James Weldon Johnson strives to create the textualization of the black image, that is, to make the black image "less picturesque," Larsen strives to resituate the black body, making it less recognizable by exploiting the intangible value given to small details. Characters such as Larsen's Clare Kendry and Irene Redfield exploit the seeming rigidity of race by highlighting the details so frequently read as "natural" for one race rather than another.

A Reference Made in Passing

In *Passing* Larsen seems to suggest that identity is a hazy fiction one tells but which outward appearances and surface events only partly confirm. Rather than directly stating their thoughts, characters communicate through an exchange of looks—particularly her two light-skinned female characters, Irene and Clare. These subtle forms of expression heighten the sense of uncertainty throughout the novel. The reader never learns explicitly the reason for Clare's fall from a window, the reality of a homosexual longing between Clare and Irene, or the true nature of the relationship between Clare and Irene's husband. This indeterminacy extends to the racial identity of Larsen's characters, an identity not always easily discernible because of the characters' mixed racial background and their inclination to "pass."[4] Without adequate markings or clues, any reading, whether of identities or situations, is flawed or incorrect.

A brief, almost offhand remark Irene makes refers to a legal trial in which these issues of knowledge, passing, and the gaze combined to interrogate the race and veracity of a woman. "The Rhinelander case" was an annulment proceeding in the 1920s in which wealthy white Leonard Kip Rhinelander sued his wife, Alice Beatrice Jones, for fraud. Leonard claimed he did not know that his light-skinned wife was "colored," the daughter of a white woman and a dark-skinned cab driver.[5] Larsen refers to the Rhinelanders only once, near the end of the novel, after Irene has come to suspect that her husband, Brian, is having an affair with Clare. Irene wonders what would happen if Clare's white husband discovered not the affair but that Clare has "colored" blood: "What if Bellew should divorce Clare? Could he? There was the Rhinelander case."[6] Married on October 14, 1924, in New Rochelle, New York, the Rhinelanders were featured in newspaper articles that described them as contented newlyweds and quoted Leonard on his lack of concern about his wife's racial background: "We are indeed very happy. What difference does it make about her race? She's my wife, Mrs. Rhinelander."[7] It was not long, of course, before Leonard realized the "difference" race—and class—made to his prominent family. In late November 1924, at the demand of his father, Leonard filed an annulment suit, claiming that Alice had lied about her race and deceived him into marrying her. Although this contradicted his earlier statement to reporters, Leonard filed the suit with the help of his father's lawyers, and the trial began on November 9, 1925. What caused the trial to escalate to the height of drama was the role played by the nonwhite body. Alice's body literally became evidence in the case when she was forced to disrobe in front of the judge, lawyers, and the all-white, all-male jury to prove that she had never lied to her husband about her race, that in fact any man who had been intimate with her could "see" her color.

Although Irene's casual remark has been received as simply a historical reference, her citation is ironic, for not only are there uncanny similarities between the major figures of the novel and those of the trial, but also the novel critiques the methods and conventions that assume a central import in the Rhinelander case. Etiquette and performance, the forms of behavior on which the prosecution and the defense relied in the trial to authenticate race, are subversively used by Irene and Clare in *Passing*. Examining the trial in relation to the novel helps us to interrogate the cultural practices that enable and complicate the identity politics of race; both narratives illuminate the use of social and racial codes to evaluate, through the look, the female body. Abstract and elusive in the salons of *Passing,* the social and racial conventions are reified in practice in the courtroom, demonstrating the violence of such codes and reading processes in the creation of symbolic meaning. The defense's strategy ironically resembled a black modernist one: Alice's lawyer attempted to concretize the subtle, elusive elements of race, class, and gender into recognizable and readable protocols.

The concepts of readability and representation are central to both Larsen's novel and the Rhinelander case. If, as Foucault states, the body is an inscribed surface, "imprinted by history" and bestowed with what Judith Butler calls a cultural "intelligibility," *Passing* challenges (while the case depends on) those meanings traditionally associated with the black female body.[8] Foucault's writing metaphor is, as Butler points out, problematic, for it assumes a prediscursive body that is "figured as a ready surface or blank page available for inscription"—a concept Foucault argues against in *The History of Sexuality, Vol. 1.*[9] His statement presents a more disconcerting paradox when considered in light of African American bodies. Hortense Spillers's psychoanalytic "Mama's Baby, Papa's Maybe" is perhaps the most insightful critique of the narrative function often assigned to black bodies, figures necessary for, but not full members of, a discourse Spillers refers to as an "American grammar," the "ruling episteme that releases the dynamics of naming and valuation."[10] Black bodies in these "symbolic paradigms" appear not too far removed from the blank pages Butler critiqued—only in this case the exterior surfaces are inscribed to reflect a relation to whiteness. Portuguese slave traders, for instance, categorized captives as "white enough," "less 'white like mulattoes,'" and "black as Ethiops"—a grammar of "declension" based on skin color.[11] The black body is perceived as a vacuous object, given meaning and signification only through a difference from whiteness. The paradox is that this empty object is, at the same time, all body, reflecting the negative value in the too familiar mind/body dichotomy, too much body to achieve privileged abstraction.

Foucault's reading and writing metaphor suggests not only the visual appraisal of readily apparent surface attributes of the body but also the process of making meaning and forming knowledge out of those physical clues, a process inherent in the Rhinelander trial and a strategy Larsen's characters employ. *Passing* undermines the grammar of racial language communicated through and by the body, those signs of "intelligibility" that help to make meaning possible. Both the novel and the trial center on the assumption of an always decipherable, easily readable black body. The novel disrupts a racial and sexual "legibility," the meanings derived from stereotypes, by simultaneously hindering the reader's act of interpreting Clare while making the reader question Irene's interpretive practices—just as the jury in the Rhinelander trial must decide to which racial category Alice belongs and judge Leonard's ability to "read" his wife. Reading the woman's body in both the novel and the trial is a delicate act because of the uncertainty of "race" with the light-skinned body. In *Passing* this uncertainty is further heightened by the potential for ambiguity in the decorated, stylized female form, the "masquerade" and remaking of the self available through fashion and cosmetics.[12] Indeed as Larsen presents them, racial passing and fashion are curiously related; there is an easy confluence between the two because of their reliance on the subtleties of vision. Depending on the appearance of the mixed-race female body, the subject who passes can elide categories determined by race; and clothes can "camouflage" the body for those special times when "we don't want to be seen—or when we don't want our true selves to show through."[13] Irene's and Clare's *performance* of a certain type of femininity, with fashion as their costumes and middle-class etiquette as their stage directions, helps the women to accentuate the ambiguous visual demarcations of the light-skinned African American body and enables them to pass as white more successfully. Fashion and passing are forms of reinventing the self in the novel, ways to restyle how the black or the black/white female body can be read, or indeed ways to deny any reading at all. This chapter highlights the adornment of the body not only to show the characters' "attempt at identity construction," as described by Meredith Goldsmith, but also to reveal how the characters strategically confuse the spectator of the black female body.[14]

This idea of performance is shaped by Butler's writings on gender performance, or "the effect of gender . . . produced through the stylization of the body, . . . the mundane way in which bodily gestures, movements, and styles of various kinds constitute the illusion of an abiding gendered self."[15] But is race equally performative? Are there certain "gestures, movements, and styles" that are readily perceptible as an "effect" of race? Is it a subversive act or merely a type of performative essentialism when one acts out or plays up movements associated with a race? Larsen's novel suggests that, indeed, there are codes that are not "essential" qualities of a race but are easily imitated, mastered, and performed and just as easily signify one race (or gender or class) rather than another.

Expanding on Butler's ideas, Amy Robinson has written engagingly about sexual *and* racial passing. Directing us to view "identity politics as a skill of reading," Robinson suggests that we examine not the veracity of the passing performance but the appearance of veracity to others. This subtle distinction shifts the objective of reading the passing performance from an ontological to a spectatorial inquiry. Robinson's argument highlights just how intertwined the spectatorial and ontological positions are in relation to those women of color who do not pass.[16] Alice's lawyer surprised Leonard's legal representatives by admitting, during the first day of the trial, that she had "colored" blood. But had she withheld that information from Leonard? Could a man "know" his wife intimately and yet not know her race? The fact that Alice had to disrobe in court, the belief that one could *see* her race and hence *know* her race, suggests how spectatorial knowledge constitutes ontological knowledge in relation to nonwhite femininity. For nonwhite women the two epistemological positions are violently aligned: Alice's disrobing situates her into a long line of women of color who have had their bodies, literally and figuratively, placed on trial. In addition, Larsen complicates any notion of readily interpreting the black or black/white female body. Indeed, as if punning on the difficulties of "reading" blackness, Larsen gives a crucial role to letters in *Passing,* just as letters played a significant role in the Rhinelander trial. In both there is a comparison of written letters to the body, but Clare's body and letters refuse a clear reading, whereas Alice Jones Rhinelander's body and letters are subject to the violence of the look. In the Rhinelander trial the body also takes the place of Alice's words, her testimony to the jury.

One of Larsen's acquaintances once remarked, "Nella was an actress; she knew how to pose for a picture."[17] Her performative abilities equally excelled in her writing. Studying the facts of a trial suffused with the theatrical, indeed a trial that, as we shall see, summoned a major Broadway figure of the time, helps us to appreciate more thoroughly Larsen's lexical production. Her textual play conceals and reveals, tempts and teases not only Irene Redfield in her various acts of reading Clare but the novel's reader as well. By subtly referring to one of the most sensational trials that took place during the Harlem Renaissance, *Passing* dramatizes racial and social performance and demonstrates how to stage the body to convey or deny a particular reading—all while uncovering some of the elements of black modernism.

Manners for Moderns

Visuality and appearance are central issues in *Passing.* An exchange of glances between and among women occurs repeatedly in the text—glances that the main character, Irene, can never fully comprehend. Irene's acts of looking at

Clare question her friend's "mysterious and concealing" eyes and admires her charm and "indifferent assurance" (*P*, 161). Her evaluations of Clare are almost obsessively concerned with minute details of clothing. She frequently fears that she can never quite measure up to Clare's beauty and style, feeling "dowdy and commonplace" in comparison to her friend (*P*, 203).

Several discussions of women, fashion, and the fashion industry provide clues to the exceptional attention Irene gives to Clare's attire and suggest the significance of fashion to women who occupy the boundaries of race. In Leslie W. Rabine's study of the "two bodies of women" (one caught in a system that negatively defines what a woman should look like and one engaged in a process of self-invention and transformation), she notes how clothing can mask the class of the wearer: "With the rise of commodity capitalism, workers could dress like the wealthy bourgeois, and so clothing became a masquerade that could *signify* any role in the absence of a referent, instead of *designating* a fixed place in a scale of positions. It ambiguously revealed or concealed the social identity of its wearer."[18] It is this "absent referent," the absent "markedness" traditionally associated with blackness, that both Irene and Clare call attention to through their use of fashion.

While Rabine points out the democratization made available by clothes and commodity culture, Diana Fuss in "Fashion and the Homospectatorial Look" examines the processes of identity construction that occur when women look at the idealized, perfect women captured in the photographs of fashion magazines. Fuss uses Julia Kristeva's notion of the homosexual maternal facet to explain why women are attracted to these images. According to Kristeva the mother's face is the first object that the child looks at and identifies with while still in the pre-oedipal stage. As the child forms her own identity, the mother's face becomes a lost object: "For the girl, such a loss is a double [loss] since the mother's image is [also] her own." By looking at fashion magazines, particularly at ads that employ close-ups, a woman may get "special pleasure" from seeing the face of a woman, as this offers the "fantasy" of replacing the lost object, of recapturing the mirror image of the mother.[19] Fuss argues that the woman who looks is supposed to identify with the model, not to possess her; that is, these ads encourage the spectator "to desire to be the woman [in the ad] so as to preclude having her."[20] This leads her to conclude that "the entire fashion industry operates as one of the few institutionalized spaces where women can look at other women with cultural impunity. It provides a socially sanctioned structure in which women are encouraged to consume ... the images of other women."[21] Read with attention to the notion of an unarticulated desire, Fuss's argument supports Deborah McDowell's influential analysis of homoeroticism in this novel, her proposal that Larsen "flirt[s], if only by suggestion, with the idea of a lesbian relationship" between Clare and Irene.[22]

Just as clothes reinvent the exterior of the body, offering a type of costume, etiquette helps to finish the performance. Etiquette manuals offered instructions and prohibitions on how to move or stage one's body in social settings. With the proper awareness and training, anyone could occupy a certain desired social space, or at least give the appearance of doing so. As Marjorie Ellis Ferguson McCrady and Blanche Wheeler put it in *Manners for Moderns,* "the behavior of the $12 a week stenographer can be just as becoming as that of the $50,000 a year lady."[23] One early etiquette manual "dedicated to the colored race" was the 1920 *National Capital Code of Etiquette.* In it Edward S. Green advised his black readers "How to Dress," doling out advice such as avoiding loud colors "that fairly shriek unto Heaven" (*Q,* 14).[24] Both *Passing* and Larsen's earlier novel *Quicksand* critique advice such as Green offered. As a teacher, Helga Crane in *Quicksand* tries to abide by her school's and Green's idea of "good taste" but rebels because of her love for rich colors (*Q,* 3). She considers marrying into a black "first family," but she flees her school and the South because "she hadn't really wanted to be made over" (*Q,* 8, 7). Throughout *Quicksand* Helga tries to balance her wish for the appearance of social poise, such as etiquette offered, with her more sensual, indecorous feelings.[25]

It is intriguing, then, to read *Passing* not only as a tale of black-white intrigue and discreet homosexual longings but also as a black modernist tale of manners, a subtle style manual that at times both promotes black middle-class "performance" and displays the contradictions embedded in such acts. Irene, for instance, initially reads Clare through the language and lens of fashion. The first encounter between them resembles a descriptive excerpt from a women's magazine. Irene sits on the balcony of the upscale Drayton Hotel. When Clare first enters, Irene notices a "sweetly scented woman in a fluttering dress of green chiffon whose mingled pattern of narcissuses, jonquils, and hyacinths was a reminder of pleasantly chill spring days" (*P,* 148). The correspondence between scent and color, between a woman's perfume and her clothes, is, as Goldsmith points out, reminiscent of the language of advertising.[26] Clare recognizes Irene first and bluntly stares at her. Irene is initially disturbed by her stare but then feels guilty because she thinks the woman knows she is a black person sitting in a socially segregated space.

The reference to clothing calls attention to what it can either hide or highlight beneath. Clare's gaze makes Irene conscious of herself, it is as if Irene "suddenly has a body."[27] She becomes aware of her own attire and anxious about how she may appear to others: "What, she wondered, could be the reason for such persistent attention? Had she, in her haste in the taxi, put her hat on backwards? Guardedly she felt at it. No. Perhaps there was a streak of powder somewhere on her face. She made a quick pass over it with her handkerchief. Something wrong with her dress? She shot a glance over it. Perfectly all right. *What* was it?" (*P*, 149). To Irene, Clare's steady look could only be the result of a blunder in her application of makeup, a lapse in her fashion sense. These assumed fashion and beauty faux pas force her to "verify herself endlessly," to reexamine her body and clothing in bits and pieces.[28] Fuss's homospectatorial look, then, can also be a regimental tool. However innocuous the exterior look is, it can be internalized and made to operate punitively, especially for black women.

J. C. Flügel provides another reason why attention to clothes is so important for Irene, Clare, and other women who may pass. In *The Psychology of Clothes,* an examination of the cultural and psychological meanings attached to fashion, Flügel asserts that clothes augment one's identity, endowing one with a bodily presence: "Clothing, by adding to the apparent size of the body in one way or another, gives us an increased sense of power, a sense of extension of our bodily [selves]—ultimately enabling us to fill more space."[29] Fashion's ability to strengthen a sense of identity is important for these two women whose identities are so fragmentary and fragile. For Irene and Clare clothes are not only a metaphorical extension but also the means of deception: their well-dressed bodies allow them to occupy a privileged social space that, if they were recognized as black, would not be available to them. Although their fashions leave their racial identities in flux, their ability to dress well enables them to heighten the perception that they belong to one race rather than another, thus enabling them to pass as white more successfully. In her analysis of the novel Butler remarks on how blackness is not an immediately evident way of classifying bodies, since "what can be seen, what qualifies as a visible marking, is a matter of being able to read a marked body in relation to unmarked bodies, where unmarked bodies constitute the currency of normative whiteness."[30] The scene on the balcony of the Drayton reveals that the "markings" can be concealed, played with, or heightened to achieve a certain effect. Indeed Clare's and Irene's fashion skills allow them to evade being considered "marked" at all.

This episode at the Drayton is just the first of several scenes in which the women exchange glances, in which Clare's look implies some knowledge that she has but that Irene, for some reason, cannot or will not understand. Additional scenes of visual exchanges reveal Clare's paradoxical status in the novel: while everyone imposes his or her definitions on her, she remains inscrutable, her gaze "unfathomable." Although she is always the center of attention, no one really knows her, a result of her objectification as well as of not knowing to whom her "having" gaze is directed (Irene or Brian?). One scene of subtle reading and heightened unknowability occurs when Irene visits Clare's apartment for tea. Irene arrives, unaware that Clare has invited another former classmate, Gertrude Martin. Most interesting about the reunion is what is not said but is merely implied or suggested about reading bodies and performing femininity and how the narrative communicates these issues through visual ambiguity, the light-skinned black female body passing as white.

This scene inevitably encourages comparisons, as Irene compares her life choices to her friends' and finds herself outnumbered, feeling a "sense of aloneness, in her adherence to her own class and kind" (P, 166). For like Clare, Gertrude has married a white man. And although she does not pass with her husband, Gertrude, in both her speech and actions, maintains a "dutiful eagerness" to be perceived as white (P, 171). The quality that plagues Irene throughout the narrative, "loyalty to a race" (P, 227), and implicitly deception of one's race, underlies the scene and briefly rises to the surface in their discussion of a "black Jew" (P, 169). Is one "authentically black" if one marries a black man and passes only occasionally, as Irene does? Or does one, like Clare, stay "true" to the race by periodically surrounding oneself with blacks? Or is the most "honest" position the one that is in fact represented by Gertrude, a position in which everyone, including your husband, knows you are black, although you try hard to convince others that you are white "in spirit"? Larsen makes us ponder these essentialist, though for her characters significant, questions through what is considered to be that most feminine of interests, and perhaps the easiest and most superficial claim to legitimacy, clothing and decoration. The three women, through their attire and social skills, enact their own "performance" in an attempt to become "bodies that matter," bodies that not only give the appearance of having successfully contended with marriage and children but that also have used racial ambiguity to obtain social status. Subtle, strategic, and unspoken alliances are made and unmade among the women as each seems to ponder the lives—and clothes and bodies—of the two others.

Larsen immediately sets up the relation among fashion, décor, and the body when Irene enters Clare's apartment and is confronted with "startling blue draperies" and "gloomy chocolate-coloured furniture" (*P*, 165). Clare manages to coordinate with her room by wearing "a thin floating dress of the same shade of blue, which suited her and the rather difficult room to perfection" (*P*, 165). The other member of the tea party does not harmonize as well. In fact this person seems to disappear into the room, for at first "Irene thought the room empty, but . . . she discovered, sunk deep in the cushions of a huge sofa, a woman staring up at her." While Clare's body coordinates, Gertrude's body disappears. Irene subjects Gertrude to a thorough yet subtle look and judges her, in contemporary parlance, a fashion victim. Her former schoolmate wears an "over-trimmed Georgette crepe dress [that] was too short and showed an appalling amount of leg, stout legs in sleazy stockings of a vivid rose-beige shade" (*P*, 167). Irene's gaze establishes a distinction between Clare's fashionable body and Gertrude's bodily excesses.[31] Although her body initially disappeared, Gertrude seems on closer inspection to have too much body, for "she had grown broad, fat almost," with aging "lines on her large white face" (*P*, 167). What is significant about this scene is the subtle theory Larsen posits about the very ability to read appearances. Irene and Clare are women attuned to each other's class codes, with Clare able to read Irene better than Irene wishes. In fact, Fuss's homospectatorial look can be redefined as a feminine-directed look or, as Brian succinctly describes Irene's feelings toward Clare, something "so subtly feminine that it wouldn't be understood by [men]."[32] Poor Gertrude, however, the woman who cannot read either fashion or people well, remains oblivious to the visual dynamics occurring between her two old friends.

This scene reveals another disparity between fashionable and unfashionable women and the significance of etiquette in the intangible skill of "class passing." Both Irene and Clare are adept at social theatrics and etiquette, knowing the proper words to say and when to say them; and they are comfortable dispensing the banal amenities that count as social grace and poise in the world of Larsen's novel. Gertrude, however, lacks skill in hiding social discomfort: "She was, it was plain, a little ill at ease" (*P*, 166). Indeed Gertrude's biggest crime is that she is a shade too obvious, a shade too *readable.* Clare's illegibility is part of her fascination. But Gertrude does not pass muster in Irene's eyes, for she "looked like her husband might be a butcher" (*P*, 167). If there is any doubt about this, about the difference between Clare and Gertrude, this scene offers one of the few times when Irene becomes a reliable narrator, for "it did seem to her odd that the woman that Clare was now should have invited the woman that Gertrude was" (*P*, 166). Gertrude Martin, despite her strenuous efforts, simply cannot perform.

In this scene Larsen offers three competing visions of the black woman who passes, if only occasionally as Irene does. The women become reflectors of their husbands' wealth and position, their husbands' success written on their female frames. But as Irene notes to herself but constantly fails to remember, "appearances . . . ha[ve] a way sometimes of not fitting facts" (*P*, 156). Although Clare and Irene are both fashionably proper and socially skilled, beneath these surface appearances Irene may have more in common with the unknowing Gertrude than with the perceptive Clare; for Irene continually enacts misreadings of herself. Irene, for instance, never completely recognizes her class consciousness. Perturbed that Clare may show up at a black middle-class resort, she explains away her trepidation by thinking, "It wasn't . . . that she was a snob, that she cared greatly for the petty restrictions and distinctions with which what called itself Negro society chose to hedge itself about" (*P*, 157). But Clare, the most astute reader of them all, easily detects Irene's elitism while observing her contemptuous glance at Gertrude's "plump hands [that] were newly and not too competently manicured—for the occasion probably" (*P*, 167). Irene's most significant self-deception involves her attitude toward women who pass, women who, like Clare and Gertrude, lack "that instinctive loyalty to a race" (*P*, 227). Yet Irene overlooks her own unfaithful moments when she tells a friend that she never passes, "except for the sake of convenience, restaurants, theater tickets, and things like that," as well as the fact that at the moment when she becomes reacquainted with Clare, she is passing (*P*, 227). One cannot help but wonder if the resentment Irene feels toward Clare throughout the novel originates from her admiration of Clare's freedom from racial allegiance, the "thing that bound and suffocated her" (*P*, 225).

Only Clare emerges from this reunion scene with a sense of mystery intact. Indeed there is an element of Clare's look which is so strange that Irene keeps thinking about it long after she leaves Clare's home: "Irene Redfield was trying to understand the look on Clare's face. . . . Partly mocking it had seemed, and partly menacing. And something else for which she could find no name" (*P*, 176). Although she finally decides that the look is "unfathomable, utterly beyond any experience or comprehension of hers," it does not prevent her, as well as the reader, from continually wondering until the end of the novel, how should one read or interpret Clare Kendry?

Subtly playing on the notion of interpreting and misinterpreting blackness, of reading and decoding signs of race such as "finger-nails, palms of hands, shapes of ears, [and] teeth," the narrative seems to urge us to view Clare's body as an *un*readable text (*P*, 150). McDowell's analysis of *Passing* examines the relation that encourages a reading of the body as a letter and letters as a body. She notes that "the novel's opening image is an envelope," to which she refers as a "metaphoric vagina."[33] McDowell draws on both Irene's reluctance to read Clare's letter and what we will later know about Clare's "furtive" and "peculiar" qualities (*P*, 143). Clare's inner femininity is concealed within the envelope and not legible; and Clare's insistent letter writing propels the action of the story, just as her body attracts others' looks. This central and primary image of Irene reading Clare, literally and metaphorically, is significant because it is what Irene will attempt to do for the rest of novel.

But Irene's partial readings never allow her or the reader to develop concrete conclusions about Clare. Notably, Larsen delays revealing Clare's actual words in the letter, focusing first on the letter's surface qualities, its appearance. The letter, like Clare's fashion style, is "a bit too lavish, . . . a shade too unreserved in the manner of its expression" (*P*, 182). When Larsen finally quotes this "second letter of Clare Kendry's" (*P*, 181) (Larsen once again confuses the reader, beginning the novel not with the first letter but with the second), it is disclosed not in full but only in parts, as if Irene can contend only in sections with the intensity of her feelings for Clare. We never get the "full" Clare Kendry, even at the beginning of the novel. In fact Irene's perusal of Clare's second letter mirrors her examination of Clare two years earlier on the balcony of the Drayton Hotel in Chicago, where she made only "instinctive guesses" about the woman before her (*P*, 145). Irene destroys the letter, just as she will remove Clare from her life. After reading it, she tears it up into little pieces and "drop[s] them over the railing." Foreshadowing Clare's plunge out of a window, the letter "scatter[s], on tracks, on cinders, on forlorn grass, in rills of dirty water" (*P*, 178).[34] This technique of partial disclosure should be familiar to those accustomed to the representations of femmes fatales, for the limited knowledge and visibility of a siren are part of her attraction to others. Like the presentation of Gilda's body in Charles Vidor's 1946 film of the same name, Clare's words are alternately concealed and revealed. As Mary Ann Doane notes, "The fascination of a Gilda is the fascination of the glimpse rather than the ambivalent satisfaction of the full, sustained look."[35] The erasure of words, a withholding, acts as a kind of lexical striptease; the presence and absence of certain words only heighten the erotic effect of the letter. As I make evident later, this "complex dialectic of concealing and revealing" is one of the novel's central reversals of the Rhinelander trial, in which the "full sustained look" is imposed on Alice Jones Rhinelander.[36]

Clare, then, remains an enigma even at the end of the novel. Although she is always the center of attention at various gatherings and in Irene's thoughts, she remains unknowable. Irene and the reader's shared inability to develop concrete conclusions about Clare allows her to depart as a puzzle, "indecipherable, unfathomable" (P, 176). John Bellew has the satisfaction of at least knowing that Clare did in fact have some African American blood and of learning for himself one secret about his wife. When Clare does become "known," when her husband discovers her secret, she dies.

The Rhinelander Case

What would have happened had Clare not fallen out the window? Although my reading suggests that Irene pushed her to her death, the ambiguity of the ending allows for the possibility that Clare chose this dramatic way to make her exit. Knowing the potential violence of her husband, a man who has a "latent physical power," Clare may have thought that the best solution was not confrontation but death (P, 170). If we agree with Irene that Clare is inherently selfish, then her death is not an accident but a deliberate act that enables her to escape the explanations and recriminations of lying to her white husband.

It is the uncertainty of what would have happened to a woman such as Clare that makes one ponder that fleeting mention of the Rhinelander case. The striking similarity between Clare's and Alice's positions brings history into the fiction of the passing woman. In his brief essay on the use of the trial in *Passing*, Mark J. Madigan notes that Larsen's reference to it is noteworthy because it acts as "a metaphor for the central concerns of the novel."[37] Although no records exist that indicate whether Larsen was deliberately trying to rewrite the trial, there is a more subtle and ironic significance to the reference to the Rhinelanders, for the novel problematizes the basic premises of the trial and undermines the concept of performing race or class through appearance, fashion, or the codes of etiquette. As in the novel, clothes, or the lack of them, shape the perception of others. Clare "dresses up" to conceal her racial identity and make it less certain, while Alice was forced to disrobe to prove that she was honest. In addition, letters exchanged between Alice and Leonard were introduced as evidence and contributed to the sensational, voyeuristic aspects of the trial.

Although the two maintained a rigid distance in the courtroom, the Rhine-landers' correspondence with each other "embodied" their relationship, allowing observers to peek into their bedroom. Whereas Irene attempts to read Clare's body metaphorically through her unreliable vision, as if Clare were some undecipherable letter, Alice Jones's body is more literally read. Her body acts metonymically in the context of the trial. Because Alice never appears on the witness stand, her body, as well as her letters, stand in for her testimony. The Rhinelander trial, which occurred four years before *Passing* was published, centered on issues of racial knowledge, representation, and performance. As several crucial exchanges in the trial demonstrate, the outcome of the trial depended not only on Alice's body but also on Leonard's inability to "perform," through etiquette, the actions associated with wealthy white masculinity.

Indeed Leonard's marriage itself was considered a breach of proper decorum. His position in New York society was strong enough to get Alice listed in New York's Social Register of 1924, and then, as her race became known, ambiguously "de-listed." Responding to numerous complaints, including one from Mrs. Emily Post, the editor of the list somewhat embarrassingly stated that Mrs. Rhinelander was " 'in but not of' the Social Register" and hoped that this qualification would settle the matter: "To an arbiter of social etiquette such as Mrs. Emily Post has proved herself to be . . . this should indeed be final, and yet now that a touch of the tar brush has dimned [*sic*] the lustre of the Social Register, who knows?"[38] It was not, however, enough for Philip Rhinelander, the head of the Rhinelander clan, who reportedly threatened to disinherit his son. Several weeks after the marriage of Leonard and Alice, the suit for annulment was made public, and the trial took place a year later in 1925.

From the beginning the trial was a battle to represent the particulars in the best possible light. Both the prosecution and the defense attempted to identify the other party as the aggressor in the courtship and marriage. While the defense argued that Alice was an innocent, hardworking "little girl" defiled by a wealthy playboy, the prosecution, led by Leonard's lawyer Isaac Mills, presented "Kip" as a weak, easily influenced young man.[39] The assertion that he was "mentally backward" supposedly helped to explain how he was seduced and deceived by Alice: "We shall show that he was suffering from a physical ailment. He is tongue-tied. Sometimes he can hardly get a word out of his mouth." And yet although Leonard suffered from slow thinking, he was mentally alert enough to know not to associate his name with questionable people, refusing "to confer undying disgrace on the family by an alliance with colored blood."[40]

The prosecution also attempted to show that Alice was more sexually experienced than Leonard, that it was she who led Leonard astray. His team of lawyers relied on the stereotype of the sexually promiscuous black woman, arguing at one point that Alice had lied about her age and "seduced" the younger Leonard. Alice's lawyer, Lee Parson Davis, countered by questioning Leonard about Alice's attire before they were married. Leonard denied that "he had asked [Alice] to wear long sleeves" and that he carried a "powder puff" when they went on long trips.[41] In this way her lawyer attempted to show that if Alice was guilty of deception, it was under the direction of a man who knew about her biracial background.

As with *Passing,* the trial was suffused with ambiguity and uncertainty. During an hour-and-fifteen-minute opening statement, Leonard's lawyer focused the jury on four key questions that surrounded the Rhinelanders' courtship, marriage, and case for annulment:

Is the defendant colored and of colored blood?
Before the marriage did the defendant represent herself as white?
Did Leonard marry her believing her to be white?
Did he enter into the marriage with full knowledge of her ancestry?[42]

The nature of these questions, their concern with ascertaining knowledge of a person's race and Alice's representation of her race to others, suggests the pressure to unveil the "vamp."[43] But the prosecution's case was hindered from the start, not only because of the statements Leonard had given to reporters after the wedding in which he acknowledged Alice's racial background but also because he had frequently associated with the darker-skinned African American members of Alice's family before the marriage. The prosecution tried to diminish the significance of these facts by focusing on what the *Chicago Defender* called Alice's and her sister's "independent" qualities: "Due to the independence acquired because of their early start in earning a living, Alice and Grace eventually became identified with that vivacious feminine set so often referred to as 'flappers.' They are said to have sought gayety and found it."[44] During the trial the jury was informed of Alice's taste for alcohol and her expertise at poker.

In addition, Mills focused on a key point in the Rhinelanders' courtship to reveal Alice's familiarity with the opposite sex and to suggest her propensity for baiting a man and enticing him away from his moral codes. In December 1921 Leonard and Alice spent several nights in a New York hotel, the Marie Antoinette, where they registered as Mr. and Mrs. Smith. Leonard stated that the hotel was Alice's suggestion and that it took only twenty minutes to persuade her to let him stay with her. Through his own lawyer's questioning, he revealed that they had sexual intercourse several times while they stayed there. Yet under cross-examination by Alice's lawyer, Leonard admitted that he had lied when he claimed it was Alice's suggestion. This crucial admission comes at an otherwise light moment in the trial, when even Alice laughs at the idea that he was sexually unschooled:

> Q[uestion]. You weren't so frightfully innocent when you met Alice, were you?
> A[nswer]. I was.
> Q. You made love to Alice.
> A. Yes.
> Q. You weren't so innocent about that, were you? (Loud laughter.)
> A. I was. (Alice laughed.) [45]

Taken literally, this exchange supports the prosecution's portrayal of him as a hapless young man led into lovemaking by a more experienced woman, but Davis eventually got Leonard to admit that Alice was "perfectly ladylike" until they arrived at the Marie Antoinette. The image of male innocence conveyed in his answers raised skepticism about both his veracity and his masculinity. In a crucial exchange regarding how Leonard's lawyers had obtained Alice's private letters, not only did the defense question his manliness, but Leonard himself seemed to question it as well:

> Q. You promised this little girl you'd keep them sacred?
> A. Yes.
> Q. But as long as it would benefit you to spread them on the record you were willing to break your promise?
> A. By the advice of counsel.
> Q. And you still consider yourself a man?
> A. I can't answer that. [46]

Both of these exchanges illustrate how Leonard's behavior during the trial contributed to a perception of emasculation. At times he "gave the impression of being driven indomitably by something outside of himself," although he was revealing the most intimate details of the courtship of his wife. [47] Leonard's hesitant admissions and erroneous testimony, and his frequent contradictions and weak, unmasculine presence, made him an unreliable witness. As the *New York Times* bluntly put it, "Rhinelander had been held up to ridicule on the very things which he might have been expected to know most about, little matters of social etiquette." [48] According to Barthes's discussion of taste and distinction, it is just such "little matters" that do indeed count in reading a person's status. As he notes about the detail, "it is precisely this 'nothing' which is the radiant nucleus."[49] The social and racial codes that assist Irene and Clare in *Passing* eluded the hapless Leonard. The conventions that would seem to validate Leonard's claims instead functioned to undermine his lawsuit. "Kip," a man in a position of not having to "class pass," could not perform the power of white masculinity attributed to men of his class. Under Davis's cross-examination Leonard admitted that he had pursued Alice, that he had had frequent contact with the Jones family, including Alice's brown-skinned African American brother-in-law, and that his father's lawyers had lied in written statements to the court.

While the dissolution of both Leonard and his case was achieved by putting him on the stand, both the defense and cross-examination of Alice took place without her ever speaking a word. Her presence on the witness stand was not required. Her body, and her letters, would "speak" for her. Although I do not want to minimize the amount of attention Leonard received, Alice appears to have been not only more literally exposed but also more emotionally unveiled than Leonard. Alice suffered through a dual exposure, the intimate revelations and expressions of her love for her husband by the prosecution and the viewing of her nude body by the judge and the jury. Even Leonard's letters opened her to inspection. Two letters Leonard had written that were read in court were considered so "shocking" that women were asked to leave the courtroom before they were read.[50] The *Pittsburgh Courier,* however, decided to let its readers protect themselves; the paper printed excerpts from the "scarlet letters," which implied that Rhinelander sexually satisfied himself after reading Alice's notes: "Last night, sweetheart, after writing three full pages to you, I undressed and scrambled into bed, but not to go to sleep. No, baby, do you know what I did? Something that you do when my letters arrive at night."[51] Read closely, however, the letter implies that Leonard only did what he had learned to do from his lover; and so the revelations of Leonard's private letters further vilified Alice.

Unlike Leonard's notes, Alice's writings had a more unstable resonance in the context of the trial. The prosecution would read from Alice's letters immediately after one of Leonard's weak testimonies, a point-counterpoint plan of attack, or without attempting to place them in context. Her declarations of love for the man she would marry sounded incongruous in the public courtroom. In an obvious attempt to make Leonard jealous, she used exaggeration and hyperbole in several of her love notes. In one letter written while they were apart, Alice named the blackface entertainer Al Jolson as one of the many men who flirted with her and threatened to take Leonard's place in her affections. The prosecution brought in Jolson as a witness to refute this, showing that she was prone not just to embellishment but also to outright lies.[52] Because Alice never testified during the trial, her letters to Leonard became the only documentation of her words and the first means by which the jury appraised her veracity.

Although the letters were a source of humor for court spectators and a diversion for the prosecution as Leonard stumbled through his testimony, they may have inadvertently helped Alice's case. According to a *New York Times* reporter, she wrote "poetry with a truly negro rhythm which was so superior to her ordinary forms of expression that it seemed as if she must have copied the lines from a popular song."[53] Alice's letters were framed in terms of the primitive, a quality the article referred to as one of "unrestrained vulgarity." To the reporter, they were "the fervid, illiterate letters of a woman to whom Rhinelander was a Prince Charming."[54] Alice's writing became for others a confirmation of her racial heritage, her written notes serving as a sign of her race. Other excerpts from her letters displayed spelling mistakes and grammatical errors and were taken as both class and racial signs of her eighth-grade education and her previous occupation as a maid.[55]

The appraisal of the letters became a preparation for the examination of her body, the disrobing scene which took place as if one could visually authenticate race. Ironically it was Alice's own lawyer who ordered that she display her body in order to refute any possible assertion that "Rhinelander was color blind."[56] He sought to demonstrate that in having sexual relations with her before the marriage, Leonard would have had the opportunity to see her skin. Her body was thus offered as visual "proof" of her mixed racial identity and of the impossibility of misrepresenting her race to him.

The moment of disrobing took only a few minutes, in the jury room, away from photographers, reporters, and other courtroom spectators. Although reporters were not allowed into the room, varying accounts of what took place appeared in the press.[57] The *Chicago Defender* offered the most vivid description of the event:

> The court, Mr. Mills, Mr. Davis, . . . the jury, the plaintiff, the defendant, her mother, Mrs. George Jones, and the stenographer left the courtroom and entered the jury room. The defendant and Mrs. Jones then withdrew to the lava-

tory adjoining the jury room and after a short time again entered the jury room. The defendant, who was weeping, had on her underwear and a long coat. At Mr. Davis' direction she let down the coat so that the upper portion of her body, as far down as the breast, was exposed. She then, again at Mr. Davis' direction, covered the upper part of her body and then showed the jury her bare legs up as far as the knees.[58]

The reporting of the disrobing incident, as well as the court's and lawyers' decisions about what to allow to be read in open court, recalls the omissions in Clare's letter in *Passing*. The description of what is concealed and revealed heightens the sensual elements of the trial for courtroom spectators and newspaper readers. But unlike Clare's body, Alice's body receives the "full sustained look" from the jury, the interrogative gaze available only to those whose bodies are denied abstraction.[59]

More significant is what the act of disrobing suggests about the relation between "knowing" the black female and seeing her body. The disrobing casts the ambiguous Alice as "black"—or at least affiliates her with other women of color who have had their bodies, or their words, put on trial, such as Sojourner Truth, for instance, who bared her breast to a white audience to put an end to the rumor that she was a man.[60] These scenes of verification highlight the demand for the visual display or public disclosure of the black woman, either to prove herself or to justify her words, as if only through the sight of black femininity can one judge the black woman's truth, her "essence," her "authenticity." Alice's trial links her to other women of color who are judged in situations in which "the black woman [appears] as mere body, whose moral and emotional sensibilities need not be treated with consideration."[61] It is this association between visuality and the attempt to gain knowledge about the black woman, between the public unveiling of black femininity and the divination of a black woman's character, sexuality, and experiences, that *Passing* ruptures with the presentation of Clare. Alice's jury room exhibition reified the assumptions of race, class, and gender into the knowable, accessible black woman's body, a sedimentation of black femininity that Clare Kendry dismantles. Larsen's novel denies ready access to both the external and intimate aspects of a black woman, rendering ineffective any reading of black femininity based solely on a woman's body or appearance. The jury, however, did read Alice's body: the twelve white men ruled that Leonard had knowledge of Alice's race before the marriage and denied his suit for annulment. Alice's juridical success was ambivalent at best. One member of the jury, a Mr. Henry M. Well of Elmsford, revealed that there had been strong sentiment among the jurors in favor of Leonard, telling the *New York Times,* "If we had voted according to our hearts the verdict might have been different."[62]

Notably, a historical sense of Alice Jones herself remains absent. Having been interpreted, read, analyzed, and perused, the woman at the center of the trial remains something of a mystery. Her reluctance to testify at her trial and the large cast of characters involved in the event combined to keep her in the background. What becomes memorable is not so much the woman herself but rather what she represents—because of her blackness and femininity—to the spectators in the court, to the readers who followed the trial in the newspapers, even to more contemporary commentators on the case such as myself. Reading through the newspaper articles, one finds the "real" Alice Jones to be elusive, on the margins, not quite center stage. It is this unknowable aspect of Alice Jones Rhinelander that mirrors the obscurities of Clare Kendry and the ambiguities in Larsen's novel.

Despite critics' celebration of "undecidability" in the novel, analyses of *Passing,* including this one, often reveal the reader's complicit desire "to know."[63] In this sense the novel raises metacritical concerns of reading, language, and interpretation. There is a continual deferral of knowledge and facticity in *Passing,* unlike the disrobing event, which attempted to determine racial identity at the moment of disrobing. As Ann duCille notes, who one decides is the "novel's central figure" determines not only the interpretation of the ending but other aspects of the novel as well.[64] With whose reading skills, for instance, does one wish to align oneself? One detects with Clare and Gertrude an opposition between two types of reading. Gertrude reads too literally, and Irene, according to one possibility that duCille suggests, never learns how to read at all until it is too late; she is " 'the last one to know' wife who has been blind to a friend's play for her husband."[65] Clare, however, almost seems to enjoy the havoc she creates by playing with her image and the visual signs and gestures of an upper-class white femininity; she knows only too well the multilayered potential meanings of language, gestures, and acts. If anything suggests that this is Irene's story, it is the fact that Larsen continually places her in a familiar position, that of the questioning reader who must try to piece together a narrative based on partial clues.

In a book-length treatment of the Rhinelander trial, Earl Lewis and Heidi Ardizzone note that Alice's death certificate "left her race mysteriously blank."[66] Whether an accidental omission or a silence deliberately crafted, the absence is an unsatisfying but fit conclusion. For this finale to the Rhinelander case eerily echoes the ambiguous fatal endings in Larsen's narratives, in which readers and spectators are denied complete knowledge and left on their own to contend with the gaps. If there is anything comforting about this delitescent conclusion, it is that it asserts, however slightly, Alice's prerogative not to reveal herself, even in her final representation.

In a pivotal exchange between Irene and Hugh Wentworth in *Passing,* Irene notes the ephemeral quality of blackness that cannot concretely be named or expressed. Looking at Clare on the dance floor, Hugh cannot tell if Clare is in fact passing as white, and Irene attempts to reassure him:

> "Well, don't let that worry you. Nobody can. Not by looking."
> "Not by looking, eh? Meaning?"
> "I'm afraid I can't explain. Not clearly. There are ways. But they're not definite or tangible."

Like the chroniclers of the spirituals, Irene has difficulty placing blackness in a specific statement or recognizable forms. Irene's inarticulateness discloses a less embodied form of black modernity and counters rigid and static conceptions of blackness, even while she and Clare exploit the presence of rigid codes of race so that they may pass for white. George Schuyler's hero Max Disher similarly takes advantage of stagnant conceptions of race in order to pass racially, but where Larsen's style is discreet and subtle, Schuyler in *Black No More* uses extreme caricatures in order to disrupt ideas about race and gender and to expose the absurd contradictions prevalent in American culture.

Some years ago we wrote a novel in which we made one of the characters say that colored writers in the United States took the Negro question too seriously. . . . [I]nstead of employing methods of argument or denunciation they should make use of ridicule and satire. . . . Such phases of the race question offer a great deal for some colored writer who could employ the methods used by H. L. Mencken in attacking various foibles of civilization in general and of the American people in particular.

James Weldon Johnson, "Satire as a Weapon," *New York Age*

Most Negro publications, then as now, were solemn and serious, containing little wit and humor except in comics. To me nothing was above a snicker, a chuckle, a smile or guffaw.

George Schuyler, *Black and Conservative: The Autobiography of George S. Schuyler*

Surface Effects

Satire, Race, and Language in George Schuyler's *Black No More* and "The Negro-Art Hokum"

IN 1933 James Weldon Johnson found himself in an awkward position. Two black writers, one George Schuyler and the other Claude McKay, wrote to him requesting a recommendation letter for a Guggenheim Fellowship. Johnson explained his dilemma to the administrator of the prestigious grant. Although both were stellar enough to receive the award, if only one of the two men could receive it, "Schuyler should be the one; for he has not yet had a real chance to show what he may be able to do." Johnson was particularly impressed with Schuyler's skill in a style of writing infrequently employed by the younger group of African American authors: "He has made use of irony, satire, and ridicule. These are literary weapons that the Negro writer has made very little use of, but there are few that could be used with more deadly effect."[1] W. E. B. Du Bois reviewed Schuyler's first novel, *Black No More,* in the *Crisis* and, like Johnson, praised Schuyler's satirical skills, despite Schuyler's caricature of the well-known scholar and leader in the novel. "A writer of satire," wrote Du Bois, "is always misunderstood by the simple. So much so, that periodicals, like the *Crisis,* are almost afraid of using satire, even in the smallest doses." Noting how the genre alienates those prone to read metaphorical language literally, Du Bois declared, "If we should speak of the long ears of a certain Mr. Smith, some literal reader would write in and tell us that by exact measurement Mr. Smith's ears were less than three inches in length."[2]

Satire, as Du Bois's tongue-in-cheek statement suggests, depends on an experienced audience. The reader must deftly negotiate the literal and the allegorical; and, unfortunately for Schuyler, not all of his readers were as proficient and appreciative as James Weldon Johnson and W. E. B. Du Bois. There is a burden placed on the reader of satire, particularly when the topics parodied involve the always sensitive economic and political uses of race; and Schuyler's readers, repelled by his over-the-top criticisms of African American leaders in the 1920s and throughout his career, may have been reluctant to bear such weight.[3] Schuyler's use of satire in *Black No More* and in his best-known essay, "The Negro-Art Hokum," is significant, however. Both texts encourage the reader to look beneath the fragile veneer of race and question common conceptions about blackness, whiteness, the body, and visuality. *Black No More* in particular clarifies the ways in which language and the visual inform accounts of America, indeed the ways in which America needs and creates a myopic citizenry. Schuyler's hero, Max Disher, becomes a political figure by exploiting the national fantasy of a blackless America, a fantasy that depends as much on language as it does on a visual epistemology of race.

Schuyler's hyperbolic efforts to challenge conventional black representations creates a different resonance of black modernism in his works in comparison to the writings of James Weldon Johnson and Nella Larsen, which privilege the nuance and complexity valued in "high" modernism. Unlike Johnson, for example, Schuyler claims that there is no unique African American aesthetic. In both "The Negro-Art Hokum" and *Black No More,* Schuyler maintains that language and cultural expressions are regional rather than racial. And yet Schuyler is important to a discussion of black modernism in the 1920s because of his decided views on black representation and art and his disruption of the commonly held equations between blackness and the body.

BLACK NO MORE is a sociological and political satire, as well as a tale of science fiction. Dr. Junius Crookman invents the "Black-No-More" whitening process, a procedure to lighten the skin of African Americans through "electrical nutrition and glandular control."[4] As a result of the process, new methods for "reading" race are required, for by the end of the novel, the fake whites are much paler than the real ones: "The new Caucasians were from two to three shades lighter than the old Caucasians. . . . What was the world coming to, if the blacks were whiter than the whites? Many people in the upper class began to look askance at their very pale complexions. If it were true that extreme whiteness was evidence of the possession of Negro blood, of having once been a member of a pariah class, then surely it were well not to be so white!" (*BNM*, 177). Although the visibly black body disappears in *Black No More*—the Crookman method changes not only the skin color but also the physical features commonly associated with blackness, such as the lips, nose, and hair—there remains a subtle division of groups in the world of the novel into the whites and the "too whites." Although the process alters the physical features of the person under-going the treatment, there are several elements that cannot be changed. The Black No More process has no effect on the speech patterns of the participants, nor does it affect a child born to a person who has undergone the process. As will become clear, these two exceptions are significant. First, as the learned Dr. Crookman explains to his colleagues about African American speech—and as Schuyler asserts in "The Negro-Art Hokum"—"[t]here is no such thing as Negro dialect, except in literature and drama" (*BNM*, 14). It is a fiction, as make-believe and invented as the idea of a pure white race, a concept used to manipu-late racial differences in the country. The second exception—the fact that brown and black babies continue to be born, despite the parents' visible whiteness—causes anxiety among both white and newly whitened Americans; but it is an anxiety that several groups in the novel—including black "race men," white supremacists, American politicians, and Dr. Crookman himself—are able to exploit and manipulate for their own purposes. Taking aim at eugenicist and scientific practices, the arguments of white racial supremacist organizations, and common assumptions about black art, *Black No More* challenges one of the ideas prevalent during the Harlem Renaissance: that the concept of race is an adequate category on which to base an artistic or political movement. Schuyler suggestively demonstrates how a "New Negro" aesthetic may be only an aes-thetic of the surface, dependent on narratives of bodily and racial difference.

In previous discussions of the novel, the conversation has inevitably turned to the infamous "debate" in 1926 between Schuyler and poet Langston Hughes which took place within the pages of *Nation* magazine. Although Hughes has usually been viewed as the "winner" of the debate, or at least the more "authen-tically black" of the two, Schuyler's ideas foreshadow poststructuralist concepts of race which are now widely accepted. Schuyler's essay, "The Negro-Art Hokum," and Hughes's essay, "The Negro Artist and the Racial Mountain," reveal that questions about the biological versus the social construction of race appeared long before the debates about essentialism and constructionism that formed a significant aspect of the investigation of identity politics in literary studies in the 1980s and 1990s. The Schuyler-Hughes exchange posited two different views of what constitutes the "uniqueness" of African Americans and their art and can be read as an early version of that academic dialogue of the late twentieth century, albeit in a different form. While Hughes believed that there was an "eternal tom-tom beating in the Negro soul," Schuyler, in stating that the "Aframerican" is "merely a lampblacked Anglo-Saxon," suggested that only superficial, innocuous qualities distinguished Caucasians from black Americans.[5] According to Schuyler, Americans whether black or white are simply Americans; the mixture of races and cultures in the United States makes the boundaries between racial categories indistinct; and art, in whatever form, should be distinguished according to the nationality of the artist rather than his or her race. A second "symposium" of the Harlem Renaissance, the *Nation* essays offer a nuanced and influential exchange on black representation, a debate the *Crisis* symposium had initiated several months earlier. In this chapter I seek not to reiterate the already well-rehearsed encounter between Schuyler and Hughes but instead to take Schuyler's critique of surface appearances as a starting point for discussing the role of language and the visual in the formation and, as will become clear, the continuation of race and nationality, and to uncover a complex modernist narrative about race and gender, nationality and politics, narrative and the act of reading.[6] Schuyler's use of satire functions as a criticism of the American politician's manipulation of language and America's reliance on the visual as a determinant of race and citizenship.

The Surface Story

Schuyler's satirical target was democratic; no one was exempt from his pen because of race. The question whether to portray the educated black elite or the black exotic, the implicit poles defined by the *Crisis* symposium, was irrelevant for him because it assumed static representations of two types of blackness. Schuyler's strategy for contending with the question of black representation was to exaggerate, to parody any and all groups that sought to exploit race for any motive, a style not often practiced in early African American fiction. In editorials, short book reviews, and "man in the crowd" pieces in black news-papers such as the *Pittsburgh Courier* and the *Messenger* and essays in the maga-zine *American Mercury,* Schuyler mocked and deflated the earnestness of what he termed the "so-called Negro Renaissance" and in the process distinguished himself from the coterie of young black writers becoming popular in New York. Consider, for example, Rudolph Fisher's two novels, *The Walls of Jericho* (1928) and *The Conjure Man Dies* (1932). Both deride, with understated humor, the New Negro elite and the concern for skin color and class. Fisher uses two black male characters, Jinx and Bubba (who appear in both novels), as the vehicle for most of this humor. Through them Fisher states with detachment some of the prejudices long held by African Americans regarding skin tone, racial hierarchies, and economic opportunities. Wallace Thurman has a very different take on these same issues. His two books, *The Blacker the Berry* (1929) and *Infants of the Spring* (1932), wallow in despair and rejection. At the end of the first novel, the dark-skinned Emma Lou Harris abandons a developmentally challenged child, and one of the main characters in *Infants* com-mits suicide. Unlike the gentlemanly humor of Fisher and the claustrophobic portrayals of Harlem provided by Thurman, Schuyler's satire injected some levity into the serious discussion about black representation and mocked mediocrity wherever he found it. Although he was not always consistent in his ideas, he did stress that African Americans were just as talented, and sometimes just as un-talented, as other Americans, a belief that rendered questions such as those posed in the *Crisis* symposium problematic. Schuyler's solution was to articu-late his own question, basic and unsettling, to the growing audience for black fiction: What would it mean if artists, intellectuals, and writers recognized the logic of the Harlem Renaissance, as defined by the *Crisis* symposium, to be as intolerable as other forms of racism? What if they acknowledged that creating a movement based on difference, however "positively" that difference was defined, was unwarranted, unwanted?

Black No More challenges Harlem Renaissance conventions by satirizing the way language can construct racial identities. The main character self-consciously uses narratives of whiteness and blackness to con others and to affect a white masculine identity as a patriotic national figure. Moreover, there is a certain irony in Schuyler's concept of "lampblackness," if it is taken as an indictment of the privileging of surface appearances, of confirming race and citizenship by looking at bodily surfaces. Satire depends on apprehending the difference be-tween the literal representations of a narrative and its more latent, metaphorical interpretations. Schuyler thus exploits a genre that relies on a skilled reader, one who can temporarily suspend disbelief for the satirical critique to function yet can recognize significance underneath cursory external readings. If we read beneath the surface, *Black No More* warns us against the dangers of misreading, of relying too heavily on external differences such as skin color. The novel becomes a reflexive narrative about the visual economy of race and the difficulties of reading race and nation in modern America. *Black No More* demonstrates how, in the hands of politicians, racial identity can be affected by language, and is therefore open to manipulation and artifice. One could argue, however, that in one respect the author fails to look closely under the satirical surfaces he himself has created. That is, Schuyler's keen reading of the uses and abuses of language and of racial divisions and identifications does not extend to gender. Instead, by the end of the novel the black female body functions as a guarantee for the male racial identity made so supple by language. The novel strives to contest the racial parameters of the Harlem Renaissance, yet by failing to acknowledge the significance of the feminine, it undermines Schuyler's structuralist arguments.

Despite this miscalculation, *Black No More* challenges some of the basic premises of the Harlem Renaissance and indeed contributes to conceptual points that are still in contention in African American literary studies today.[7] By deriding Americans' overemphasis on skin color, one of the period's most strident critics foregrounds the paradoxical aesthetic terms of that period. How should the Negro be portrayed in art? Schuyler's answer is: the way one would portray any other American—as humorously and as absurdly as possible.

The Mencken Model

Schuyler had a model for sharp, hard-hitting political writing that also parodied the customs and mores of the average American citizen: the critic and editor H. L. Mencken.[8] In a 1927 letter to Schuyler, Mencken lamented the cautiousness with which African American writers skewered the foibles of white Americans: "A while back I made some effort to get an article showing how the whites look to an intelligent Negro. Various dark literati of my acquaintance tried their hands at it, but all of them, it seemed to me, miss it. They couldn't get rid of politeness."[9] Echoing his own response in the *Crisis* symposium a year earlier, Mencken urged Schuyler and other black writers to write about the "hilarious spectacle" often presented by whiteness.[10] Fortunately for Mencken,

Schuyler cared little about either politeness or social etiquette; when writing he often threw "politeness into the garbage can," as he informed Mencken in a letter.[11] Schuyler did in fact disturb expectations and rupture niceties in print, both in newspaper columns he wrote for the *Messenger* as well as in his fiction. Using Mencken as a model for the possibilities of satire, Schuyler exposed through language the artifice of American behaviors, the most artificial being those associated with race.

H. L. Mencken was fascinated by the contrasting possibilities of language—the way certain words and phrases reflect a distinctive national culture and yet sustain the most hypocritical of national rhetoric. Two of Mencken's more groundbreaking writings, the essay "The Sahara of the Bozart" and the study *American Language,* explored the opposing sides of this dichotomy and, when examined with Schuyler's writings, appear to have influenced the younger writer. The editor infamously lampooned the customs and lack of aesthetic sensibilities among white Southerners in his polemic "The Sahara of the Bozart," first published in the *New York Evening Mail* in 1917.[12] Writing about the South, Mencken proclaimed that despite "its size and all its wealth and all the 'progress' it babbles of, it is almost as sterile, artistically, intellectually, culturally as the Sahara Desert." Because of the death of a large number of Confederate soldiers during the Civil War, the South, according to Mencken, "has simply been drained of all its best blood" and has "left the land to the harsh mercies of the poor white trash, now its masters." African Americans, however, fared better in his appraisal: "It is not by accident that the Negroes of the South are making faster progress, culturally, than the masses of the whites. It is not by accident that the only visible esthetic activity in the South is in their hands." According to Mencken, even the effects of miscegenation worked to the disadvantage of lower-class white Southerners: as a result of the "preference of the southern gentry for mulatto mistresses . . . the poor whites went unfertilized from above, and so missed the improvement that so constantly shows itself in the peasant stock of other countries."[13] After reappearing in book form in 1920 the essay provoked anger among white Southerners but applause from African Americans such as James Weldon Johnson.[14]

There are several intriguing similarities between "The Sahara of the Bozart" and Schuyler's controversial "Negro-Art Hokum." Not only do the two essays use a similar strident style in order to make their points, but also thematically, "Sahara" and "Hokum" address an analogous danger: bad writing. Comparing "Sahara" and "Hokum," one notices first a similar critical appraisal of art and writing—in Mencken's essay the art and writing of the South and in Schuyler's that of "Aframericans." Both Mencken and Schuyler identified and reprimanded in their respective subjects what one may call a "literary boosterism," the enthusiastic and at times uncritical praise of a piece of writing from an author of a specific group—not because the author was any good but simply because he or she was from that group.[15] Insincerity and pretentiousness in literature deserved to be uncovered; and when in the presence of literary "hokum," the reader should ask, to use Schuyler's question, "How come" (NAH 663)? How and why did the writing escape the literary gatekeepers and make it into print? Finally, Mencken's influence can be seen in Schuyler's descriptions of a white lower class in *Black No More.* Preaching to lower-class white factory workers about the dangers posed by African Americans and communists, the whitened hero of *Black No More* appraises the workers, who appear bovine and easily malleable: "They were a sorry lot, under-nourished, bony, vacant-looking, and yet they had seen a dim light. Without suggestion or agitation from the outside world, from which they were almost as completely cut off as if they had been in Siberia, they had talked among themselves and concluded that there was no hope for them except in organization" (*BNM,* 94). Schuyler's Southern white factory workers appear to be direct descendants of the poor whites lampooned in Mencken's "Sahara."

Mencken was a contributor to the study of language and speech through his detailed book *American Language,* first published in 1919. Mencken's purpose in *American Language* was to document the differences between "standard" British English and the English used throughout the United States, particularly as spoken by the average American. The study attempted to identify what made American language unique, how language "prods deeply into national idiosyncrasies and ways of mind."[16] A thick philological survey, the study was revised four times with two supplements before Mencken's death in 1956. As a "sketch of the living speech of these States," the volumes celebrated the variety of American communication, even when that communication was grammatically incorrect. Mencken desired to puncture the veil of academic snobbery that covered American colloquial speech and sought to celebrate a vibrant vernacular culture as poorly recognized by British writers as it was by American intellectuals. Mencken's gift for playing with language reveals itself in his tendency to generate provocative terms, most notably the term *boobus Americanus,* a reference to the biological classification system which drew upon his interest in eugenics, the topic of several Mencken articles.[17] In its ability to vex, the phrase calls forth Schuyler's term for goading African Americans, "lamp-blacked Anglo-Saxons."[18]

Reading George Schuyler with an awareness of Mencken's influence emphasizes the satirical elements of Schuyler's writings. This is not to suggest that Schuyler was simply imitating Mencken. As Jeffrey Ferguson points out in his biography of Schuyler, the belief that Schuyler simply copied Mencken mischaracterizes their fruitful correspondence and friendship, which began in the 1920s and continued until Mencken's death in the 1950s.[19] Mencken demonstrated how effective humor could be in pointing out the contradictions embedded within American culture. Schuyler developed his own demonstrations of such contradictions by lampooning sensitive and highly charged racial dilemmas. Mencken's experiences with a vocal and oppositional audience may have prepared Schuyler for a similar type of audience. The reaction to "The Sahara of the Bozart" demonstrated that the position of sarcastic truth-teller was a thankless job as well as a dangerous one, and both Mencken and Schuyler received harsh reactions to their writings.[20]

An appreciation for satire is needed when reading Schuyler's most controversial statement in "The Negro-Art Hokum"—that "the Aframerican is merely a lampblacked Anglo-Saxon" (NAH, 662). The lack of readerly skill or appreciation may help explain the strident reaction to this statement, which conjures up images and associations of blackface minstrelsy. Taken literally, the term suggests that the African American is a masked white American and implies not an equality between the white and black races but rather imitation and mimicry on the part of African Americans. More figuratively, the term emphasizes the degree to which skin color is an artificial distinction, as superficial as makeup, as recognizably "fake" as the burnt cork that minstrel stars once wore. In "The Negro-Art Hokum" as in his other writings, Schuyler makes use of exaggeration, and the reader must see through the bombastic rhetoric to discover what he is satirizing and critiquing.[21] In editorials and articles for black newspapers Schuyler routinely emphasized the absurd, to the point where readers—*skilled* readers—were able to discern what Rudolph Fisher termed a "Schuyleric opinion."[22]

For example, a frequent target of Schuyler's pen was what we might call a racializing look, the visual appraisal of the body which accepts the illusion of difference on the basis of skin color and ranks such differences accordingly. Schuyler foregrounds the prevalence of such readings at the very beginning of *Black No More* with his tart preface dedicated to "all Caucasians" who can "confidently assert that there are no Black leaves, twigs, limbs, or branches on their family trees" (*BNM,* xxvii). Schuyler's writings invite a consideration of the nation's preoccupation with codifying such looks; that is, his work encourages us to see how reading skin color to determine identity is itself a racialized American practice. In his essay "Our Greatest Gift to America," Schuyler ridicules the foreign newcomer's transition from racial immigrant to white American. The erasure of ethnic differences takes place not in the naturalization courts or through the rigorous immigration laws of the 1920s but simply through the expectation of American citizenship granted by whiteness. Schuyler argues this point most effectively in his caricature of "Isadore Shankersoff," a fictionalized immigrant from Russia newly arrived in New York:

> Over night he has become a member of the superior race. Ellis Island marked his metamorphosis. For the first time in his life he is better than somebody. Without the presence of the blackamoor in these wonderfully United States, he would still know himself for the thick-pated underling that he is, but how can he go on believing that when America is screaming to him on every hand that he is a white man, and as such entitled to certain rights and privileges forbidden to Negro scientists, artists, clergymen, journalists and merchants.[23]

Citizenship applies even to those who are new to America's shores because "race reading" privileges visual appearance. The presence of white skin, regardless of birthplace or length of time spent in the country, determines who can exercise the rights of American citizenship. "Reading the body" is an interpretive act, a process that places bodies into prescribed narratives of nationality and race. National and racial narratives in turn are based on the faulty premise that one can always correctly read blackness or whiteness and on an analogy that equates any form of whiteness with American citizenship.

Reading Schuyler's "lampblack" comment in this way, with an awareness of the satirist's hyperbolic language designed to irritate and provoke, focuses the discussion on an element of Schuyler's argument that is infrequently acknowledged, and that the best-known response to "The Negro-Art Hokum" fails to counter: the vital position African Americans play in the formation of American identity. In his essay Schuyler reframes the question of race and ethnic identity into one of nationality or geographical location within the United States: "Aside from his color . . . your American Negro is just plain American. Negroes and whites from the same localities in this country talk, think, and act about the same" (NAH, 662). The problem with Schuyler's position, however, is the overwhelming significance he attributes to national identification. On the one hand, this emphasis serves to demonstrate that black Americans are a significant, if often undervalued, part of the American nation. On the other hand, Schuyler's patriotism is reflected in a too optimistic assessment of how readily African Americans are able to participate in American democracy. He lists, for example, a host of activities in which all citizens, black and white, supposedly participate, concluding that "when [the black man] responds to the same political, social, moral, and economic stimuli in precisely the same manner as his white neighbor, it is sheer nonsense to talk about 'racial differences' between the American black man and the American white man" (NAH, 663). If one takes this statement literally, without an eye to Schuyler's satire and sarcasm, an initial response would be to wonder how Schuyler can overlook the differences between education and environment for black and white children in 1920s America, that is, the powerful effect of segregation in education and housing. Rather than describing a democratic moment in the Harlem of 1926, when "The Negro-Art Hokum" was published, Schuyler paints a picture that would not be realistic for a majority of African Americans until the last quarter of the twentieth century. In "The Negro Artist and the Racial Mountain" Langston Hughes counters "The Negro-Art Hokum," but does so without mentioning this particular aspect of Schuyler's essay. Despite his moving response, Hughes fails to address explicitly the element of nationality, which is both a strength and a weakness in "The Negro-Art Hokum" and Schuyler's other writings. Hughes instead critiques a type of upward mobility that requires hiking over the aesthetic "racial mountain" of white standards.[24]

But the reaction to the "lampblacked Anglo-Saxon" charge changes when the term is reread as an indictment not so much of white or black Americans but rather of the privileging of certain colors, a privilege recurrent in stories and myths about America.[25] The construction works not as an epithet but as a call to question superficial appearances and surface readings. When read with an awareness of Schuyler's style and within a critique of the way the visual is constitutive of race and national identity, "lampblackness" functions as a satirical retort to the very American practice of "reading the body" and of assumptions of unambiguous whiteness or blackness. The term is not a derogatory epithet for African Americans who have "sold out," but a rhetorical construct that exposes the privileging or devaluing of visual whiteness or blackness and the stories or policies constructed from such valuations, or as Schuyler phrases it, "making skin color the gauge of worth and the measure of citizenship rights."[26] Race, to put it in more contemporary terms, is not simply black or white;

instead, by portraying people and situations that present race in such a blunt, one-dimensional manner, Schuyler demonstrates the absurdity, and sometimes the humor, of these debates.

Schuyler's hero in *Black No More* reinvents himself as a credible white spokesman by manipulating American mythologies and by exploiting the invisible role blacks have played in the structure of these myths. More subtly, *Black No More* demonstrates how the acts of reading and seeing inform racial and national identities. Schuyler's character demonstrates a facility with language, particularly an ability to generate empty slogans as significant, surface-building rhetoric which conditions and structures a national gaze.

Reading Lessons: *Black No More*

Black No More parodies a familiar American narrative according to which the economic and political life of the nation needs blackness to define whiteness. Max Disher, the streetwise insurance salesman of Schuyler's novel, sometimes makes unskilled readings. Disher thinks that whiteness will enable him to enjoy the full benefits of being an American citizen, for he believes in, if not the inherent superiority of whiteness, then the happiness that comes with being a white man in America with access to all rights and privileges. But once Max becomes a white American, he must rethink the beliefs he held as an African American and come to terms with the ordinariness of being a white man. This transition, as well as his success at maintaining a new white identity, depends on his acquiring a command of language with which he can assert an essentialized narrative of race, nation, and masculinity and thereby exploit the American tendency to assign social value and political power to white skin. In the process of portraying a character who obtains and utilizes these skills, Schuyler satirizes the common assumptions of the period.

According to Max, whiteness is the condition from which all forms of American privileges can be exercised, a belief revealed painfully to him on New Year's Eve.[27] On that night Max is rebuffed twice, first by a group of slumming white Southerners who do not invite him to join them even after he obtains liquor for them; and second by the beautiful Helen, a member of the group who rudely refuses his offer of a dance. The thought of Helen stays with Max, and he dreams about her later that night. He envisions "dancing with her, dining with her, motoring with her, sitting beside her on a golden throne while millions of manacled white slaves prostrated themselves before him" (*BNM*, 9).

The wishes expressed in his dream recall what Max and his friend Bunny identified earlier as the "three things essential to the happiness of a colored gentleman: yellow money, yellow women, and yellow taxis" (*BNM*, 4)—or cash, pretty women, and mobility. The dream, however, turns into a nightmare of a lynch mob. Undeterred by either Helen's rebuff or the nightmare, Max undertakes a quest to find Helen again, a quest that will depend on his becoming white, which would also enable him to take advantage of the privileges of being an American citizen: "As a white man he could go anywhere, be anything he wanted to be, do most anything he wanted to do, be a free man at last." In other words, "science [would] succeed where the Civil War had failed" (*BNM*, 10), allowing him to achieve the three critical elements necessary for happiness. Becoming white would enable Max to enjoy the full power of American citizenship, a power that he will later learn is in fact a myth, for the nation has difficulties living up to its ideals, even for white Americans.

In order to become white, Max approaches Dr. Crookman and volunteers to be the first black American to be "black no more." As the newly whitened Max moves through New York with all the apparent privilege of whiteness, it also becomes apparent that nothing is "natural"; the happiness he assumed would be his because of his new features is fictitious. At another cabaret Max feels a pang of nostalgia while gazing on the sight of white bodies straining to move in time with the music. According to Max, these white bodies labor excessively in a fraudulent act of displaying fun. The dancers, "out of step half the time and working as strenuously as stevedores emptying the bowels of a freighter, were noisy, awkward, inelegant" (*BNM*, 22–23). These struggling white bodies appear inauthentic and forced. Coming soon after Max watches the group of white Southerners slumming in a Harlem cabaret, the scene has an air of mimicry that surprises even Max. To his eyes "there was something lacking in these ofay places of amusement or else there was something present that one didn't find in the black-and-tan resorts in Harlem" (*BNM*, 22). Max finally "sees" a subtle lack in white bodies, but only when they imitate blackness. Initially believing that the anonymity of being white, of being "indistinguishable from nine-tenths of the people of the United States," sustains the privileges of whiteness, Max becomes a better reader of the tenuous nature of superficial appearances when he joins his previous experiences as an African American man with his new experiences as a white man and realizes that whites were "little different from the Negroes, except that they were uniformly less courteous and less interesting" (*BNM*, 43). Max uses this realization of the deceptive power of appearances to tell a story about the nation through one of its most revered concepts, the democratic system of government, and through one of the culture's most revered figures, the white woman.

Renaming himself Matthew Fisher and looking for employment, Max/Matthew travels south and becomes a leader in the Knights of Nordica, or K.O.N., a parody of the Ku Klux Klan.[28] Max reinvents himself as Matthew through a series of speeches and rises to a leadership position because of his power of verbal expression. As Matthew, he successfully uses abstract, at times superficial, language. Schuyler's character excels in the rhetoric of political optimism, particularly an ability to generate empty slogans as surface-building rhetoric. Such language has power because of its potential for applying to all people, even those who are most excluded from opportunities for social or economic advancement. Both Matthew and the Rev. Givens, the head of the Knights of Nordica, use generic language that resists specificity. For example, according to Matthew, posing as an anthropologist from New York, anthropology is the study of a false narrative consisting of "the Word of God, the sanctity of womanhood and the purity of the white race" (BNM, 54). His language masks the reality of inequalities of class, instead emphasizing the supposed hierarchy of races. While attending his first Knights of Nordica meeting, Matthew realizes that "these people would believe anything that was shouted at them loudly and convincingly enough. He knew what would fetch their applause and bring in their memberships and he intended to repeat it over and over" (BNM, 54). Matthew's previous occupation as a salesman has given him dexterity in delivering speeches. He "sells" himself through simple nationalistic rhetoric and convinces the Rev. Givens that he shares Givens's racial beliefs.

One place where Matthew exploits the power of superficial language is Paradise, South Carolina, a factory town full of poor white Americans who turn to the Knights of Nordica to help them unionize. Unbeknownst to the workers, however, the factory owners have also turned to the Knights of Nordica, for Matthew's "trade" involves breaking strikes and supporting the interests of business owners. He brings secret operatives into the town who, while organizing the low-paid workers, spread rumors about the racial background of union leaders. These leaders have to prove not that they are white but that they are not black. As the residents of Paradise discover, the two conditions are not the same, for the paradoxical logic of the Black No More process, as well as the history of race mixing in America, ensures that anyone can appear white, but no one can "confidently assert" the absence of black familial ties.

Consider, for example, the union leader Swanson. One of Matthew's operatives implies that Swanson was originally an African American from South
Carolina. Swanson's admission to one part of the rumor, that he once lived in
South Carolina, is enough to confirm the second part, that he is a black man
who appears white because he has experienced the Black No More process. The
factory workers are only too willing to listen to such stories and accept them as
credible. With no experience of or knowledge about challenging these tales, the
workers accept them unquestioningly. Matthew exploits the fallacies and frauds
made possible when people are illiterate—literally, when they cannot read, and
figuratively, when the only narratives they know are the ones taught to them by
men like Matthew, who look at lower-class whites "with cynical humor mingled
with disgust" (*BNM*, 94). With a new discourse for articulating their racial
ideas, the workers overlook concerns about salaries, work hours, and the quality
of life. The rhetoric instead brings white workers together in a racially essentialist solidarity. By the end of Matthew's union-busting operation, Paradise is
forever changed: "Rumors continued to fill the air. People were always asking
each other embarrassing questions about birth and blood" (*BNM*, 99). Matthew
displays little guilt over his con man's game; rather his sense is that anyone
gullible enough to believe the stories deserves to be taken. Paradise is an Eden
only for the factory owners; for the workers, paradise is just a myth founded
in racial superiority. Empty generic rhetoric binds the white citizens together,
seduces the workers into complacency, and masks the reality of their unfortunate
circumstances. Matthew exploits the fact that racial identity is not always and
inevitably visibly written on the body. Race becomes subject to rumor and
speculation, to language. The episode in Paradise shows what can happen when
stories, in the form of gossip and innuendo, contaminate a community.

Max's speeches to the Knights of Nordica members repeat national and racial concepts backed by little factual evidence; his lectures are indeed notable
for their vacuousness: "He reminded them that they were men and women;
that they were free, white, and twenty-one; that they were citizens of the United
States; that America was their country as well as Rockefeller's" (*BNM*, 94–95).
Newspapers and sermons become the forums for disseminating his fake origi-
nary narratives; by using "one-syllable word editorials," he convinces a group of
white laborers that communists, who may have undergone the Black No More
treatment, are trying to steal the laborers' jobs. His successful prevention of
a strike involves creating analogies in the mind of a Southern white public
that were never there before ("Harlem and Negro became synonymous") and

leading the illiterate workers to think in terms of essentialist, superficial arguments, thus preventing more rigorous appraisals of their situation, for "so long as the ignorant white masses could be kept thinking of the menace of the Negro to Caucasian race purity and political control, they would give little thought to labor organization" (BNM, 97, 44). At Matthew's prodding, Givens also uses generic language. Speaking to a radio audience, Givens lectures on "The Menace of Negro Blood." He "talked for upwards of an hour during which time he successfully avoided saying anything that was true" (BNM, 116).

The generic language of American ideology helps Matthew solidify his position as a national leader and pervades the swindle he perpetrates against the members of the Knights of Nordica, German factory owners, poor white Southerners, and other African Americans. By playing with "official stories" in newspapers and on the radio, Matthew becomes the master narrator, manipulates the "citizen-readers," and nearly places Rev. Givens at the pinnacle of the government, the United States presidency.[29] His verbal con depends on difference, the difference Schuyler dismisses as lampblackness in "The Negro-Art Hokum." Matthew is a trickster figure, using stories to create his identity, deploying rhetoric in an attempt to become a race leader. In Black No More racial identity and national identity are not bodily based; rather they become an effect of language, a story one tells and sells, and a conditioned way of seeing. Matthew's "pitch," his salesman's croon, is to get people to *not* look under the surface, but to act and think according to perceived differences.

"Race Patriots": Mothers of the Race

Matthew Fisher affirms his racial and national positions through narratives and language, but there is another way American narratives are created, given shape and form. *Embodied.* Matthew's second way of conning the Knights of Nordica and other white Southerners is not so simple, because he himself believes in the basis of this other swindle. It is only toward the end of the novel that Matthew questions this belief—his preference for white femininity. This reevaluation occurs in part because of two black female characters, who, though on the periphery of *Black No More,* pose the direst threat to Matthew's newfound national self. One woman, Sisseretta Blandish, is initially reluctant to undergo the Black No More process, and another, Madeline Scranton, decides not to experience the process at all. Both Sisseretta and Madeline disturb Max's attempts to authenticate his white body and national status. To confirm his white masculinity, Max needs whiteness, and he obtains that whiteness by discarding his relationship to the black family, symbolically represented in the novel by the two black women.

A turn to Hortense Spillers and Laura Doyle may help clarify the analysis here and illustrate the significance of Sisseretta Blandish and Madeline Scrantoon as surrogate mothers in the novel. In "Mama's Baby, Papa's Maybe: An American Grammar Book" Spillers demonstrates how the black mother affirms race and guarantees a black identity even if the father is white—the one case in which the Name of the Father does not project itself onto kin.[30] Though Doyle does not specifically refer to Spillers, the race-determining status of the black mother figures prominently in Doyle's reading of Ralph Ellison's *Invisible Man*. She argues that Ellison's unnamed character is an example of an "interruptive narrator," a narrator in modernist fiction who avoids the mother and the inheritable qualities of race that the mother passes on to the child.[31] She notes that there are very few African American women in *Invisible Man* and that the section of the novel that does include a black woman (Mary in chapters 11 and 12) is a revision of a section Ellison edited out of the novel, in which Mary had a more central role.[32] Published in 1963 as the short story "Out of the Hospital and Under the Bar," this original segment presented Mary as the figure who administers aid to the disabled narrator when he is temporarily paralyzed by an explosion at a paint factory.[33] In chapter 12 of the novel, however, Ellison rewrites the recovery scene so that anonymous white doctors, not the maternal Mary, heal the Invisible Man with the use of cold, sterile machines. Doyle argues that by rewriting the scene so that the white doctors "mother him in place of Mary," Ellison allows the narrator to evade his problematic past.[34] In Doyle's analysis, the mother's absence in *Invisible Man* provides for an articulation of black identity that escapes female influence or intrusion. Although she does not remain with him to the end of the novel, Mary offers the narrator a brief connection to a black folk past and presents a race-affirming link, or in the narrator's words "a stable, familiar force like something out of my past which kept me from whirling off into some unknown."[35] Doyle's analysis is pertinent in relation to *Black No More* because in both Schuyler's and Ellison's novels, the absence of the black mother enables the black male protagonists to reinvent themselves. In Schuyler's novel it is not only the mother who is absent but the black family as well, one of the traditional means of passing down culture. After Max undergoes the Black No More process, for instance, he heads to Atlanta, where he was raised. When he arrives, he decides: "He wouldn't hunt up any of his folks. No, that would be too dangerous. He would just play around, enjoy life and laugh at the white folks up his sleeve" (*BNM*, 29). The creation of a new identity occurs in the absence of familial ties, for Schuyler implies that one result of the whitening process is the near eradication of the black family as it was previously known. Once millions of African Americans turn white, merchants and businesses begin to suffer losses, "reporting their inability to locate certain families or the articles they had purchased on time" (*BNM*, 38). A second "Great Migration" occurs, not west or north, but one in which African Americans move anonymously into the white race.

A possibility for a surrogate black family resides with Sisseretta Blandish, who bears some narrative similarities to Ellison's Mary. Max's landlady and Harlem's best hair stylist, Sisseretta challenges Max's insouciant journey into whiteness and stirs in him a brief moment of doubt and hesitancy. Like Dr. Crookman, Sisseretta is an entrepreneur, and her hustler's spirit is every bit as opportunistic as Max's; but in a novel filled with salesmen pitching various wares, her products are the only ones with a semblance of integrity. She offers hair straightening and tan powder, services and items that create only temporary changes to the body. Sisseretta appears, at least initially, as a "race patriot," a woman committed to the race. Her patriotism awakens unusual feelings of culpability and disloyalty in Max when he reveals his new identity to Sisseretta, who is suspicious of a white face in her building:

> "Well," she sighed, "I suppose you're going down town to live now. I always said niggers didn't really have any race pride."
>
> Uneasy, Max made no reply. The fat, brown woman turned with a disdainful sniff and disappeared into a room at the end of the hall. (*BNM*, 28)

Sisseretta Blandish offers not nostalgia, as Mary does for the Invisible Man, but guilt, and her gender prevents her from celebrating the possibilities of becoming white, as Max does. Her practical way of looking at the changes caused by the Black No More process demolishes assumptions about white femininity and fragility. Even as a white woman Sisseretta would be neither the woman on the pedestal nor the Helen who belongs on a magazine cover but an ordinary low-wage-earning domestic: "She had lived long enough to have no illusions about the magic of a white skin. . . . She had seen too many elderly, white-haired Caucasian females scrubbing floors and toiling in sculleries not to know what being just another white female meant" (*BNM*, 40). Sisseretta sees clearly behind the national fantasy of whiteness. While Max's new white life appears to guarantee him the rights of a white male—"At last he felt like an American citizen" (*BNM*, 29)—Sisseretta's perception of life as a white female reveals the economic realities of gender, age, and class.

Crookman's advertisement outside the Black No More sanitarium is a humorous but effective sign of the possibility to remake oneself without recourse to the mother or the family. Consider Crookman's advertising sign:

> A large electric sign hung from the roof to the second floor. It represented a huge arrow outlined in green with the words BLACK-NO-MORE running its full length vertically. A black face was depicted at the lower end of the arrow while at the top shone a white face to which the arrow was pointed. First would appear the outline of the arrow; then, BLACK-NO-MORE would flash on and off. Following that the black face would appear at the bottom and beginning at the lower end the long arrow with its lettering would appear progressively until its tip was reached, when the white face at the top would blazon forth. After that the sign would flash off and on and the process would be repeated. (*BNM*, 33)

The science that produced the skin-lightening process and the art that creates the larger-than-life advertising sign coalesce in Crookman's trademark. Significantly, the process is repeated. Although the name of the product promises just a single application (black "no more"), the sign itself denies the permanence of this race-erasing system. The sign reflects the continual displacement of the past: only the present and the future can be represented by the electrified arrow and faces. Crookman's logo exemplifies the absence of the past represented by the mother or the family, an absence acknowledged throughout the post–Black No More America of the novel, particularly by an Al Jolson–like singer who performs "Vanishing Mammy" over the radio ("You went away, Sweet Mammy! Mammy! one summer night / I can't help thinkin,' Mammy, that you went white" [*BNM*, 115]). Dr. Crookman's sign suggests a non-embodied temporality, a new sense of time in relation to the manufacturing of identity. His large advertisement is an announcement of the product's ability to erase, and quite literally de-face, the discrimination endured by blacks over the past century.

In one other sense the Black No More process replicates itself. As more people undergo the process, there is a rash of black babies being born to "white" couples: and "the blame for the tar-brushed offspring in the public mind always rested on the shoulders of the father, or rather, of the husband" (*BNM*, 88), Schuyler's subtle insinuation that a woman's husband may not always be the father of her child ("mama's baby, father's *maybe*"). And yet this natural act of birthing becomes another opportunity to make money for Dr. Junius Crookman and his associates when they establish the appropriately named "lying-in hospitals," places "where all prospective mothers could come to have their babies. . . . [W]henever a baby was born black or mulatto, it would immediately be given the twenty-four-hour treatment" (*BNM*, 89). The crisis of a post–Black No More America is one in which patrimony and race are rendered uncertain. By removing the black mother, the pretense of having definitive knowledge of one's race can be maintained.

With only newborn babies needing the process near the end of *Black No More*, the privileging of white skin color is reversed, and a dusky brownness becomes the new desired quality. A "Down-With-White-Prejudice-League" is founded, state legislatures create "separate schools for pale children," and a scientist writes a book "proving that all enduring gifts to society came from those races whose skin color was not exceedingly pale" (*BNM*, 178). In short, the familiar hierarchy of color returns. Schuyler creates a circuit of time that leaves one wondering, as Max does, if it is the beginning or the end (*BNM*, 17).[36] Ultimately, then, Crookman's electric arrow is not correct, for an arrow suggests a linear development of time, going in one direction. The lights on the neon sign, however, show that the process returns to the place from which it started. The symbol on the sign should be, in the words of the Invisible Man, "not . . . an arrow but a boomerang."[37]

In *Black No More*, then, the reinvention of the black male's body into a white one occurs without the black mother. Reconceiving oneself in the absence of the black mother removes the black male subject from charges of illegitimacy, as well as the weight of the body and the certitude of race the black mother passes on. Racial reproduction occurs without the black woman, outside of the body, and is dependent on technology and science. By relegating the burden of the body to black women, Max and other men avoid this function. The absence of the basic familial group disturbs the ordinary process of racial readings.[38] The Black No More process disrupts and establishes new familial relations, a new family tree; and by the end of the novel, as conservative white racists are forced to recognize, "we're all niggers now" (*BNM*, 155).[39] In the absence of a clearly identifiable demarcation of races, new divisions evolve, demonstrating the nation's reliance on difference to create social and cultural meaning.

AND YET it is a black female figure that unwittingly complicates Schuyler's premise. Although Schuyler erases the black body, it does not completely disappear in his narrative. By the end of the novel a different meaning of race imposes its force, for the book charts the disappearance of the black body only for it to reappear subtly in the presence of an African American woman who rejects the Black No More process. Represented in a photographic image, this figure provides the other characters with a stable racial referent.

This second challenge to Matthew's American whiteness is posed by a female character who, except for a newspaper photograph at the end of the novel, appears in name only. This woman not only causes Matthew to question his concept of white femininity and his earlier skin-color ranking of black women but also challenges the novel's social-constructionist goals. Matthew's friend Bunny receives a telegram about the lynchings of white politicians from a woman identified only as Madeline Scranton:

> "Who's this Scranton broad?" queried Matthew in a whisper, cutting a precautionary glance at his wife.
>
> "A sweet Georgia brown," exclaimed Bunny enthusiastically.
>
> "No!" gasped Matthew, incredulous.
>
> "She ain't no Caucasian!" Bunny replied.
>
> "She must be the last black gal in the country," Matthew remarked, glancing enviously at his friend. "How come she didn't get white, too?"
>
> "Well," Bunny replied, a slight hint of pride in his voice. "She's a race patriot. She's funny that way."
>
> "Well, for cryin' out loud!" exclaimed Matthew, scratching his head and sort of half grinning in a bewildered way. "*What* kind o' *sheba* is that?" (*BNM*, 156)

This one black woman inspires the type of romantic interest similar to that which drove Max to the Black No More sanitarium at the beginning of the novel. Schuyler locates the promise and potential of the race, the *future* of the race, in Madeline Scranton. The "race patriot" is the new origin of racial differences; and by the end of the novel, although no one character is racially "pure," she maintains an "authenticity" that no other character in the novel possesses.[40]

This visual certainty is further confirmed with the novel's final image: a photograph of the major characters in a newspaper perused by Dr. Crookman. "All of them, he noticed, were quite as dusky as [Matthew's son] who played in a sandpile at their feet" (*BNM*, 180). By placing these figures in a photograph, Schuyler forces a stability and finality to the subject of race. The photograph visually anchors the succession of racial identities and forecloses, for the time being, the rapid changes in identity. The sight of the brown bodies confirms and attests to a racial identity less questionable than before. Schuyler appears to draw on the concept that photographic representation equates with a verifiable identity or presence.

And So On . . .

Despite its status as satire, there are moments in *Black No More* that, rather than merely describe racial unease, actually appear to enact it. These are moments that other scholars have called "frenetic" and "misanthropic," when the novel ceases to be funny, when Schuyler's satirical narrative takes a sudden, brief turn toward realism and the anxiety of racial absence results in death.[41] I close this chapter by examining one such moment in detail and suggest that the anxiety occurs because of the difficulty of "reading" race and the tenuousness of visually acquired racial knowledge in the novel. This marked moment of non-humor occurs near the end of the novel, when the book's grotesquery veers toward violence, black becomes white and then black again, and the referents for the signs of blackness are up for grabs.

Only the pertinent details of this otherwise confusing section are recounted here. Snobbcraft and Buggerie, the two leaders of the Anglo-Saxon Association and members of the Democratic Party, have found out, through genealogical research, that they, along with most of the white population in the United States, have African American blood. Their black ancestry thus derails their election campaign based on racial purity. Trying to escape angry mobs at their homes, Snobbcraft and Buggerie hide their identities by rubbing black shoe polish over their faces and hands and attempt to pass as "rare" Negroes in Mississippi. (Schuyler presents us with quite literally "lampblacked Anglo-Saxons.") They encounter a lynch mob of "Christ Lovers," a whole community of uneducated white Southerners, while still wearing the black shoe polish. How effective is language in Happy Hill, Mississippi, a place where most of the residents are illiterate? There is a sign in the center of town outside the general store that says, "NIGER REDE & RUN; IF U CAN'T REDE, RUN ENEYHOWE" (*BNM*, 165). The sign, though misspelled and grammatically incorrect, still functions, still manages to interpellate the correct subjects: there are no blacks in Happy Hill. The two politicians wash off the polish and eventually convince the mob that they are indeed white. This, however, brings back the threat of lynching, for the congregation cannot read but they can see: they identify Snobbcraft and Buggerie from their pictures in the newspaper; learn of the politicians' black ancestry from a more literate white citizen; and, since "a newspaper wouldn't lie" (*BNM*, 174), the angry crowd decides to lynch the Democratic candidates anyway. The incident is described in detail by Schuyler: "The two men, vociferously protesting, were stripped naked, held down . . . and their ears and genitals cut off with jack knives and the fiendish cries of men and women. When this crude surgery was completed, some wag sewed their ears to their backs and they were released and told to run" (*BNM*, 175). This rapid exchange of racial categories and racial affiliation serves to question the *spectator's* race:

> There were in the assemblage two or three whitened Negroes, who, remembering what their race had suffered in the past, would fain have gone to the assistance of the two men but fear for their own lives restrained them. Even so they were looked at rather sharply by some of the Christ Lovers because they did not appear to be enjoying the spectacle as thoroughly as the rest. Noticing these questioning glances, the whitened Negroes began to yell and prod the burning bodies with sticks and cast stones at them. This exhibition restored them to favor and banished any suspicion that they might not be one-hundred-per-cent Americans. (*BNM*, 176)

Schuyler here explicitly portrays whiteness and violence as requirements to being "one-hundred-percent American." Performance trumps traumatic memory, and the attempts to secure the meanings of whiteness are repetitively denied. If "it takes one to know one," that knowledge itself is predicated on reading practices that privilege visual signs over language.[42] Visual signs take over linguistic ones; and at this moment even Schuyler seems to be at a loss for words. The section ends somewhat abruptly with the narrative intrusion of "AND SO ON AND SO ON" (*BNM*, 176), as if Schuyler was uncertain, after such vivid brutality, how to return to the lighthearted sexual innuendo that initiated the scene and characterizes other sections of *Black No More*.

The anxiety that emerges here is an anxiety precipitated by racial *absence*, the unease that results when, after a "blackless America" is achieved, "reading" race is no longer a possibility.[43] By the end of the novel, racial hierarchies are upended, with white signifying black and a return to the privileges of color that marked the beginning of the novel. Forced to reject the claims of essentialism yet still needing to demonstrate the compulsory, repetitive nature of racial bias, the latter portion of *Black No More* descends into the grotesque. The problems associated with racism—discriminatory practices, stereotypes of groups, national leaders and politicians who use race to mobilize a base—recur with an incessant banality. The end of *Black No More* demonstrates that in the absence of real social change, the physical erasure of the black-white hierarchy accomplishes little, and America becomes "definitely, enthusiastically mulatto-minded" (*BNM,* 179). Hierarchies are needed, both despite and because of the absence of physically different races.

LANGSTON HUGHES, commenting on the genre of satire in his autobiography *The Big Sea,* claimed that "except [for] the obvious satire of George S. Schuyler's *Black No More,"* African Americans lacked an appreciation for irony.[44] Hughes criticized those African American readers who, in any writing regarding the race, wanted only unambiguous denunciations of discrimination, clear calls to improve conditions for black Americans, and obviously "positive" images, representations that, in equating language and referent, recall the *Crisis* symposium's questions. Hughes suggested that their displeasure with ironic wit keeps black people from locating subtle meanings in satirical humor and from appreciating the strategic possibilities of satire, of the "joke," as Ralph Ellison puts it, "that always lies between appearance and reality."[45] The modernism of *Black No More* resides in its effects, by separating the signs and meanings of blackness from the body. But the somewhat depressing aspect of the novel is that there is nothing beneath Schuyler's lampblack, satirical makeup. Schuyler's race-erasing narrative is one only of surface effects.

Hughes's statement that "the strange inability on the part of many of the Negro critics to understand irony, or satire" was made in reference to Carl Van Vechten and his novel *Nigger Heaven.*[46] The need to read "beneath the surface" of Schuyler's writings perhaps applies even more succinctly to Van Vechten and his novel. In letters to friends and family members, Van Vechten stated that he wanted the title to resonate ironically with readers. When the book was released, black New Yorkers not only did *not* read beneath the surface; they refused to read beyond the title. And yet Van Vechten does manage to capture some form of modernism in his representations of African Americans. Those representations, as we will see in the next chapter, are found not so much in his book as in his photographic portraits.

Any coherent domain of collective activity is always strategic and selective.

James Clifford, *The Predicament of Culture*

We are now in a better position to appreciate the structure of the system of possession: a given collection is made up of a succession of terms, but the final term must always be the person of the collector.

Jean Baudrillard, "The System of Collecting"

Collectin' Van Vechten

The Narrative and Visual Collections of Carl Van Vechten

CARL VAN VECHTEN'S 1926 novel is most famously known for linking a racial epithet with a sanctified space. The very title, *Nigger Heaven,* was, and still is, offensive enough to dissuade one from glancing at the pages within the covers.[1] After perusing the novel, after doing what critics of the novel advised against— that is, reading the pages behind the intemperate name—one discovers several possible motivations for choosing the appellation. The most objective reason is geographical: the phrase refers to Harlem's location uptown in New York City, "above" white New Yorkers downtown. In the mouths of some of Van Vechten's characters, the phrase signals both the unique possibilities and the problems of this predominantly black space. "Nigger Heaven" is either a term of endearment for the area or an ironic reference to the harsh labor conditions for the black workers of the city. More provocatively, the title suggests the segregated theater: "Nigger Heaven" is the cramped balcony or gallery which overlooks the spacious whites-only orchestra seating. One character, Byron, uses the phrase to suggest that although the orchestra section supposedly offers the best seats in the house, the view is limited:

Nigger Heaven! Byron moaned. Nigger Heaven! That's what Harlem is. We sit in our places in the gallery of this New York theatre and watch the white world sitting down below in the good seats in the orchestra. Occasionally they turn their faces up towards us, their hard, cruel faces, to laugh or sneer, but they never beckon. It never seems to occur to them that Nigger Heaven is crowded, that there isn't another seat, that something has to be done. It doesn't seem to occur to them either, he went on fiercely, that we sit above them, that we can drop things down on them and crush them, that we can swoop down from this Nigger Heaven and take their seats.[2]

Byron's monologue exposes the different perspectives on the theatrical performance available to the white and to the black audience and, more important, the compromised position of power of the segregated whites in the orchestra seats. In his description, the white spectators are at a distinct disadvantage, for with only a limited view of those behind and above them, they cannot determine when they might become the object of violence. Moreover, in order to see what is behind them, they must turn their heads awkwardly; the black audience members, in contrast, can quite easily "swoop" down from the gallery and usurp the whites' seats. The partitioning of space in Byron's metaphorical theater reflects a familiar dualism, a doubled quality that appears repetitively in relation to several key issues surrounding the novel, in both contemporaneous and later assessments of the text and its author, and in the period of the New Negro Movement itself. These issues appear to be prejudged according to the race of the reader or spectator. As Charles Scruggs has suggested, publisher Alfred A. Knopf capitalized on the contradictory assumptions a reader might draw from the title because of his or her race. Analyzing Aaron Douglas's two publicity drawings for the novel, he argues that the title reveals Harlem as the "metaphor" for a desired heavenly space in the eyes of white readers but as a "myth" of self-sufficiency to black readers, noting that the publisher used the two pictures to promote the book differently in the white and the black press.[3]

Like the disparate reactions to the title, division emerges in the critical evaluations of the white presence within the New Negro Movement, those occasional moments when, in Byron's words, the whites in the orchestra turned their gaze "to laugh or sneer." Either white philanthropy helped black writers and propelled the Harlem Renaissance forward, or white assistance promoted "primitive," exotic ideas about blackness and stifled the creativity of emerging young artists. Whereas Langston Hughes stated that Van Vechten did more for the race than anyone else in the period, the poet Sterling Brown argued that

Van Vechten "corrupted the Harlem Renaissance."[4] Competing perspectives arose yet again when the black writer picked up his or her pen. James Weldon Johnson, recalling Du Bois's articulation of double consciousness, described the contradictory expectations sometimes faced by the early black writer hoping to portray his or her race while reaching a wide (and white) readership: "It is more than a double audience[,] it is a divided audience, an audience made up of two elements with differing and often opposite and antagonistic points of view."[5]

What becomes evident in this series of debates in which two positions are always so neatly and concisely available is that the doubled responses mask less neat, less clear-cut studies of complicated figures and cultural processes. While it is easy to argue for or against any one side, the presence and influence of Carl Van Vechten during this time are not as transparent as any two positions may suggest. Van Vechten, unlike some other white writers on black themes, had a uniquely privileged position both with white publishers and with prominent black literary and artistic personalities. Van Vechten had a range of friendships which varied from the well-to-do Alfred and Blanche Knopf to the sometimes unabashedly broke Ethel Waters. And while he helped get black writers published, Van Vechten also, as becomes obvious in his correspondence with the Knopfs in the 1940s and 1950s, prevented some black writers from making it onto Knopf's booklist.[6]

Ironically, the preeminent white writer of the period experienced the dilemma of the dual audience that James Weldon Johnson described and that was so common among early African American writers. Black writers may have felt hindered by trying to serve a contradictory readership, but Van Vechten, I would suggest, nourished such contradictions. He positioned himself as a mediator, as the guide between the black and white literary worlds, the bridge between uptown Harlem and Central Park. As with Knopf's publicity for the book, exploiting this division in spectatorship or perspective was key to the construction of the novel. Although *Nigger Heaven* is a pedagogical book serving two disparate audiences, one must resist such binary thinking, even though, or indeed because, such dualisms form a core component of the novel. Such dualistic thinking misses the larger arguments the book makes, not only about black representation but also about the black body, the phenomenon of a "renaissance," and modernist narrative itself.

While the title invokes the metaphor of the theater, the novel as a whole displays the subtle use of a different metaphor that more accurately suggests Van Vechten's aesthetic practices, that of the collection. In what follows I read

Van Vechten through the two elements that have most influenced his controversial and ambivalent position in African American literary history: his collection of African American arts, letters, and photographs and his contributions to and patronage of the Harlem Renaissance. I examine the specific, concrete products of this nexus of collection and contribution: his "Photographs of Blacks," and what he quite confidently calls in correspondence to friends "my black book," *Nigger Heaven*.[7] I seek not to condemn or to apologize for Van Vechten but to explain several taken-for-granted contradictions concerning his role and his best-selling novel: why, for instance, some of the most prominent and now canonical black writers of the period lauded the book, particularly the black writers who form the core of this study, and why better-written novels by African American writers on similar "low" subjects failed to do as well as Van Vechten's. Van Vechten presents Harlem as a museum attraction, an assemblage of black bodies on display. *Nigger Heaven* functions as a discourse of collecting, a narrative of his consumption of black culture and a way for him to promote and stage a certain desired representation of black artists while also educating a white public unfamiliar with the New Negro. As forms of the visual, the collection and the photograph help Van Vechten establish and reinforce the signs and symbols of a "renaissance." Problematically for Van Vechten, however, the collection and the photograph are also modes of cultural remembrance that, in celebrating a culture, also risk reducing that culture to predetermined types, to a group's supposed "essentials," which for African American culture has frequently been the body. Only in the photographs does this reduction to particular types—to bodies—convey the ironic distance necessary to enable the viewer to "appreciate" Van Vechten's collecting practices.

Van Vechten's presence during the Harlem Renaissance and his subsequent collection devoted to black culture resonate with debates about Western institutions' owning or collecting objects from non-Western cultures. James Clifford has detailed the "predicament" such institutions and ethnographers face when observing, writing about, or collecting objects or data that purport to reflect a group. Regardless of whether the items reside in systems of art or science, the resultant "assembled codes and artifacts [are] always susceptible to critical and creative recombination."[8] That is, the collector or the curator can impose or invent the system by which to organize the objects. As Jonathan Weinberg has noted, the act of collecting and reassembling was a significant part of Van Vechten's personality.[9] In order to create his numerous personal scrapbooks, Van Vechten clipped innocuous newspaper and magazine text and rearranged the cuttings to reflect his point of view, usually creating a humorous, pornographic reading. Van Vechten's practice of assembling and rearranging characterizes just one of the many "crises" of representation within the Harlem Renaissance. Indeed, after the question of "The Negro in Art—How Shall He Be Portrayed?" the other important aesthetic dilemma was whether or not white authors had the "right" or the creative ability to represent the New Negro. Reading *Nigger Heaven* as a collection foregrounds the contested nature of black artistic representation and problematizes the charges of appropriation that arise so frequently when white authors are discussed in this period: Who "owns" the representation of the New Negro? What is the "proper" relation of the white writer to black subject matter? Van Vechten is significant—and problematic—to the Harlem Renaissance because of his role in determining which "codes and artifacts," to use Clifford's words, should achieve currency in African American aesthetics and how these elements should be structured.

An analysis of the collection is particularly appropriate in a discussion of Van Vechten because he consciously sought to preserve elements of black culture and the personal history and mementos of the black writers with whom he came into contact, valuable materials that would later define twentieth-century African American culture. In early correspondence between Van Vechten and Langston Hughes, for instance, Van Vechten asked the twenty-four-year-old, minimally published poet for a favor: "Will you do something for me? I want you, if you will, to write me out the story of your life—detailing as many of your pregrinations [*sic*] and jobs as you can remember." Hughes demurred, asking: "Wouldn't you be satisfied with an outline? I am still enmeshed in the affects of my young life to write clearly about it. I haven't yet escaped into serenity and grown old yet." Four days later, after Knopf decided to publish Hughes's collection of poems that would be called *The Weary Blues,* Van Vechten explained to Hughes why he had made the request. He "felt convinced that these things [the publication of his book and poems] and other things, would happen and . . . wanted to be prepared."[10] The "other things" included the publication of Hughes's poems in *Vanity Fair* and the recognition of Hughes as one of the brightest "new" black writers then becoming well known on the East Coast. Van Vechten's premonition of Hughes's eventual successes enabled him to claim that he had foreseen and guided the young poet to fame.

Van Vechten's "intuition" would be repeated throughout the 1920s, usually with artists already well known and acknowledged by African American audiences, a tendency to tardiness that may have led to Countee Cullen's remark to a friend that "Carl is coining money out of the niggers."[11] But Van Vechten's recognition of black artists was significant because he propelled these artists toward a wider audience and brought increased attention to their achievements. Van Vechten's help was, to put it politely, "acquisitive": as with Hughes, he collected information about the artists, for a variety of future uses, while his collections helped to ensure his significance to the Harlem Renaissance. Van Vechten "studied" black culture for several months before attempting *Nigger Heaven,* and in the process he performed the compromising, nonobjective roles of the collector, the tourist, and the agent.[12] Acting as a travel agent, Van Vechten provided tours to white curiosity seekers and guided them to the best spots. Through his efforts as a press agent, the novelist publicized the works of black writers such as Hughes, Zora Neale Hurston, and Nella Larsen. And in several cases Van Vechten felt authorized to act for or in the place of African American writers and leaders, particularly, as we shall see, within the pages of the consummate mass-circulation modernist magazine, *Vanity Fair.* His role as a mediator between the white and black literary worlds allowed him to offer suggestions to white editors and black writers about the subjects that would most engage white publishers and a white reading public.

Reading *Nigger Heaven* as a collection more clearly exposes the roles Van Vechten assumed in relation to black writers and conveys the significance of the visual in his brand of modernism. The collector shares with the tourist an interest in recognizing and accumulating signs.[13] Both the tourist and the collector, for example, play on the epistemological and ontological power of the visual: seeing is believing, as long as one has signs that are authentic, in terms of the souvenir, or selective, in terms of the collection. The tourist becomes the collector: having gathered up the best signs, he displays them for an accessible meaning, in this case a narrative or plot; and Van Vechten, with the assistance of Nella Larsen's friend Dorothy Peterson, organized what he considered the most representative instances of Harlem life, a collection that now resides at Yale University.

But *Nigger Heaven* is a collection, not a tourist's souvenir, a distinction that is particularly important in terms of the narrative possibilities of each. The souvenir functions as a "trac[e] of authentic experience"; it reminds the possessor of some moment, some context, some city; and it "reports" on one's individual experience of an event: "Such a narrative cannot be generalized to encompass the experience of anyone; it pertains only to the possessor of the object."[14] Unlike the souvenir, which functions as a narrative of a private moment, the collection relies on public display.[15] It conveys one's taste and consumption of objects; it reflects on the "selectivity of the collector" and the collector's ability to provide a narrative or a new context for the objects.[16] In addition, the collection fills in the space of one's environment with objects not of use value but of aesthetic value which mark the collector himself. As Susan Stewart notes, "when one wants to disparage the souvenir, one says that it is not authentic; when one wants to disparage the collected project, one says 'it is not *you.*'"[17] The collection, then, works not in the place of some event, metonymically, as does the souvenir, but rather metaphorically, as a reflection of the collector. In short, the distinction between a souvenir and a collection is that the collection's narrative is that of the collector himself.[18] The James Weldon Johnson Memorial Collection at Yale's Beinecke Library is a testament to Van Vechten's amazing ability to collect the Harlem Renaissance: the people, things, objects, and manuscripts that have influenced how the period is studied and remembered. Yet it is precisely because of this collecting spirit that he occupies such an ambivalent position. My aim is to apply pressure to the question of why Van Vechten occupies this conflicted position; in so doing I attempt to move beyond the question posed by the title of the narrative itself and its representations of blackness. Although *Nigger Heaven* celebrates the "mecca of the New Negro," it is, in fact, more about Van Vechten himself—or at least his ideas on the black modern. As we shall see, the novel that is supposedly about the New Negro becomes in effect a novel about Van Vechten, specifically about his ideas on how to represent the New Negro.

If we agree with Mieke Bal that collecting is not "a process about which a narrative can be told, but . . . itself a narrative," then Van Vechten's collection of black arts and letters tells us the story not only of Carl the Collector but also about the narrative of black representation in the 1920s, as well as how that narrative has been received as the history of the "Harlem Renaissance."[19] Which signs will Van Vechten select as representative, as readable and knowable to those within and outside the space? Which signs are authentic and "true" to the people he wants to place on parade? How does he keep the audience—the spectator, the tourist, or the theater patron—interested in the performance? Reading Van Vechten's relation to black culture through the discourse of the collection offers a way to comprehend his highly problematic presence during the Harlem Renaissance as well as the incomparable legacy left by his voyeuristic interest in black culture. The concept of the collection is appropriate to a study of Van Vechten's novel as well because *Nigger Heaven,* as with the "best" collections, seeks to educate and entertain, and the narrative accomplishes this through the gaze and the body. *Nigger Heaven* reads the space of Harlem as a place of sexual experimentation, one dependent on knowing and showing the body. The novel privileges those Harlemites who know how to use their bodies and the bodies of others. The "codes and artifacts," the signs dispersed throughout the novel that would come to represent, positively or negatively, the Harlem Renaissance, are all bodily inflected.

Van Vechten's *Vanity (Fair)*

Van Vechten had few qualms about inserting himself into the debate over what a New Negro was and what his or her art should be; and in fact he helped to push the issue into the magazine pages of white America. In several articles and brief notes in *Vanity Fair,* Van Vechten stated his unapologetic interest in the more salacious aspects of black life and urged a variety of black artists, including writers, theater producers, and musicians, to "exploit" this subject matter or else risk having white artists do it for them. Covering a variety of black aesthetic life, the articles articulate a New Negro program, that is, Van Vechten's theory of collecting and cataloguing. He selects and orders the signs of blackness that will come to represent authentic blackness to non-Harlemites and to readers of his novel. The articles delineate his strategy of black modernism, which is stated frequently and didactically in *Nigger Heaven.*

Van Vechten selected one of the most appropriate venues to discuss his interest in the New Negro and to introduce an unknowing white public to the artistry and modernism that resided in black culture. In the 1910s and 1920s *Vanity Fair* and its editor, Frank Crowninshield, epitomized urbane, sophisticated New York; the magazine in fact helped launch several trends that would come to define the modern. The risk-taking monthly published photos of African and African-influenced European art before an appreciative Western audience developed. Crowninshield was the "unofficial publicity agent" for the groundbreaking Armory Show of 1913, and *Vanity Fair* was one of the earliest American journals to reproduce the work of artists from the show.[20] As owner and publisher Condé Nast later reminisced, Crowninshield's attention to modern art nearly ruined the magazine, for the editor's "interest in the modern French art movement, at first, did us a certain amount of harm. We were ten years too early . . . in talking about Van Gogh, Gauguin, Matisse, Picasso, etc. At first . . . people took the ground that we were (presumably) insane." Crowninshield also published several new young writers, including e. e. cummings, Aldous Huxley, and Dorothy Parker. By the 1920s *Vanity Fair* had become the magazine of social get-togethers, the journal that covered "the things people talk about at parties—the arts, sports, theatre, [and] humor."[21] Thus the appearance of Van Vechten's articles in the magazine was more than fortuitous. The journal offered a frame, a guide for readers on how to anticipate the innovative and how to appreciate the latest modern fad, including this intriguing figure called the "New Negro." Van Vechten's brief notes and articles, written throughout the peak years of the Harlem Renaissance, presented a series of platforms to educate white readers. The essays not only introduced a white public to the literary and artistic New Negro but also tested Van Vechten's ideas about the modern and provided an extended marketing opportunity for his "Negro novel."

Van Vechten's earliest *Vanity Fair* articles specifically devoted to the New Negro were "notes of introduction" to two of the emerging black poets of the time, Countee Cullen and Langston Hughes. Listing a "who's who" of New Negro writers, musicians, and dancers, Van Vechten christened Cullen "one of the best of the Negro writers" and likened him to Alexander Pushkin, because "he is able to write stanzas which have no bearing on the problems of his own race."[22] Van Vechten provided a short lesson on Cullen's literary style, suggesting how the poet should be read: Cullen has a "passionate eloquence," but "a satiric or bitter aftertaste is likely to linger in his most ostensibly flippant verse." Van Vechten's note on Langston Hughes emphasized the descriptive and the exotic: "His cabaret verses dance to the rhythm of Negro jazz; now he mourns for the hurt of the black man; again he celebrates the splendor of the women of Mexico or the savage beauty of the natives of the African coast."[23] *Vanity Fair*'s practice when publishing black poets was different from that of other magazines during the 1920s. The *Atlantic Monthly,* for instance, published African American writers such as George Schuyler and Rudolph Fisher; and H. L. Mencken's magazine *American Mercury* also published black writers, but their essays appeared on their own, without a statement of explanation or "introduction" by someone like Van Vechten. Van Vechten's notes on the two black poets, however, functioned in much the same way as his introduction to the 1927 edition of James Weldon Johnson's *Autobiography of an Ex-Colored Man,* which Siobhan Somerville and John Young compare to the authenticating essays by white editors of black-authored slave narratives.[24] The notes speak of a group new to the *Vanity Fair* reader and to which Van Vechten had privileged access. Moreover, Van Vechten had some influence on which poems the poets sent to the journal. In a letter to Hughes, Van Vechten instructs him to "send as many jazz and cabaret things as you happen to have on hand."[25] Van Vechten's advice helped Hughes get published, advanced the sale of the magazine, and contributed to black readership of the white journal. After *Vanity Fair* published four of Hughes's poems in the September 1925 issue, Hughes informed Van Vechten that "Vanity Fair is having an unprecedented sale in the colored colony here in the last few months. Colored shop keepers who had never heard of the magazine a short while ago are displaying it now and I've already autographed no less than six copies on the page containing my poems."[26]

Although the brief notes proclaimed Van Vechten's "finds" of Cullen and Hughes, it was in a series of *Vanity Fair* essays that Van Vechten revealed the possessive drive of the collector and identified the specific qualities of blackness that would characterize his conception of the black modern. The qualities were, for the most part, elements that the educated New Negro refused to develop because of "an explicable tendency on the part of the Negro to be sensitive concerning all that is written [or sung] about him."[27] Repeating a claim that appeared the same month as his *Crisis* symposium response, Van Vechten quite candidly admitted his interest in the salacious side of black life, as well as his premonition that white authors would exploit this infrequently used material. As he observed in "'Moanin' Wid a Sword in Ma Han': A Discussion of the Negro's Reluctance to Develop and Exploit His Racial Gifts," the "low-life of Negroes offers a wealth of exotic and novel material while the life of the cultured Negro does not differ in essentials from the life of the cultured white man." For Van Vechten, the underside of black life was more worthy of creative energy; and it provided material that, like other artifacts from a culture perceived to be exotic, was capable of being possessed. Van Vechten argued that the extreme sensitivity about how the African American is represented might actually hinder the development of black art. Notably, his guidelines for producing successful black art echo Alain Locke's call for objectivity in the preface to *The New Negro*. Van Vechten wrote, "Until novels about Negroes, by either white or coloured writers, are regarded as dispassionately from the aesthetic standpoint as books about Chinese mandarins, I see little hope ahead for the new school of Negro authors."[28] Van Vechten's essays promote the perception of African American life as property or a heritage that the black artist may forfeit without proper usage, warning that white men "who have a nose that senses demand" would take traditional black art forms such as the spirituals and "ma[k]e them enough their own so that the public will be surfeited sooner or later with opportunities to enjoy them."[29]

Until a "chocolate Ziegfeld" could be found, Van Vechten offered "a few hints" to the black producer or director in the essay "Prescription for a Negro Theatre." He provides specific, bodily advice for what he personalizes as "my spectacle," selecting distinctive signs that would suggest an image of black "authenticity."[30] In a somewhat surprising discussion of skin color and black women, Van Vechten notes the importance of the proper shade of skin color in casting a chorus line. Where current Negro cabarets failed, according to the writer, was in refusing to employ dark-skinned dancers; using light-skinned women, he predicted, would "likely have the ultimate effect of destroying the last remnants of general public interest in these revues." Light-skinned black chorus girls "disappoint" a white audience and deny the possibility of a vividly pleasing image. Indeed, "a fascinating effect might be achieved by engaging a rainbow chorus: six black girls, six 'seal-browns,' six 'high yellas,' and six pale creams."[31] Published in October 1925, precisely when expatriate Josephine Baker was starring in *La Revue Nègre,* "Prescription for a Negro Theatre" un- cannily describes Baker's show in Paris, particularly when Van Vechten details how he would stage the high point of the entertainment: "a wild pantomimic drama set in an African forest with the men and women as nearly nude as the law allows. There, in front of a background of orange-tinted banana fronds and amethyst palm leaves, silhouetted against a tropical blue sky divided by a silver moon, the bucks, their assegais stabbing the sky[,] . . . and their lithe-limbed, brown doxies, meagrely [sic] tricked out in multi-hued feathers, would enact a fantastic, choregraphic [sic] comedy of passion."[32]

Van Vechten's aesthetic directives are corporeal and gendered: black produc- ers should include a wide range of black women, not because it would reflect more accurately the shades of blackness that constitute "Aframerica" but be- cause it would create a more pleasurable and, one could argue, sensual vision of a "rainbow." Van Vechten's meticulous and extensive details do not challenge "the national mental attitude," as James Weldon Johnson suggests the "true" black art will do.[33] Rather Van Vechten argues that black writers, painters, and producers need to be less resistant to portraying what he calls the "picturesque" elements of black life, urging that "the true artist speaks out fearlessly. The critic judges the artistic result; nor should he be concerned with anything else."[34] Van Vechten's cunning method of self-plagiarism functioned as a mode of publicity for his "black book." " 'Moanin' Wid a Sword in Ma Han,' " pub- lished four months before *Nigger Heaven,* used imagery that would appear in the novel, specifically the language that contributes to Byron's metaphor of the theater and, hence, the novel's title. Commenting on a black musician's classical music recital, Van Vechten notes the audience's unenthusiastic response: "There was, to be sure, perfunctionary applause, but we, who sat in the orchestra chairs, were not moved to make any excessive demonstration of spontaneous appreciation."[35] Writing in response to this disappointing black performance, Van Vechten urges African American artists to reject whatever sounds artificial in favor of the more authentic sounds of black life, an injunction stressed throughout *Nigger Heaven.*

Additional articles by Van Vechten developed his theories about creating a popular, commercial black entertainment in the theater or indelible portraits of black life in novels and songs. In order to do this, the black artist had to take advantage of the difference offered by blackness and shape such difference into a better black art. Van Vechten teased and prepared the white reader for what was coming in *Nigger Heaven.* His theatrical devices, such as jazz music and cabaret dancing halls, came to symbolize the primordial, instinctual nature of the black which intrigued proponents of the white American modern. The essays, in short, selected, ordered, and made credible Van Vechten's criteria for a Negro art. His "powerful discriminations"—why a chorus should have both dark-skinned and light-skinned women, for example—were made sensible to the *Vanity Fair* reader, if not the New Negro artist.[36] Determined and dissected in such a public space as the magazine with an estimated circulation of 100,000 readers, the signs picked out by Van Vechten were also signs that were, at the least, looked for by the developing white audience of the New Negro.[37] His articles provided the starting point for his larger project of assembling his collected artifacts and his various experiences into, quite literally, a narrative. This is not to say that it was only Van Vechten's articles that identified the signs of the Harlem Renaissance, but that Van Vechten's pre–*Nigger Heaven* writings influenced the evaluation of such signs.

Harlem Bodies

Nigger Heaven is Van Vechten's compilation of knowledge, a grouping of African American types that introduced Harlem to outsiders. Although this accumulation of events and types was, after the title, the greatest source of complaints about the book (Charles Larson calls Van Vechten's plot "hardly more than a string of thematically related events"),[38] the large number of items, what Baudrillard calls a "succession of terms," helped Van Vechten to instruct both the white and the black reader.[39] The characters' dress, style, and activities promote a New Negro aesthetics and develop Van Vechten's "prescription" for creating African American art, a cure that contradicted the theories about a better black art posed by James Weldon Johnson. Van Vechten and Johnson were good friends (along with Alfred Knopf, the two shared the same birthday of June 17, and for several years after their first meeting celebrated the day together with close friends and family), and Johnson was one of the earliest African Americans to take Van Vechten around Harlem, yet the two differed significantly in terms of portraying the "New Negro." Both Johnson and Van Vechten were aware of the nexus of the body and the visual in African American art. While Johnson sought to rupture that division, however, Van Vechten called attention to it. *Nigger Heaven* divides Harlemites by their use of the body and grants victories and romantic or personal success to those who know best how to use their bodies in navigating the black, urban and modern space.

The reason why *Nigger Heaven* disappoints is in part because Van Vechten's "prescriptive" features, the aesthetic injunctions stressed in the *Vanity Fair* articles, dominate the novel. Just as Van Vechten's ideas on black art devalue the ordinary for the more visually pleasing, *Nigger Heaven*'s study of the sensational side of Harlem mitigates any "positive" focus on educated New Negroes. The novel, separated into two sections, can be read as a compendium of two "reports" of embodied Harlem, peopled with characters who supposedly reveal all facets of Harlem life. The bodies are types, "collected" and presented not for their individuality but for representing preconfigured ideas of the black New Yorker. The first section, which centers on the "New Negro," features Mary Love and Byron Kasson, characters who are removed initially from the body and its "natural" instincts. The second section, concerning a stylish hustler and a beautiful female dancer amid scenes from Harlem's cabarets, revels in the body and risqué entertainment. These doubled pairings help articulate Van Vechten's lessons on writing about blackness and representing the black modern; but the virginal Mary and the would-be writer Byron compete for the reader's interest with the more scandalous Lasca Sartoris and the Scarlet Creeper, both of whom, like Van Vechten himself, embody a queer subjectivity.

The first section of *Nigger Heaven* presents characters who appreciate art and the finer things in life but at the expense of their supposed sexual proclivities. For these representatives the body is controlled or static, accessible only through conventional ideas of art and beauty. Cultured, reserved librarian Mary Love, for example, represses the body and her sexual desires, for she has "an instinctive horror of promiscuity, of being handled, even touched, by a man who did not mean a great deal to her" (53). Mary and her love interest, Byron, are so far removed from black culture that they learn the accepted signs of black authenticity not from their black friends but from whites familiar with black culture: Byron learns to Charleston from white boys at his college, the University of Pennsylvania, while Mary learns "the lingo," black dialect, by reading DuBose Heyward's *Porgy*. More tellingly, Mary Love cannot admit the sensual nature of her body, in ways that foreshadow Larsen's Helga Crane of *Quicksand*.[40] She lacks the emotion that is supposedly inherent to African Americans:

> [Mary] cherished an almost fanatic faith in her race, a love for her people in themselves, and a fervent belief in their possibilities. She admired all Negro characteristics and desired earnestly to possess them. Somehow, so many of them, through no fault of her own, eluded her . . .
>
> Savages! Savages at heart! And she had lost or forfeited her birthright, this primitive birthright which was so valuable and important an asset, a birthright that all the civilized races were struggling to get back to—this fact explained the art of a Picasso or a Stravinsky. (89)

Mary identifies more readily with her blackness through high modernist art. Although she can quote whole passages from Gertrude Stein's "Melanctha," a novella about a mixed-race woman who has several intimate encounters, Mary cannot readily acknowledge her feelings for Byron. In addition, she feels an un-acknowledged sexual attraction to the other black women she meets, particularly the beautiful Lasca Sartoris. When Mary first encounters Lasca's photograph, she is struck by the other woman's beauty: "What was it, even in this dead, flat counterpart, that gave to the lady the impression of supervitality? Mary did not know. Yet she was aware at once of the abundant sex-appeal in this lithe crea-ture's body, an appeal which had filtered through the lens, been caught on the negative, and finally been stamped perdurably on this sheet of paper" (80). Mary and Lasca finally meet at the Charity Ball, a social event that attracts whites and blacks of various classes. As Mary watches Lasca flirt provocatively with Byron, her primordial instincts threaten to engulf her: "How Mary hated her! How she longed for the strength, the primitive impulse that would urge her to spring at Lasca's throat, tear away the collar of her sapphires, disfigure that golden-brown countenance with her nails" (166). Mary's emotions overwhelm her only in reac-tion to Lasca, a woman who is associated with carnality to such an extent that she inspires primal feelings from others throughout the novel.

Byron, an aspiring New Negro writer who is briefly Mary's boyfriend, does not suffer from a lack of bodily reserve. In fact we learn that Byron has not been able to keep his passions entirely in check when his father makes a passing reference to a "sordid episode" with a "servant-girl at college" (173). Byron's lack of self-discipline and inadequacy are all the more noticeable in comparison to the successes of the other men in the novel. Randolph Pettijohn, frequently referred to as "The Bolito King," makes a fortune selling hotdogs on the streets of Harlem, invests in real estate, opens a cabaret, and works the numbers. Anatole Longfellow, also known as the Scarlet Creeper, uses the Harlem street as his stage. It is the Scarlet Creeper in particular who accentuates Byron's haplessness. The Creeper exemplifies a type of man that Lewis Erenberg in his history of cabarets in America calls the "tango pirate" or the "social gangster," who inhabited the underworld of nightclubs and cabarets. These types were dangerous because they "stole" the innocence of young women. Though "willfully aggressive," they were also "effeminate, will-less, and dependent on women for money." The Creeper exudes the confidence and machismo of the tango pirate, "a man heavily involved in sensual expression, combining the traits of expressiveness, absence of work, love of luxury, and fascination with women."[41] These strutting, rakish figures emphasize the more decadent aspects of the Harlem Renaissance and a corresponding interest in the body and clothing. When we first see the Scarlet Creeper, he is wearing "a tight-fitting suit of shepherd's plaid which thoroughly reveal[s] his lithe, sinewy figure to all who gaz[e] upon him.... A great diamond, or some less valuable stone which aped a diamond, glisten[s] in his fuchsia cravat" (3). The Creeper reveals his ability to manipulate his appearance and the space around him with the jewel, ambiguously either a diamond or a rhinestone, and establishes a masculine aesthetic sensibility through fashion, clothes, and, remarkably, the color hot pink. Like the men described by Susan Bordo for whom being "festooned with sparkling jewelry is not a sign of effeminacy, but potency and social standing,"[42] men like the Scarlet Creeper can take traditionally feminine objects and display them as a sign of virile masculinity.

Throughout *Nigger Heaven* there is a strategic privileging of those who know how to parade, those who know how to position their bodies on Harlem's boulevards.[43] As James Weldon Johnson noted, "strolling" down Lenox Avenue or 135th Street in Harlem was not a hobby but an "art." The most successful were those who were dressed to compete, for "this [was] not simply going out for a walk; it [was] more like going out for adventure."[44] The Scarlet Creeper, whose name evokes his ability to saunter down the streets, embodies a more confident masculinity than does Byron. The Creeper's parade through Harlem offers the reader the first glance of the city and a brief "walking tour" of the area. He effectively navigates the space of the black capital; within seconds of starting down a Harlem street, he is propositioned by a woman. The Creeper is a figure who moves between the black upper and lower classes of the city, though he represents the underside of Harlem.[45] In contrast, Byron is ultimately unable to navigate the social and geographical spaces of either black Harlem or white New York.[46] Byron is a newcomer to the city, and while he anticipates that race will affect his immediate employment prospects, he fails to understand how class operates within an African American space. Compared to the everyday black worker, Byron fails to measure up. On his first day as an elevator operator, for instance, Byron watches his more skilled colleague work the buttons and the door: "All these maneuvers Byron, of course, had seen performed before, but with no comprehension of the difficulties they involved" (193). Perceived as acting uppity and unable to imitate a black dialect to fit in with the other working-class black men, Byron soon loses that job. The Creeper, however, never seems to have a job yet always has money, his wealth rooted in his ability to appraise the bodies of others. The Creeper and his first "conquest," Ruby, engage in an unspoken mating ritual that revolves around the male gaze and the body, enacting a "game of mutual duplicity" (10). Although the Scarlet Creeper appears only briefly at different moments in the novel, his presence tends to overshadow the text, becoming an image of powerful and attractive masculinity that we do not see anywhere else.

One problem with *Nigger Heaven,* then, is that the representatives of the New Negro do not inspire confidence; one hesitates to place the future of the race in Byron's or Mary's hands, and the fact that Mary is the only figure in the novel who likes Byron does not reflect well on either character. Indeed, Mary unintentionally describes the reader's reaction to these characters when she tells Byron, "I believe . . . that [whites] actually prefer us when we're not respectable" (148). Van Vechten's collection of the educated New Negro compels the odd sensation that, even though the first and second sections of the novel are subtitled "Mary" and "Byron" respectively, one finishes the book knowing little about them. As Wallace Thurman notes of the "vapid" Mary, "there has been no realization that Mary Love is the least life-life [*sic*] character in the book, or that it is she who suffers most from her creator's newly acquired seriousness and sentimentality, she who suffers most of the whole ensemble because her creator discovered, in his talented trippings around Manhattan,

drama at which he could not chuckle."⁴⁷ What disappoints is the lack of interest one finds in the "good" New Negroes, even though they are the ones to
whom Van Vechten may have been the most sympathetic. Significantly, then,
the most engaging figures in *Nigger Heaven* are those who demonstrate an uninhibited sexuality, and those who are most "modern" display same-sex attractions. For all of Mary Love's recitations of Gertrude Stein and William Carlos
Williams, and Byron's attempts to become a New Negro writer by osmosis,
those who challenge conventional ideas of blackness are these "other" figures.
As in Thurman's novel *Infants of the Spring,* challenging proscriptive ideas of
blackness entails an awareness of sexual difference or, at the very least, comfort
with one's sexuality.

The novel was so unforgivable to black readers such as W. E. B. Du Bois and
Sterling Brown because the ending suggested the demise of the New Negro
writer, caught between art and propaganda, too self-confident for his own
good.⁴⁸ Our final glimpse of this racial "heaven" is in fact a hell; it reads as Van
Vechten's statement about New Negro impotence and ineptitude. The ending
takes place in the mind of a now drugged and cataleptic Byron: "They stood in a
circular hall entirely hung in vermilion velvet; even the ceiling was draped in
this fiery colour. . . . [D]ancers slipped through the folds of the hangings, men
and women with weary faces, faces tired of passion and pleasure. Were these the
faces of dead prostitutes and murderers? Pleasure seekers from the cold slabs of
the morgue?" (254). Byron ends the novel spent and used up by Lasca, his claims
to art destroyed, his manhood once again in doubt.⁴⁹ He shoots Randolph
Pettijohn, Lasca's new lover, but only *after* the Creeper has first killed Pettijohn.
The final image in the novel is that of the white hand of a police officer, ambiguously either assisting or arresting Byron. This New Negro's uncertain fate further contributes to the unattractiveness of the "good" ones. Charles Scruggs
argues that both Byron and the Creeper "have been reduced to style without
substance" and are "brought low . . . through the agency of Randolph Pettijohn."⁵⁰ But the Creeper is the real hero of the story. He exhibits control of his
body, of others, and of his space. Although the Scarlet Creeper loses his "piece,"
Ruby Silver, to another collector of money, the Bolito King, he avenges his loss.
It is the Creeper who escapes the law, while Randolph Pettijohn, the self-made
businessman, and Byron, the struggling New Negro writer, are caught up in the
perils of the big city.

There is one final rationale for the black general public's disapproval of the
novel. In a book explicitly about African Americans, Van Vechten often inserts

himself disingenuously into the text. He fictionalizes himself in *Nigger Heaven*, quite literally, in the figure of the white writer Gareth Johns, and more symbolically as the fictional editor of a national magazine seeking stories about African American life. Gareth Johns, a nervous newcomer in the homes of African Americans, manages to stay in the background during a dinner party scene, listening in amazement as Mary converses in French about African sculpture and recites from memory the poetry of Wallace Stevens. But unlike Gareth, Van Vechten the writer and collector never maintains a polite distance from the subjects he writes about, never tactfully admits his status as interloper or outsider. Van Vechten cannot help but enjoin, however ironically, in his fictional text what he also states continually in the *Vanity Fair* magazine articles. *Nigger Heaven* reveals Van Vechten's uncomplicated assumption of access to black culture, black life, and the black body, as well as black phrases. Hence Van Vechten's belief that his "in the know" use of the racial epithet in the title would be unproblematic.

Moreover, when Van Vechten does attempt to acknowledge his outsider status, he does it in such a way as to deride black rectitude in writing about black urban life, suggesting just how "un-modern" the New Negro writer risks becoming. This is perhaps best demonstrated in the scene in which the character Russett Durwood, a stand-in for H. L. Mencken, repeats some of Van Vechten's theories about black writing (221–27). Calling Byron to his office after reading the writer's graceless short story, Durwood interrogates Byron's, and by extension other black authors', writing skills: "Why in hell don't you write about something you know about" (222)? According to the editor of the *American Mars,* the current crop of black writers "employ all the old clichés and formulas that have been worried to death by Nordic blonds who, after all, never did know anything about the subject [of African American life] from the inside" (223). Durwood concludes his sermon by ordering Byron to submit another story only when he becomes "a regular author and not a pseudo-literary fake" (227). Despite his disavowal of propaganda, Van Vechten preaches to the New Negro writer in this section, and the novel achieves its full realization as a metanarrative in this scene. *Nigger Heaven* continually calls attention to itself (as Van Vechten usually calls attention to himself in various fictional guises) as a narrative, as an act of writing about "writing about the New Negro." Van Vechten's satirical style and the self-conscious modernist citations call attention to the novel as a metafiction about the possibilities of the New Negro novel and the perils of leaving such a text to be written by "Nordic blonds" such as Van Vechten.

In her analysis of Harlem Renaissance novels, Emily Bernard calls our attention to the numerous Van Vechten–like characters in other works of the Harlem Renaissance. These novels present, however peripherally, a white, blond male character who is often a writer interested in the Negro—books such as Larsen's *Passing,* Thurman's *Infants of the Spring* and *The Blacker the Berry,* Rudolph Fisher's *Walls of Jericho,* and Countee Cullen's *One Way to Heaven.* Bernard argues that white characters serve several narrative functions in black-authored Harlem Renaissance novels, such as acting as "mediators in relationships between black characters" and serving to "authenticate" fictional portrayals of a Harlem Renaissance frequented by white slummers.[51] It is also important to point out that Van Vechten's own novel provided the origin and model, the starting point, if you will, for the subsequent presence of this "exceptional" white figure in black fiction.[52] The presence of so many Van Vechten–type characters in black Harlem Renaissance fiction does more narrative work than simply demonstrate the influence of Van Vechten and his novel. They not only function as yet another "signpost" and an easy invocation of the zeitgeist of the Harlem Renaissance. These narrative "nods" to and acknowledgment of Van Vechten also suggest, however slightly, how some black authors contended with Van Vechten's "instructions" to the New Negro and subtly reveal what they thought about the influential white author and his book. Walter Thurman's Campbell Kitchen in *The Blacker the Berry,* for example, is "quite sincere in his desire to exploit those things in Negro life which he presumed would eventually win for the Negro a more comfortable position in American life." Similarly, in his review of *Nigger Heaven,* Thurman observes that "Van Vechten was rendered sincere during his explorations and observations of Negro life in Harlem."[53]

In Countee Cullen's 1932 novel *One Way to Heaven,* however, the Van Vechten–like character is a source of some amusement. Mattie, the black maid for the wealthy, black Constancia Brandon, falls in love with Sam, a hustler. Walter Derwent, a white author, is not invited to Mattie and Sam's wedding because Mattie does not approve of racial mixing. Derwent does, however, provide a nice wedding present, sent in absentia, for as Constancia informs Mattie, "Walter Derwent has coined enough money on his articles about us [Harlem's African Americans] to afford a handsome donation to the gift table." This comment, a near echo of Cullen's statement about Van Vechten to a friend, suggests that if white authors like Van Vechten exploit African Americans, the exploitation can at least go both ways. Earlier, at one of Constancia's mixed-raced parties, she introduced Derwent to a black author, bluntly letting him know the author's opinion that "your frequent visits to Harlem have an ulterior motive, that you look upon us as some strange concoction which you are out to analyze and betray." Later at the party, Cullen writes, "Walter Derwent sat in a corner and took notes, already shaping in his mind some clever sentence which he would employ in his recital of the affair." Although the Van Vechten–like character here makes only brief appearances, Cullen subtly reveals his distaste for certain aspects of Van Vechten's writing practices.[54]

In the frequent use of such characters, we see how Van Vechten's "succession of terms" leads back to himself. Miguel Covarrubias's famous caricature of Carl Van Vechten as a black man, "A Prediction," plays a specific role in Van Vechten's collections (figure 4.1). The drawing depicts for white readers the promise held out by *Nigger Heaven* and the lure of Van Vechten's other "black" compilations: that the white body can turn black through exposure to black culture. Covarrubias's sketch uniquely reflects the temporal element of collections and the sense of progression or followed sequence. "A Prediction" captures a future moment, the constantly deferred end result of the collection. For the concluding element of a collection is the collector, "the one who dictates [the collection's] signifiers—the ultimate signified being, in the final analysis, none other than himself."[55] Van Vechten, as Covarrubias implies, and as *Nigger Heaven* suggests, makes his collections into his own image. The circularity and self-reflexivity of the collection becomes apparent in the novel's avant-garde, parodic style, as well as in its "Glossary of Negro Words and Phrases."[56]

Van Vechten aggressively presents his version of the New Negro in *Nigger Heaven,* his characters embodying his type of black modernism. This is the final paradox of the book and one of the central contradictions of the contemporaneous reception of it: a novel that revels in presenting a metacommentary on the Harlem Renaissance being read "realistically," a claim made by both prominent and up-and-coming black writers and artists of the time. In his glowing review of *Nigger Heaven,* James Weldon Johnson noted that Van Vechten was the only white author who never "viewed the Negro as a type, who has not treated the race as a unit, either good or bad," though in fact these two "units" perfectly reflect the division of the novel into two sections. Charles Chesnutt claimed that the novel displayed "brilliancy and obvious honesty."[57] Eric Walrond enthused that "the Harlem it describes is accurately creditably glamorously enshrined." Nella Larsen wondered of herself and other black writers "why couldn't we have done something as big as this for ourselves," a

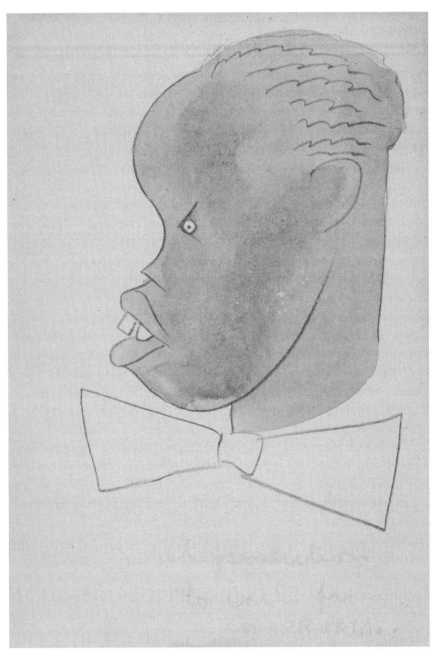

Figure 4.1. "A Prediction" by Miguel Covarrubias (1925). National Portrait Gallery,
Smithsonian Institution/Art Resource, NY. © Maria Elena Rico Covarrubias.

sentiment echoed by the editor of *Opportunity,* Charles Johnson.[58] Alain Locke called the book "a brilliant novel of manners," and Aaron Douglass told Van Vechten, "You have not only written a great and beautiful novel, but you have also pointed the way very clearly and definitively to young writers of color."[59] George Schuyler also praised *Nigger Heaven* and its author. Schuyler wrote a profile of Van Vechten for the black journal *Phylon,* having been recommended for the job by Harold Jackman, as well as a brief introduction for the 1950s Avon paperback edition of *Nigger Heaven* in which he declared the novel to be an "uncannily accurate portrait of Negro urban life in sophisticated New York."[60]

How are we to take these black writers' admiration for the novel? One wonders if the praise some bestowed on *Nigger Heaven* was not for the book itself but for what it opened up a space for them to accomplish. Harlem and its more prominent residents who are caricatured in *Nigger Heaven* were ripe for parody, something that the serious responses to the *Crisis* questionnaire and Du Bois's "Criteria of Negro Art" did not acknowledge.[61] By playing with Harlem as a referent, expanding what it stands for and being willing to poke fun at the area and its residents, Van Vechten in *Nigger Heaven* expands the possibility of representing Harlem and encourages (even as a negative example) future writers of the city to take some representational risks. Here, within the pages of *Nigger Heaven,* the concept of "Harlem" changes: it is not only a place now but also a narrative, the literal and literary site of Van Vechten's collected objects, that is, his newfound knowledge of black life—and a space for aesthetic experimentation.

Visual Irony

Carl Van Vechten's career in photography began in 1932, by which time he had "practically abandoned the writing profession."[62] By the 1940s the Van Vechten photographic portrait, like an invitation to one of his mixed-race parties in the 1920s, had become a status symbol, a sign of one's significance in either black or white artistic circles. Although both *Nigger Heaven* and Van Vechten's photographs celebrate African American life and personalities, there are significant differences between the two regarding representational possibilities, even when one takes into account the obvious differences of form. Although the desire to promote an interest in black arts informs both Van Vechten's literary and visual collections, it is the latter that resists the totalizing appropriation of black culture which underwrites the controversies surrounding *Nigger Heaven.*

Van Vechten's photographic collection contains hundreds of images of well-known personalities and ordinary individuals.[63] I am specifically interested in an extensive grouping titled "Photographs of Blacks," most of which are held at Yale University. Black female performers dominate this compilation, particularly Ethel Waters, whom Van Vechten recognized as the "real" star of the Harlem Renaissance. His images of women provide a necessary challenge to the masculine assumption of New Negro-ness ("The Negro in Art—How Shall *He* Be Portrayed?"). As Nancy Kuhl notes, "Van Vechten portraits have come to be the preeminent pictures of particular women."[64] This is especially the case for female Harlem Renaissance writers such as Zora Neale Hurston and Nella Larsen. Indeed, two of Van Vechten's photographs of Hurston in a feathered hat, one image of her laughing, the other of her "looking mean and impressive," now function not only as definitive images of Hurston but also as a larger metonym for the literary Harlem Renaissance itself (figure 4.2).[65] Similarly, Van Vechten's photographs of Larsen are reprinted in nearly every post-1980s biography and edition of her work. In what is a more than ironic reversal, the man who authored the most scandalous novel of the Harlem Renaissance is responsible for creating the visual images and documenting the personages that have come to define the period. His photographs quite literally shape our perceptions of the period's participants.

The Van Vechten photographs, taken for the most part outside the conventional time period of the Harlem Renaissance, reflect a type of black modernity. In fact several photographs dating from the post–Harlem Renaissance era reveal the irony and mockery that elude *Nigger Heaven*. The photographs do something that the narrative cannot: they embody and visualize irony. They invite, at times demand, reading and interpretation. Densely layered with multiple meanings, Van Vechten's photographs do not simply document the period and its personalities; they cite and parody the symbols of a black modernism he himself helped fashion and promote. The photographs foreground his often questionable appropriation of black culture, but they offer a better opportunity than *Nigger Heaven* to undermine the common reading practices that establish the black figure as consisting of merely and only body. Moreover, they reveal a larger point—that the visual can effect a disruption of the "more picturesque." That is, they can challenge the stereotypical, one-dimensional misreadings of and assumptions about blackness.

I have been, to use Roland Barthes's word, "pricked" by the photographs that display one of Van Vechten's frequently used props, what appears to be an

Figure 4.2. Zora Neale Hurston (1934), photograph by Carl Van Vechten. Yale Collection of American Literature, Beinecke Rare Book and Manuscript Library, Yale University. Reproduced by permission of the Carl Van Vechten Trust.

African mask (figures 4.3–4.5).[66] The photographs echo more familiar images that center on race, gender, and irony. Their content, a subject posing with a putatively African mask, appears to cite visually Man Ray's well-known 1926 photographs of Kiki of Montparnasse, collectively titled "Noire et blanche" (figures 4.6, 4.7).[67] Van Vechten heightens his ironic citation of Man Ray's heavily made-up white female by selecting as his subjects not a white woman but a black singer—Billie Holiday—also heavily made up, and an apparently nude white man.[68] The repetitive presence of the mask calls attention not to the person in any one photo but to the object in its various positions. The mask in Van Vechten's photos, however, does not have the sharp lines of traditional African masks. Instead the full, protruding lips and round cheeks constitute a sort of generic representation of the African, that is, the *Western* idea of Africa and the African. It is a romantic signpost of the continent, what a (white) American would think an African mask to be. This false reference to Africa in the photograph becomes an ambiguous sign that resists specification, typecasting, stagnation. Through the use of this artifice, Van Vechten foregrounds a sense of inauthenticity, in a way similar to his ironic and self-conscious citation of modernist literature in *Nigger Heaven,* a strategy that heightens the effect of fiction.

The photographs emphasize familiar stereotypes of the primitive, but the subjects seem to mock their familiarity. This is particularly evident in the Holiday images (figures 4.3, 4.4), in which Van Vechten deliberately poses the singer to mirror one of Man Ray's images (figure 4.7).[69] But instead of gazing at the African mask with reverence, as Man Ray's female subject does, Holiday in one photo stares at the viewer apathetically, an arched eyebrow conveying disaffection or boredom. Whereas Man Ray's image suggests a kind of seduction by Africa, Van Vechten's image derides such provocation. The juxtaposition of Holiday and the mask invites not seduction but comparison, and the mask fails to match up or hold the viewer's interest. A satire of Man Ray's image of white femininity gazing on blackness with longing and reverence, Van Vechten's photograph appears to challenge such adoration.

Ambiguous signifiers such as the mask help to account for the photographs' non-reduction to the body, that is, their adherence to the "less picturesque," in contrast to the novel. The photographs do not make the body specific or essential to blackness, a reduction that does occur at times in *Nigger Heaven* with the portrayal of the sensual Creeper and Lasca Sartoris. The photographs, however, collect irony and mockery, so that one must step back to fathom the

Figure 4.3. Billie Holiday (1949), photograph by Carl Van Vechten. Yale Collection of
American Literature, Beinecke Rare Book and Manuscript Library, Yale University. Reproduced
by permission of the Carl Van Vechten Trust.

Figure 4.4. Billie Holiday (1949), photograph by Carl Van Vechten. Yale Collection of American Literature, Beinecke Rare Book and Manuscript Library, Yale University. Reproduced by permission of the Carl Van Vechten Trust.

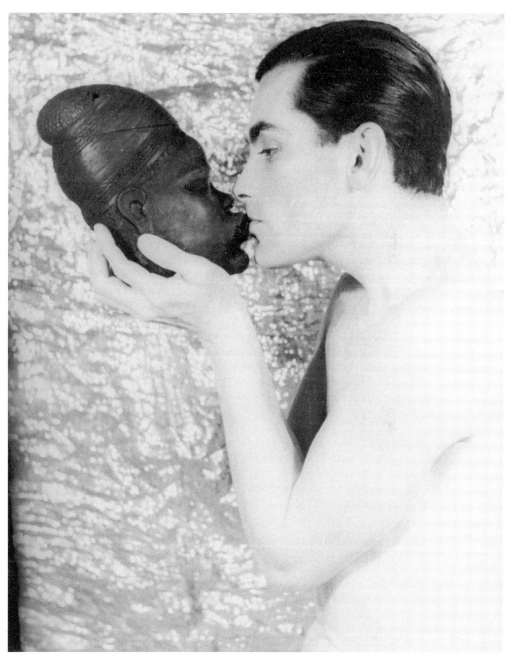

Figure 4.5. Hugh Laing with mask (1942), photograph by Carl Van Vechten. Yale Collection of American Literature, Beinecke Rare Book and Manuscript Library, Yale University. Reproduced by permission of the Carl Van Vechten Trust.

Figure 4.6. Man Ray, "Noire et blanche." Man Ray (1890–1976) © ARS, N.Y. 1926. Gelatin silver print, 6 ¾ × 8 ⅞". Gift of James Thrall Soby (132.1941). The Museum of Modern Art, New York, N.Y. Digital Image © The Museum of Modern Art/Licensed by SCALA/Art Resource, N.Y. © 2009 Man Ray Trust/Artists Rights Society (ARS), N.Y./ADAGP, Paris.

meaning intended by the accumulation of photos and poses. In another frequently reproduced photograph Bessie Smith seems to mock the vogue for all things African. A dark head with stereotypically comic African features sits on her shoulder, grinning. Smith looks askance, mirroring the eyes of the figure, and her eyebrows are furrowed in what appears to be an expression of bemusement (figure 4.8). Smith's attempt to mimic the figure (or Van Vechten's direction that she do so), and her quizzical expression produce a lighthearted effect. Like the others, this photograph works by embodying irony as a (modernist) style and by citing the "codes and artifacts" of black modern culture.

Figure 4.7. Man Ray, "Noire et blanche." Man Ray (1890–1976) © ARS, N.Y. AM1987-885.
Musee National d'Art Moderne, Centre Georges Pompidou, Paris. Photo Credit: CNAC/
MNAM/Dist. Réunion des Musées Nationaux/Art Resource, N.Y. © 2009 Man Ray Trust/
Artists Rights Society (ARS), N.Y./ADAGP, Paris.

Figure 4.8. Bessie Smith (1936), photograph by Carl Van Vechten. Yale Collection of American Literature, Beinecke Rare Book and Manuscript Library, Yale University. Reproduced by permission of the Carl Van Vechten Trust.

The distinction between the bodies in *Nigger Heaven* and the bodies in the photographs becomes more apparent when we examine the Van Vechten images next to those by another individual who helped memorialize Harlem, the African American photographer James Van Der Zee. There is a "straightness" to Van Der Zee's photos that the Van Vechten images do not aspire to, a literalness that helps explain Barthes's pronouncement in *Camera Lucida* that he finds Van Der Zee's photograph of a well-dressed African American family "touching by reason of its naiveté."[70] What Barthes reads disconcertingly as innocence may be perceived as a forthrightness, a frank desire to achieve American ideals, no matter how illusory those ideals may be. As we will see in chapter 5, Van Der Zee's photographs unambiguously capture African American hope and desire, the quest for an American dream in the face of legal restrictions that continued after World War I, despite the contributions of African Americans to the war effort. Van Der Zee's photographs are notable for this always present dichotomy of hope and pragmatism, what one may call a photographic depiction of double consciousness. In contrast, Van Vechten's photographs and scrapbooks are infused with an ironic, sardonic attitude.

This reading of Van Vechten and his two "collections" is not to suggest that there is nothing problematic about either his photographs or his book. Significantly, as the deliberate poses of some of his photographic subjects imply, Van Vechten exerted control over the space captured by the lens, usually the New York City apartment he shared with his wife.[71] Nor do I want to suggest that any appropriation, visual or literary, is permissible as long as the intention or effect is wry. But recognition must be paid to the way the visual images captured by Van Vechten, many of which have never been published, display an awareness of the present and future canonicity of the marketable signs of black culture, particularly the commodifiable Harlem Renaissance.

THE PROVENANCE of a collection is never uncomplicated. As Mieke Bal notes, "only retrospectively, through a narrative manipulation of the sequence of events, can the accidental acquisition of the first object *become* the beginning of a collection."[72] And indeed Van Vechten's version of the origins of the Harlem Renaissance displays a partiality that would give some—Alain Locke, Charles Johnson, and perhaps even James Weldon Johnson—pause. In 1962 Van Vechten offered a "self-congratulatory report" of the Harlem Renaissance in a letter to Blanche Knopf: "You started something when you published a book by Walter White.... Well what we started has eventually progressed....

The Negro has at last learned to say what is really on his mind[,] ... and I am proud that you and I started a movement that has become so lusty."[73] Van Vechten's letter to Knopf reveals a questionable interpretation of the beginning of the Harlem "collection." In Van Vechten's mind, he clearly had a groundbreaking role in the creation of the Renaissance. Reading Van Vechten as a collector helps us contextualize both the benefits and the problems in his motivations for mentoring and collecting black artists. It is because of his aggressive consumption that we have many significant manuscripts and artifacts from the Harlem Renaissance, but it is debatable whether Van Vechten was what James Clifford would call a "good collector," one who is able "to gather things around oneself tastefully, appropriately."[74]

Nigger Heaven suggests the importance of making people aware of spaces with which they may be unfamiliar, of making orchestra seat patrons and those in the gallery acknowledge each other. Van Vechten was attuned not only to the significance of the collection's content but to the space it defined as well, and he had astute motives for selecting the eventual repositories for his collections. He gave his black collection to Yale University in Connecticut and his music collection to Fisk University in Tennessee: "The idea was for whites to study black culture, and for blacks to study white culture. He was particularly delighted by the idea that white scholars would have to travel south to a black institution to study the music collection."[75]

Notably, Van Vechten's photographs rarely capture the actual physical space of Harlem, whereas Van Der Zee's and Aaron Siskind's photographs are rooted in Harlem as a locatable place. Van Vechten's images capture the irony that the pictures of both Van Der Zee and Siskind eschew. And yet, as I show in the next chapter, these two photographers evoke a nostalgia for Harlem and create other narratives of the black space that compete with each other's visual stories as well as Van Vechten's.

I have a disease: I *see* language.
Roland Barthes, *Roland Barthes*

A Photographic Language

Camera Lucida and the Photography of James Van Der Zee and Aaron Siskind

THERE IS a compulsion to interpret certain forms of visual representation literally. In photography, for instance, the instinct is to take the photograph at face value, that is, as a readily apparent truth. Roland Barthes notes in his classic discussion of photography that viewers often take the photograph "immediately or generally" for its referent, and the "photographic referent" is "the necessarily real thing which has been placed before the lens, without which there would be no photograph."[1] The photograph offers a type of guarantee, a visual proof, of an object's or a person's presence at a specific moment, and the supposed transparency of photography contributes to its evidentiary value.

To be without ambiguity or ambivalence, immediately evident and apparent: if the description of the perceived fact of photography sounds familiar, it is because we have encountered similar assumptions in discussions of race, particularly in discussions about blackness. The "there-ness" of blackness, "the fact of blackness," as Frantz Fanon would say, has often consisted of an unquestioned belief in the lower value of blackness compared to whiteness, because

145

after all, one can see the difference with one's own eyes. Through a quick glance, it is thought, one's racial identity—and moral integrity—are perceptible. Thus Alan Trachtenberg in *Reading American Photographs* notes that the belief in photography's palpable display of character fueled the fashion for phrenological and eugenic portraitures such as those by J. T. Zealy in the 1850s.[2] The assumed literalness of photography makes it an excellent platform for revealing the structure and function of racial representations and for clarifying a crucial component of such representations, the referent.

In earlier chapters I discussed two elements of the image that appear repetitively in narratives which may be described as "modern." In the works of writers such as James Weldon Johnson, Nella Larsen, and George Schuyler, the materiality and abstraction of the black image are negotiated in order to contest the assumptions of knowable, hyper-visible, hyper-*visualized* blackness. Through a process of making black representation less familiar, less comforting, less, to use Johnson's phrase, "picturesque," while simultaneously capturing some form of the elusiveness of blackness, the writers enact an early version of African American modernism. Yet in Carl Van Vechten's literary and photographic representations of blackness, his photographic images appear to perform black visual modernism more than his narrative images of blackness in *Nigger Heaven.* By calling attention to the codes of blackness that are ripe for multiple readings and parody, the photographic images contest the assumptions about blackness that Van Vechten unfortunately replicates in his novel.

In order to continue to elucidate these qualities of the image and to suggest their significance to black representation in its visual and narrative forms, I want to look further into photography, an expressive system that wrestles with these double versions of the image: the photograph holds the photographic referent, the "what's there" of the picture, and its abstract figuration, the interpretation that is possible with any photograph.[3] In photography and in readings of race, the referent maintains significance, for the literal reading of a photograph echoes the reading of racial stereotypes. Photography and the racial stereotype share a "deictic" function: they both "point a finger." In Fanon's *Black Skin, White Masks,* for example, one repeatedly encounters the exclamation "Look, mother, a Negro," an utterance that echoes a line in Barthes's last book published in his lifetime, *Camera Lucida* (1981): " 'Look,' 'See,' 'Here It Is.' "[4]

Despite its didactic and deictic quality, the photograph contains an element that escapes definitive representation, an element best suggested through writing. Both Trachtenberg and Michael North begin their studies of photography with an analysis of the various terms once used to denote photography, all of which are suggestive of the act of writing.[5] In *Camera Lucida,* however, photography is often posited in opposition to writing. Discussing the confidence one assumes about photographic representation, Barthes notes that "no writing can give me this certainty. It is the misfortune (but also perhaps the voluptuous pleasure) of language not to be able to authenticate itself" (85). Photography, it would seem, provides what writing lacks. The polysemous nature of language contrasts to the literal "fact" of the photograph.

But what of writing *about* photography, a genre in which one does not want to risk being too literal, a genre in which a delicate negotiation must occur between literal and figurative reading? How do you balance an interpretation of a photograph with what actually appears in the picture? What licenses a surplus of reading? In one sense this chapter is not just about photography. It is also, as with the book itself, about writing, about the work of writing and the images that compel us to write—about a fascination with both language and images and a desire to understand how one form of meaning and communication influences the other. Carl Van Vechten quite consciously turned to photography after retiring from writing. Rather than examining the influence as a choice that must be made between the two, I turn to a question that is more interesting to me: How do writing and photography motivate each other? Why is it that when one writes about photography, one's own writing processes become (uncomfortably) foregrounded? And how, finally, does the attempt to represent blackness elucidate the potential and the limits of both expressive systems?

Speculation here becomes dangerous. The threat of supposition inevitably arises when one is writing about the photograph because the events not captured by the lens are open to conjecture: What took place before and after the moment that was captured? Studio "portrait" photographs deny even more knowledge: Who came up with the pose, the photographer or the subject? How long did it take to get the picture "right"? As Martin Jay notes, although photographs have a "meaningful, communicative, connotative 'obviousness,'" they also "contain an 'obtuse' meaning that defies description in linguistic terms."[6] And yet language is one of the best alternatives to capturing that elusive element. The "close reading" of a photograph requires a careful balance of obviousness and obtuseness, fact and supposition: what led to this photograph being taken there, at that moment, on that day, by this person—"facts" of the photograph weighed against the speculation that close reading animates.

There is, then, a paradox about photography, one that is perhaps most fully evident when one is attempting a lexical interpretation of the photographic image: the photograph appears to be factual and truthful, but the ambiguous quality of photography becomes apparent through language, in writing about the referent it so obviously portrays. This, significantly, is also one method to mitigate racial referents, as Harlem Renaissance statesmen such as James Weldon Johnson and Alain Locke believed.

Barthes parenthetically admits to the "voluptuous pleasure" of the potentialities of language in comparison to the photograph; but there are moments in *Camera Lucida* in which the multiplicity is stabilized—fixed—through both the image of blackness and its lexical counterpart. *Camera Lucida* examines within a discrete location both the photographic images of blackness and writing *about* the photography of blackness. Barthes's aphoristic reflections on photography and language—as well as the referent in both forms of expression—thus provide a way to discuss the use of language and the use of the image to fracture the rigidity of racial stereotypes, a formative goal of black modernism.

Looking for the Referent

Barthes's *Camera Lucida* is not the most obvious choice for inclusion in a study of black modern images, but what makes it an ideal text for examining black representation is its discussion of the referent, which, as I suggested in earlier chapters, informs and marks the stereotype. *Camera Lucida* reshapes the binaries made familiar by my own discussions. Barthes's book elucidates not only the image proper/proper image binary but also the more global binary of writing and photography, the poles on which this book rests. If one considers *Camera Lucida* to be an intriguing delineation of the referent and the object it represents, one finds a process for dealing with the "reprimand" of the static (racial) referent.

Camera Lucida is more than a discussion of photography. It is variously a rumination on the effect of certain photographs on Roland Barthes, a tale of grief and mourning as he tries to come to terms with his mother's death, and a photographic detective tale as he sets out to discover why the Winter Garden Photograph of his mother as a young child resonates so deeply with him. *Camera Lucida* is a text devoted to photography as well as to another form of the creative act. In order to talk about photography, an art he does not practice, Barthes continually draws upon that which he does know, the art of writing.[7]

It is in this last book that Barthes reveals a clarity about himself and his tendency to move from subject to subject, enticing and provoking those who would attempt a linear narrative of his philosophies and theories. Each time he comes close to recognizable "authorship," Barthes moves on to another interest. "I was bearing witness," he notes, "to the only sure thing that was in me (however naïve it might be): a desperate resistance to any reductive system. For each time, having resorted to any such language to whatever degree, each time I felt it hardening and thereby tending to reduction and reprimand, I would gently leave it and seek elsewhere: I began to speak differently" (8). The passage states Barthes's resistance to any singular statement of purpose, an avoidance of a "hard" referent. As with Nella Larsen's efforts to disturb the reader's desire to "know" blackness in *Passing,* Barthes in *Camera Lucida* and elsewhere refuses such claims to being known. The abstractness he prefers becomes possible through the hardening of other forms in *Camera Lucida.* This passage describing a "resist[ance] to any reductive system" is moreover a short lesson on how to resist the reification of stereotypes such as the racial stereotype. Barthes "began to speak differently" by writing away or around what hardens. And yet, as I discuss shortly, despite his epigrammatic thoughts on the referent, when Barthes interprets a well-known photograph of African Americans, he briefly falls prey to the reprimand of the referent he seeks to avoid.

There is no "thesis" for *Camera Lucida,* no short synopsis that would adequately describe or represent Barthes's expansive style and tone. In order to get to the kernel of the photographic referent, the hard clarity of what makes the photograph function, he has to describe his thoughts about different photographs. Juxtaposing the material and the evanescent, Barthes develops ideas about photography through suggestive statements that resist condensed summary. There is, then, a fundamental paradox within *Camera Lucida:* Barthes is compelled by the referent, but the book he writes eludes it. The book forms its analyses by writing around various images except the one by which Barthes admits to being haunted. The one photograph that animates his discussion on photography, that initiates the questions he has, and that is for him the "essence of the Photograph" from which he "derives all Photography," the Winter Garden Photograph, never appears in the book: "I cannot reproduce the Winter Garden Photograph. It exists only for me. For you, it would be nothing but an indifferent picture, one of the thousand manifestations of the 'ordinary'; it cannot in any way constitute the visible object of a science; it cannot establish an objectivity, in the positive sense of the term; at most it would interest your *studium:* period, clothes, photogeny; but in it, for you, no wound" (73).

The absence of such an influential photograph is significant. Barthes notes early in the book that "a photograph is always invisible: it is not it that we see" (6). This invisibility is the result, in part, of analytical studies on photography. There are two forms of the study of photography, both of which he finds lacking. Studies focus on the object in close-up, to discover some technical dimension to the photograph; or studies examine the photograph "at a great distance," in order to highlight a historical or sociological element of photography (7). Hindered in both forms of analysis is the photograph itself, obscured, "irritatingly," by analyses. (As Barthes notes, "What did I care about the rules of composition of the photographic landscape, or, at the other end, about the Photograph as family rite" [7]?) What is highlighted instead is the referent. We cannot see the Photograph because "the referent adheres" (6); we see too much of it. By denying the reader the physical image of the Winter Garden Photograph, Barthes forces the reader not merely to look at the photo. Instead she must conjure the photo in her mind. The Winter Garden Photograph comes to be known, then, by its absence. We can only speculate about its appearance— and that speculation is itself compromised because of Barthes's possibly fallible description of it. By not reproducing the Winter Garden Photograph, Barthes hopes to make us actually "see" it, and see it perhaps better than if it had been visually reproduced. The reader is denied the material image of this crucial photo, and the referent of this photograph, as suggested in the earlier passage, becomes hardened elsewhere.

A form of this hardening or crystallization occurs when Barthes conflates one of the most transient elements, time, with a subject that appears fleetingly in *Camera Lucida,* blackness. Time impresses itself throughout *Camera Lucida,* but as with the reader's effort to know "Barthes the Author," when one seeks to grasp time, it gently glides away "elsewhere." This is memorably evident with the Winter Garden Photograph, which Barthes "discovers" by "moving back through Time" (71). That is, he discovers the essence of his mother not as she was when he knew her as an adult but in the photograph of her as a five-year-old child. The epitome of this sliding, swinging movement is the "there-has-been-ness," or "intersum," of the photograph. Curiously, when Barthes defines this quality of the photograph, there is a condition or limitation that undermines the certainty the photograph presents. In defining "intersum," for example, Barthes writes: "What I see has been here, in this place which extends between infinity and the subject . . . ; it has been here, and yet immediately separated; it has been absolutely, irrefutably present, and yet already deferred. It is all this which the verb *intersum* means" (77). It has been there—"and yet . . ." Reminiscent of Thomas Wentworth Higginson's inability to capture, in musical notes, the tonal nuance of the spirituals, or of James Weldon Johnson's "hesitant stammer" in one of his prefaces, there is some element of the photograph that refuses to be stabilized or fixed, that is as un-capturable as an authentic blackness—an element revealed through language.[8] When Barthes describes photographs showing African Americans, visions of blackness embody or "harden" his temporal concept of "there-has-been-ness." Barthes's book, then, exemplifies the forms of blackness—both an evanescence of blackness as well as a materialization of it. He critiques the referent, the pivotal aspect of the stereotype; he also makes us reexamine the referent to see beyond its literalness. "And yet," his reading of Van Der Zee's family portrait is problematic because it is so (uncharacteristically) stereotypical. Here, when Barthes critiques the referent, he also shows us how one can misread the referent in regard to race. Language betrays him when he writes about a photograph of blackness.

There have been other analyses of Barthes and blackness in *Camera Lucida,* such as Fred Moten's discussion of the Winter Garden Photograph in relation to photographs of Emmett Till, the fourteen-year-old African American murdered in Mississippi in 1955 because he allegedly flirted with a white woman and who was photographed in an open casket at his funeral at the insistence of his mother. José Muñoz reads Barthes in relation to the photography of Robert Mapplethorpe, James Van Der Zee, and Isaac Julien's film *Looking for Langston* (1989) to understand the links between mourning and portrait photography. Whereas Moten and Muñoz connect Barthes to specific forms of loss and black performativity, I would argue that *Camera Lucida*'s significance to blackness, and specifically the black modern, is more expansive. *Camera Lucida* both critiques and enacts the loss and elusive condition of foundational forms of black expression such as the spirituals.[9] Through its description of a well-known Van Der Zee photograph and its refusal to reproduce, as object, an image of blackness, the text both critiques and performs the materialization of blackness that has proved to be so problematic for early black American moderns.

THERE ARE several specific moments in which blackness is foregrounded in *Camera Lucida:* Barthes's discussion of the face of a former slave, William Casby, captured by Richard Avedon; a picture of A. Philip Randolph, also by

Figure 5.1. "Family Portrait" (1926), photograph by James Van Der Zee.
© Donna Mussenden Van Der Zee

Avedon; an image by the early photographer Félix Nadar of a French explorer of the Congo sitting between two young African boys; and perhaps most famously, a Van Der Zee photograph of a black family (figure 5.1).[10] There is another picture that foregrounds race, but like the Winter Garden Photograph, it is not reproduced. That is an image of slavery Barthes saw as a child:

> I remember keeping for a long time a photograph I had cut out of a magazine—lost subsequently, like everything too carefully put away—which showed a slave market: the slavemaster, in a hat, standing; the slaves, in loincloths, sitting. I repeat: a photograph, not a drawing or engraving; for my horror and my fascination as a child came from this: that there was a certainty that such a thing existed: not a question of exactitude, but of reality: the historian was no longer the mediator, slavery was given without mediation, the fact was established *without method*. (80)

Barthes's language attempts to convey the certainty of the photographic image. His language—like the photograph—repeats itself. His recollection evokes a temporal moment, a moment that has departed but still ("and yet") remains present, the quality of "there-has-been-ness" of the photograph which he describes in general. What is remembered—the "slavemaster, in a hat," the slaves wearing "loincloths"—replicates the white/black, mind/body division which is by now only too familiar. There is an almost desperate desire to confirm what the mind does not want to believe. The photograph certifies what, because of the passage of time, would be too easy to contest, and captures "without mediation," without negotiation, a past time that the Spectator's eyes would like not to see.

This disparity—between what is seen and what one does not want to see (or believe)—is echoed by the presence and absence of the photograph itself. There is a dichotomy between the durability of the magazine photograph and the wasting away of a system. A photograph is supposed to preserve images. Barthes's preservation of the image and its subsequent misplacement, despite (or perhaps because of) its being "too carefully put away," allegorizes the image of slavery, preserved momentarily in a photograph and yet later abolished.

In contrast to the absent/lost image of slavery, the other images of blackness mentioned in *Camera Lucida*—except, notably, Van Der Zee's portrait of a family, as I discuss shortly—display not only the transience of time but also time turning back on itself, retroflexive, a "falling back."[11] The temporal does not glide away but shows up on the black subject's body. The photograph of A. Phillip Randolph, for example, depicts weakened power, an aging virility. The suit and coat seem too large for this elderly gentleman; perhaps they were worn in better, glory days. The glimpse of the past inscribed on the photographic subject's face or body helps explain the power of Avedon's portrait of William Casby, "born in slavery, Algiers, Louisiana, March 24, 1963." The series of facts function, like the photograph itself, to authenticate the fact of slavery; they confirm that this body has witnessed and experienced slavery and its aftermath. Casby's portrait marks the passage of time but not the erasure of the fact of slavery. The blurred reflection in and of Casby's eyes emphasizes the sharp, clear lines of his face. What, *exactly,* have these eyes seen? (And, frankly, do we *really* want to know?)

The gap between photographic certainty and incredible fact calls attention to a subtle distinction between the kinds of factual evidence the photograph provides and the desire to disbelieve that such systems existed. Writing about lynching photographs, Jacqueline Goldsby points out that this genre of the photograph calls into question the factual nature of photography: "The violence of lynching disrupts and disproves the certainty that photographs are presumed to confer. Before images of lynching, we cannot believe that what we see actually happened. We do not want to admit that what we see existed."[12] Particularly in the image of the former slave and in the passages detailing the picture of slavery, there is a pain that is inarticulable, "unspeakable," aphasic.[13] These photographs foreground the unmediated certainty of a moment that, were it not for the "reality" of the photograph, would be unbelievable. The haunting nostalgia of such photographs arrests time during a moment that has been difficult for America to erase.

The photographs of black subjects in *Camera Lucida,* then, are both historically and subjectively marked, both signs of a verifiable moment in a nation's past and mementos of the nostalgia and the reluctant disbelief of an individual spectator, Roland Barthes. The magazine image of a slave auction and the Winter Garden Photograph are unrealized images (unrealized in the sense that they are imagined but not visualized) and resonate with suspended referents that cannot be reproduced.[14] In contrast to the marked materiality assumed of the black body, the hypervisibility believed to be available via the nonwhite form, these are irrecoverable referents that recall the "lost" sounds of the spirituals, and are only imperfectly captured or arrested by the temporal.

It is this irrecoverable, unapproachable quality of "The Photograph" (as Barthes designates the Winter Garden photo) that resembles the sign of blackness sought in the spirituals and in the sermons. Because they are "lost" or unfathomable referents, we can approach them only obliquely, or as Barthes states of his own writings, "aslant."[15] There are no referents that represent them. And it is this off-center detail, the one deliberately not centered, that defines the *punctum,* the quality of the photograph that is unexpected, unintended by the photographer, which captures the interest of the Spectator.

This "temporal effect" in Barthes (it is much too elusive to be called a strategy) provides a way to examine the image of blackness in Van Der Zee and Siskind. Both photographers wrestle with temporality, abstraction, and concretion but create quite disparate results.

Democracy and Documentaries

James Van Der Zee and Aaron Siskind, as well as Carl Van Vechten, are central to visual definitions of the Harlem Renaissance. Van Der Zee, in the 1920s and 1930s, and Siskind, in the 1930s and 1940s, portray the black body in ways that counter traditional representations of blackness, but in contrasting photographic forms. The photographers call attention to the constructed nature of "the pose" and the portrait as well as the irony suggested with those terms. By examining photographs taken by Van Der Zee and Siskind, some of which have now achieved iconic status, the visual variations of the black modern in photography become clearer. I center my analysis on photographs which appeared in collections that helped to define the photographers' style: *The World of James Van Der Zee* (1969), the first published collection of Van Der Zee's photographs, and Siskind's *Harlem Document, 1932–1940* (1981), a published version of a larger collaborative exhibition. I do not aim to privilege one photographer over the other or one style over the other. Rather I seek to understand how the photographers told a story about Harlem, how "proper" blackness presented so self-consciously by Van Der Zee achieves a different form of propriety in Siskind. The photographers help to complicate the "image proper" of the "proper" black body, and the story the photographers tried to tell is one both enabled and problematized by the constitutive nature of narrative and of the image.

As will become clear, both Van Der Zee and Siskind contend with the "fact" of blackness. For both the question becomes just what kind of "evidence" does the photograph permit or deny? Siskind's photographs document the problems and the need for creative living in an urban space; Van Der Zee's pictures offer a different kind of evidence of black and American possibility. In making blackness "less picturesque," they negotiate the claims of literal representation evoked by the photograph and enlarge the critical conversation about black modernism and its relation to the visual. This section begins, then, where Jacqueline Goldsby's discussion on lynching and photographs ends, with a consideration of how photography's ineluctable referent elicits a rethinking of the apparent "there-ness" of blackness.[16]

IN CHAPTER 3 I discussed the protagonist Max Disher's cynical recognition and exploitation of American rhetoric in *Black No More*. Although they reveal a similar awareness of American myths and symbols, Van Der Zee and Siskind elide such pessimism as displayed in that novel. Van Der Zee presents the hope for what the nation's future can bring, particularly after World War I; Siskind illustrates the depth of that failed promise in the form of a documentary indictment. Both men are united by a certain assurance extended by America, a democratic guarantee which determines their representations of blackness. For Van Der Zee it is a promise of what can be; for Siskind it is a promise that the nation has failed to measure up to. Their photographs pose the query, can one be black and American, and participate in the national ideals? The unfulfilled pledges of America are most dramatically revealed by comparing Van Der Zee's photographs of families with Siskind's photographs of interior and exterior domestic space.

Van Der Zee and Siskind, two photographic "documentarians," offer competing ways of "reading" Harlem and its inhabitants. Van Der Zee "fictionalized" portraits of ordinary African Americans, providing a narrative or story to satisfy the subject as well as himself, while Siskind practiced a type of photographic social activism by capturing features of Harlem that challenged conceptions of its romantic Jazz Age past. There are differences not only in style but also in the specific spaces photographed. Van Der Zee's interior photos are so obviously stylized, so clearly posed in his studio, while Siskind's interior shots in the published version of *Harlem Document* are of confined, constricted spaces that emphasize the subjects' lower-class status. But the pairing, once proposed, provides a productive tension. The passage from Van Der Zee to Siskind—from inside Van Der Zee's Harlem studio to Siskind's exterior images—reflects the visual movement from the concern for propriety of the Harlem Renaissance to the experimental images of black modernism. They both show less embodied blackness, as urged by James Weldon Johnson, but in strikingly different ways. The photographers demonstrate a different sense of temporality and of the object, the "necessarily real thing which has been placed before the lens." In Van Der Zee's photographs time becomes concrete, that is, time itself becomes an object; conversely, in Siskind's images the object becomes an abstraction.

The Family Portrait

Although it is difficult to document the popularization of photography in early African American culture, James Van Der Zee's career as a photographer encompasses the period in which the camera became relatively more affordable to diverse economic groups.[17] Van Der Zee took pictures from the 1890s, when he received a small camera through the mail as a reward for selling perfume, to the 1980s, when he passed away.[18] His photographs are marked by time and a sense of anachronism that solidifies blackness.

In a biographical article Ben Lifson writes, "James Van Der Zee is one of the purest examples in photography of what we variously call a folk, popular, primitive, or naïve artist—one who works intuitively, without a thought for the larger world of art or for his place in the history of his chosen medium."[19] But one must not confuse a lack of interest in world opinion with artistic innocence. For there was certainly some thought that went into his photographs, some premeditation about the image. Indeed Van Der Zee willingly admitted a penchant for actively fashioning a subject. Discussing his techniques in a 1969 interview he stated: "I tried to see that every picture was better looking than the person—if it wasn't better looking than the person I was taking, then I wasn't satisfied with it. . . . I would retouch the pictures and take out some unnecessary lines and shadows and then, before taking them, I would figure out the best angle to try to get as much light and expression and character into the picture as possible. I tried to pose each person in such a way as to tell a story."[20]

Van Der Zee's photographs are overtly, aggressively middle class.[21] Consider the images reprinted in the first published book of his photographs, *The World of James Van Der Zee,* edited by Liliane De Cock and Reginald McGhee. Images of black schoolchildren balance group pictures of fraternal and social organizations. Placed before these fairly anonymous figures are pictures of Van Der Zee's family, all very well dressed. A middle-class status is most evident on the bodies of women. There is an ostentatious photo of "Cousin Susan Porter," wearing gloves, not looking at the camera. The cross on her necklace echoes the staffs on the elaborate wallpaper, both jewelry and décor signifying a class above the ordinary. Another somewhat affected portrait is that of "Gaynella," who stares at a vase of roses with a disturbed expression on her face.[22] Even in "casual" or presumably spontaneous photographs there is a suggestion of upward mobility. In shots of marches and parades, for example, one senses an optimism, a belief in the power of peaceful protest.

Although American idealism and mythology are prevalent in Van Der Zee's street and parade photographs, my discussion centers on the studio portraits which, as the earlier quotation from Van Der Zee suggests, derive from an active insertion of a narrative interpretation into the photograph. These are the images of the anonymous subjects who entered his studio on 135th Street in Harlem, later moved to Lenox Avenue, the customers who could afford his sitting fee of two to five dollars, customers such as those pictured in the photograph discussed by Roland Barthes.

A return to the photograph of the African American family in *Camera Lucida* (figure 5.1) compels a return to language, a concern with how Barthes describes the photograph. It is an image ostensibly of three family members. A woman sits on a chair between two other figures, a man on the left and a younger-looking woman on the right. The photograph offers a way to clarify the distinction between the *studium,* aspects of a photograph with which the Spectator is generally interested, and the *punctum,* the accidental aspect of the photograph that "pricks" or wounds the Spectator.[23] Barthes describes the photograph thus:

> Here is a family of American blacks. . . . The *studium* is clear: I am sympathetically interested, as a docile cultural subject, in what the photograph has to say, for it speaks (it is a "good" photograph): it utters respectability, family life, conformism, Sunday best. An effort of social advancement in order to assume the White man's attributes (an effort touching by reason of its naiveté). The spectacle interests me but does not prick me. What does, strange to say, is the belt worn low by the sister (or daughter)—the "solacing mammy"—whose arms are crossed behind her back like a schoolgirl, and above all her *strapped pumps* (Mary Janes—why does this dated fashion touch me? I mean: to what date does it refer me?) This particular *punctum* arouses great sympathy in me, almost a kind of tenderness. (43)

Barthes's description foregrounds the nature of the "pose" in this photograph, as well as in other Van Der Zee photographs. These studio images have the stiff formality of middle-class staging or the even more artificial "caught in the moment" look. One element that becomes immediately apparent in the photograph, as well as Barthes's appraisal of it, is the representation of time. There is an old-fashioned quality to the photograph, signaled by the homemade look of the women's dresses (is that a safety pin on the belt of the standing woman's dress?). Barthes's question about the shoes, "to what date does it refer me," suggests the difference between the time evoked in the photograph and the actual year of its creation. This photograph arrests time, objectifies it: the subjects are caught in an anachronistic moment of "New Negro-ness." Although the picture was taken in 1926, the same year *Nigger Heaven* was published, these are not figures who would have been photographed by Carl Van Vechten.[24] Indeed the image contrasts strikingly with Van Der Zee's other frequently reproduced photograph, the 1932 portrait of an African American couple wearing raccoon coats and posed with an automobile (figure 5.2). The woman in the latter photo appears to be an extension of the man, another possession, and the ruffled hem of what looks to be a store-bought dress contrasts to the homemade dresses of the two women in "The Family Portrait." Van Der Zee's image of the three relatives is an ideal representation of "the pose," drawing on the term's suggestion of not only artifice or affectation but also fixing or freezing the subject in a predetermined style.

Perhaps it is the conscious formality of the photograph that led Barthes, like Lifson describing Van Der Zee, to use the word "naiveté." But from where does Barthes get the descriptive "solacing Mammy" (85)? There is nothing comforting about either of the women pictured.[25] In addition, these were not members of a family posing in their own home. The photograph was taken in Van Der Zee's studio, to judge from the rug that reappears in his other photographs and the impressionistic, painterly backdrop. There is a too evident formality to the photograph, emphasized by the telephone on the side table and the artificial roses. One almost expects to see an American flag draped somewhere in the background.[26]

What appears to be a "straight" photograph abounds with questions. Why is one woman's hand behind her back and not resting on the other woman, her mother or sister? What information does that hand withhold? Why do the members of this "family" not touch? In contrast to the woman who stands stiffly straight, the man leans slightly forward, as if bowing is a familiar function; his arm curves at his side and suggests a pliability; and his slight smile makes him appear approachable (again in contrast to the two women). He stands like an attendant, a servant, ready to fulfill one's command. More questions arise concerning the sitting woman's foot. Her left foot, crossed on top of

Figure 5.2. "Raccoon Coats" (1932), photograph by James Van Der Zee.
© Donna Mussenden Van Der Zee

the right one, rests at an odd angle. Is this the sign of a disability, a foot that could not be placed flat like the other one? Why does she wear scuffed, well-worn shoes, in marked contrast to the shoes of the woman behind her? Furthermore, the necklace that Barthes eventually identifies as what "pricked" him appears on both women, though Barthes refers only to the one on the standing woman. Finally, the women's hair is not "processed." Just how long have these subjects been in Harlem?

Barthes's statement that the image asserts a "having-been-there"-ness suggests how time is arrested in the photograph, an effect not only of the subjects' appearance but also of Van Der Zee's photographic setting. Just note his elaborate, almost Victorian studio, an antiquated room, as described by a visitor in the 1980s, containing "a freshly painted backdrop representing the terrace and windows of an eighteenth-century mansion, with a fool moon shining in a cloudy sky.... The old eight-by-ten view camera and its bulky wooden tripod in the center of the room were even more anachronistic."[27] Van Der Zee arrests formality to insist on the propriety of the black body.[28] Even in the image that so readily contradicts "The Family Portrait," that of the fur-clad couple of 1932, time itself becomes a questionable object, for how does a couple manage to display such wealth when Harlem's other black residents were entering the long decline of the Great Depression? How does the couple remain in the glorified days of the Roaring Twenties?

Van Der Zee worked to "make over" and reinvent an image. His photographs detail the aspirations of class, of an upwardly-mobile subject who either appropriates or confirms status through the middle-class privilege of sitting for a portrait. There is also a permanence to Van Der Zee's photographs. One is supposed to feel the weight and heft of these "serious" images. In contrast to Barthes's reading, which borders on uncharacteristic simplicity, this image of a family, if it is a family, is much more complicated than such an interpretation would allow. Ironically, then, Barthes's *punctum* can in fact be reread as a *studium,* as a tendency to generalize the images of blackness.[29] The *punctum* here is animated not only by the composition of the image but also by Barthes's *writing* of the image.

In Van Der Zee's photographs there is a sense of normalcy that borders on the banal and a correctness that makes them conventional. His photographs capture a reserve that contradicts every "coon" image. They are "less picturesque" and more literal. They are like grade school student pictures: only the faces change; the two-dimensional background stays the same; one has the comforting (or, conversely, discomforting) assurance that one's photo is like all the others. There is no sense of ambivalence or irony from James Van Der Zee. The photographic referent abounds in this image, and carries with it the credibility of "seeing is believing." With Van Der Zee, then, the image proper and the proper image conflate. Sign and referent are held together as one.

Siskind: The Drama of Objects

In 1936, roughly ten years after his celebration of the "New Negro" in the anthology he edited under the same title, Alain Locke wrote a distinctly sobering appraisal of the New Negro Renaissance. Sparked by the Great Depression and Harlem's riot a year before, the essay suggested some solutions to the "premature setback" of the once fruitful and productive renaissance of black arts and writing. Locke issued a harsh judgment of the assumptions that fueled the 1920s: "No emerging elite—artistic, professional or mercantile—can spread itself in thin air over the abyss of a mass of unemployed stranded in an overexpensive, disease- and crime-ridden slum." In addition, Locke claimed, "there is no cure or saving magic in poetry and art, an emerging generation of talent, or in international prestige and interracial recognition."[30] Gone was the optimistic faith in the transformative potential of art and literature. Absent was an inspiriting call to arms to the nation's black elite. Locke's piercing criticism of a "relapse" was captured and exemplified by Aaron Siskind's photographic images. Unlike the more apolitical images of Van Vechten and Van Der Zee, including even Van Der Zee's photographs of a figure as political and polemical as Marcus Garvey, Siskind's photographs carry with them a subtle political indictment, and they display a "self-consciousness" remarkably different from Van Vechten's self-aware, ironic humor.[31]

There are two genres that predominate in Siskind's photographic oeuvre: documentary and architectural.[32] My reading of Siskind concentrates on those documentary photographs taken in Harlem which anticipate his interest in architecture and which foretell a later engagement with the relation between objects and people.[33] Siskind's photographs involve a reconsideration of the object—not only the "thing placed before the lens," as Barthes writes, but also the manner and method of such placement. While such an ascetic portrayal of the object could result in the "art photograph," devoid of any political content, Siskind's representation of the object in this manner actually foregrounds an understated social critique of the post-Renaissance space of Harlem. Siskind's own words—on photography, language, and the object—help clarify this point.

Siskind achieves subtle political commentary through a constellation of language and images and by focusing the spectator's attention on the object. When he talks about the object in his later photographs, Siskind reveals a concern with getting—within the frame and before the observer—the object itself, without any extraneous information or stimuli, so as to divorce the object from its function and environment. Siskind's photographs display a conscious attention to the object: it is not just decoration but has a use, the pragmatic purpose of the household object. He does not reduce the object to an idea; rather, by photographing the object while attuned to its geometric shape, Siskind *expands* the object *to* an idea. In other words, he quite literally creates an abstraction from an object. This dematerialization of the object mirrors the process of modernizing the black image, of making the black image "less picturesque."

It may be helpful to reconsider here the different valences of the term "abstraction" as it has been used throughout this book. In relation to James Weldon Johnson, abstraction refers to the "less picturesque," the qualities of the black image that resist the accumulation of histories and meanings associated with the stereotype. George Schuyler in *Black No More* presented a version of "abstraction"—of the privileges and the rights of citizenship accorded to the white masculine body. Supposedly free from the burden of the body, white men have access to the full range of rights accorded by a representative democracy. Schuyler's novel demonstrates the extent to which the rights of Americans depend on an unacknowledged relation to the black body. In Barthes, abstraction refers to the process and the effect of "realization." Because of Barthes's decision not to reproduce the Winter Garden Photograph, one could argue that the referent for that photograph is abstracted; the referent is not solidified by physical representation.

The use of the term "abstraction" in relation to Aaron Siskind involves a slightly new resonance of the word, the "idea" Siskind conceives and attempts to represent in a photo: not the actual image but the *effect* of the image. Siskind's images of Harlem buildings, though of concrete physical objects, are evocative of a black presence, and they capture the difficulties and the improvisations necessary to live in the "Negro mecca." In several essays and interviews Siskind notes his shift in interest from concrete to abstract representation. No longer engaged with capturing the "real" object before the lens, Siskind's later photographs preserve not "things" but intangible concepts: "My early pictures revealed to me the basic duality that I felt in regard to the geometric and the organic together. They pointed at the essential ambiguity of all my pictures. In them you have the object, but you have in the object—or superimposed on it— what I call the *image,* which contains my idea. These two things are present at one and the same time."[34] Although the distinction is not specified, the image here has two forms, the material and the mental, and Siskind desires to photograph the mental image "which contains [his] idea." The image *is* the abstraction.

Correspondingly, then, Siskind's later pictures reveal a flattening-out of the photographic perspective: "I noticed that I was photographing objects in a setting. I noticed that in all the pictures I did that the total effect of the picture was such that it was a picture on a flat plane—I wiped out deep space and had objects which were organic in a geometrical setting. . . . The shift was from description to idea and meaning." Through this separation of form from meaning, object from function, the object becomes an abstraction. In other words, the abstract becomes the "thing placed before the lens," the photographic referent.

Siskind uses different terminology for the literal and the figurative, object and image: "a formal element and an organic element," qualities Siskind perceives as "symbolic of the essential duality of our nature—which was something that I was very much concerned about in the poetry which I used to write."[35] More than the other two photographers, Van Der Zee and Van Vechten, Siskind wrestles deeply and explicitly with the dynamic between images and language. This becomes evident not only in the brief essays in which he talks about the craft of photography, often describing the process of taking a photograph the way a scholar describes researching a subject or field, but also in one of his most famous collection of photographs, *Harlem Document, 1932–1940*.[36]

Harlem Document is distinguished from other photographic collections of the city. There are no nostalgic romanticizations of Harlem, its cabarets, or its rent parties. Instead the book begins with a notably somber foreword by the African American photographer Gordon Parks. The photographs, taken before and during the period between the Harlem riots of 1935 and 1943, are supplemented with interviews conducted by members of the Federal Writers' Project; and text and image feed off of each other in the creative product.[37] What becomes apparent in both the photographs and the interviews are objects and how people make use of them. The surplus of utilitarian, non-extravagant objects emphasizes the scarcity or insufficiency of quite basic household items. Siskind's photographs demonstrate that even the most banal, innocuous objects have a potentially unexpected impact, as revealed in the Harlem riot of 1935. According to most accounts, the riot was sparked by the theft of a knife, an object for domestic use which, if used outside the space of the kitchen, can initiate violence.[38] Comparing the images of Van Der Zee to Siskind's, one notes their quite different portrayal of household objects: while Van Der Zee often employs artificial, stage(d) objects, Siskind displays subjects with common items but removed from their intended use. This emphasis on objects is a way to document the economic and social conditions in Harlem. Siskind's photographs function by suggesting the dichotomy inherent in the normalcy of a familial moment rendered "off" by the unexpected use of domestic objects: a clothesline in the middle of a kitchen, for example. "Propriety" has a different valence where economic and social conditions influence daily living patterns. In addition, Siskind's photographs are unencumbered by the conventions of the pose and the portrait. There is less of a sense that the photographs are staged, as with Van Der Zee. There is a ruralness and a sense of community in Siskind's Harlem images that, paradoxically, are missing in Van Der Zee's photographs. The striking quality about Siskind's Harlem photographs, particularly in contrast to Van Der Zee's, is the intimacy of the images. We are unnoticed intruders in these people's homes, uninvited spectators of their private moments.[39]

Siskind's documentary photographs of Harlem work by highlighting a contrast between visually innocent subjects and the harsh surroundings in which they are caught. The subjects who occupy a domestic setting are marked by the objects employed in an unusual fashion in their homes. One of the photographs of *Harlem Document* anticipates the opening scene of Richard Wright's *Native Son* (1940). In this image, one in a series titled "Storeroom: There's a Rat in There," a girl stands with a dress mannequin: initially the room appears in disarray, but eventually the eye settles on the folded clothes and towels piled on top of a stack of furniture (figure 5.3). The mannequin displays both male and female clothing: a dress, an apron, a vest. The lack of space in the room creates gender familiarity, as when Bigger and his brother must avert their eyes when his mother and sister change clothes in *Native Son*. But it is the caption that offers the strongest link to Wright, that sutures the image to the (future) text of *Native Son*'s opening scene, when Bigger Thomas kills a rodent: "There's a rat in there." Overwhelmed with objects, including a small unclothed doll on top of the clothes, the room makes one wonder about living conditions in Harlem. In 1940 *Look* magazine featured some of the photographs from the *Harlem Document* exhibitions, a feature that attempted to evoke Wright's *Native Son,* although the magazine did not use the photograph that perhaps best captures the anxiety-producing opening moments of the novel. With so many objects in the room photographed by Siskind, how does one actually locate usable, functional clothing? The mannequin is overloaded with clothes, articles that appear too big for the girl photographed with them. To use Barthes's term again, the *punctum* is the paradox of the naked doll and the overly clothed mannequin. There is an absurd quality to both objects.

Siskind's terms for describing human connections are commonly used in discussing both objects and poetry. Consider, for example, the term "contiguity." Siskind writes: "I was concerned with Contiguity. The realization of how

Figure 5.3. "Storeroom: There's a Rat in There," photograph by Aaron Siskind, from "Harlem Document" (ca. 1937–1940). Courtesy of George Eastman House, International Museum of Photography and Film and The Aaron Siskind Foundation.

people feel in relation to one another; the nearness, the touch, the difference between a mother and her children, how she touches them and hovers near them, and how a father does; how two people feel sitting next to each other in a train."[40] This term is photographically represented in the image of a mother and daughter in a kitchen (figure 5.4). Although the mother is the one sitting on "real" furniture, she does not seem as much at ease as her daughter. The mother is perched on the edge of her chair as she looks at the food she and her daughter are about to eat; and her hunched position over the food contrasts with the daughter's straight back. The girl sits on a milk container that appears to read "Muller Dairies." The container is large in contrast to the relatively small milk bottle on the table. Paradoxically, we see a crowded table but there is still the sense of insufficiency, a contradiction echoed by the sturdiness of the table versus the open air through which the young girl can swing her legs. The rag on the wall contrasts with the clothes drying on the line. One notes the amazingly claustrophobic but efficient and pragmatic design of living space and the necessary inventiveness of daily life. There is an element of "adornment" here that echoes Zora Neale Hurston's analysis of the black home in "Characteristics of Negro Expression," the room with "a glut of gaudy calendars, wall pockets, and advertising lithographs." In Siskind's photograph we see the selective accumulation of objects and the necessity of improvised living: Where to dry the clothes? On a line in the kitchen. What shall the daughter sit on at the table? The dairy container is a perfect height. One is reminded of Hurston's living room in Alabama; except this time in Siskind's image, one does not "decorate a decoration" so much as make functional a decoration needed to maintain an existence.[41]

As with Hurston's description of the living room, there is a sense of surplus in Siskind's photographs, particularly in his portrayals of Harlem streets. Consider the photograph of shoeshine men on Eighth Avenue in which, for the passing pedestrian, there is a surfeit of opportunity (figure 5.5). The empty chairs may indicate a surplus of this kind of humble labor. How many shoeshine men can reasonably be stationed on one block, on one street, on one sidewalk? The photographs reveal the perverse quality of market conditions in Harlem, as indicated in Alain Locke's 1936 essay—too much of one thing (available labor) and not enough of another (prospective customers).

Siskind captures the various moods prevalent on the streets of Harlem. One image (figure 5.6) reflects the disappointed optimism of Locke's article, a feeling that augments the depressive tone of Ann Petry's novel *The*

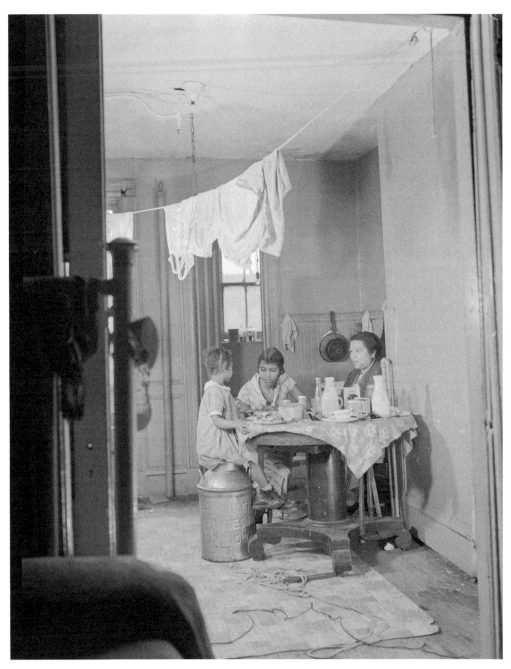

Figure 5.4. Untitled, photograph by Aaron Siskind, from "Harlem Document" (ca. 1937–1940). Courtesy of George Eastman House, International Museum of Photography and Film and The Aaron Siskind Foundation.

Figure 5.5. "Bootblacks," photograph by Aaron Siskind, from "Harlem Document" (ca. 1937–1940). Courtesy of George Eastman House, International Museum of Photography and Film and The Aaron Siskind Foundation.

Street (1946). The novel has been republished with Siskind's photograph as the cover illustration for the new edition. The title refers to malevolent 116th Street, where Lutie Johnson lives with her son, Bub. On the book's cover, Siskind's photograph has been altered: the heads of the mother and child are cut off. With only the subjects' lower bodies visible, the photo suggests malignancy. The novel, like Siskind's images in *Harlem Document,* stridently projects American possibility. The woman's sassily angled foot, clad in a fashionable shoe, bespeaks a hunger and drive, qualities also attributable to Lutie, who seeks an apartment on another, better street. But at what cost will this ambition be achieved? Frequently compared to *Native Son, The Street* offers a more subtle indictment of America and its legal and educational institutions by depicting the overwhelming influence of an urban environment. Unlike *Native Son,* which often imprisons Bigger Thomas in constricted domestic spaces, *The Street* more ably invokes the extraordinary quest for a home, also suggested in Siskind's images.

The use of Siskind's photo for the cover of *The Street* is fitting because in the published version of *Harlem Document,* images of the street appear as a natural extension of the Harlem home; and the untitled image reflects one of the more curious moments in Siskind's photographic biography, his transition to buildings and architecture. Several of the *Harlem Document* photographs demonstrate the anthropomorphic character of buildings and convey how environment affects living conditions. The image of boarded-up windows in one untitled photograph, for example, suggests the possibility of a safe home, but it is a space that is closed off (figure 5.7). The sightless eyes of the closed windows cannot see the movie posters below them. The possibility and promise of a home contrast with the dashed hopes represented by the windows. Compare this image to that of a boy standing in front of a pile of wooden planks (figure 5.8). Whereas the former photograph represents a window of possibility sealed up, this photograph offers possibility, promise, "and yet," a surplus of raw material that requires space and labor in order to create the safety and security of a home—labor that cannot be provided by such a small boy.

This photograph of the boarded-up building, like other Siskind photographs of Harlem buildings, suggests the ability to construct a domestic space in a harsh environment. The horizontal placement of the boards within the windows emphasizes the deeply horizontal lines of the photograph. The image visually exaggerates the fact that a large segment of the building has been rendered uninhabitable. And yet someone lives there: there are shades on the windows at the top left, almost but not quite out of the camera's range, suggesting a

Figure 5.6. Untitled, photograph by Aaron Siskind, from "Most Crowded Block in the World" (ca. 1940–1941). Courtesy of George Eastman House, International Museum of Photography and Film and The Aaron Siskind Foundation.

Figure 5.7. Untitled, photograph by Aaron Siskind, from "Harlem Document" (ca. 1937–1940). Courtesy of George Eastman House, International Museum of Photography and Film and The Aaron Siskind Foundation.

human presence. What appears to be a faceless façade masks the isolation of a possible existence behind the walls of the building. A second photograph is a more vertical variation on the boarded windows image. Siskind portrays the windows of a building in an alley. A contrast is apparent between the flexible curtains and the unmovable wall of bricks (figure 5.9). The eye is drawn down to some unknown dark space at the bottom of the alley. Remarkably, the viewer seems to have more space within the photograph than the resident behind one of these windows. Other than the curtains, there are no objects to beautify the space. Siskind's photographs of buildings are more evocative of the complex human dilemmas of living in Harlem than most of Van Der Zee's images. Siskind captures with his lens the anthropomorphic quality of Harlem's buildings, even, and perhaps particularly, when there are no people present in the

Figure 5.8. Untitled, photograph by Aaron Siskind, from "Harlem Document" (ca. 1937–1940). Courtesy of George Eastman House, International Museum of Photography and Film and The Aaron Siskind Foundation.

Figure 5.9. Untitled, photograph by Aaron Siskind, from "Harlem Document" (1940). Courtesy of George Eastman House, International Museum of Photography and Film and The Aaron Siskind Foundation.

Figure 5.10. "Crazy Quilt," photograph by Aaron Siskind, from "Harlem Document" (ca. 1937–1940). Courtesy of George Eastman House, International Museum of Photography and Film and The Aaron Siskind Foundation.

photographs. "Crazy Quilt," for example, showing the façade of a Harlem brownstone, embodies daily Harlem living (figure 5.10). The close quarters—a barbershop, a church, a dime store, and a beauty salon—reflect the myriad possibilities of life captured in one shot and on one block, revealing the necessity of vertical living in crowded New York.

As with Barthes's discussion of photography, Siskind's representation of a black modernism becomes apparent through the accumulation of readings. The grand effect of these readings of Siskind's photographs is to represent, abstractly, a black modernism. *Harlem Document* registers people and objects, and the relationships between them are foregrounded. Siskind's shift from object to concept, from literal to figurative, reflects the same preoccupation of writers such as James Weldon Johnson and Nella Larsen.

There is one other element that echoes the concerns of the early black moderns. Unlike Van Der Zee's photographs, which distill optimism and opportunity, Siskind's collection is permeated by a sense of failed promise. The published *Harlem Document* was created from two earlier Photo League exhibitions and projects, "The Most Crowded Block" and a previous project also titled "Harlem Document." The unpublished "Harlem Document" becomes another poignant, lost referent, for the "Harlem Document" Siskind imagined never appeared in print, and the photos were, to use John Raeburn's word, "dispersed." Ironically, as with the collected volumes of the spirituals that now survive, *Look*'s collection of the *Harlem Document* images may be only a pale version of the original because of the magazine's use of cropping and of captions that emphasized the depressing conditions in Harlem rather than the innovative forms of living. As Raeburn has discussed, the collection that has become ingrained in American culture is not the same one Siskind and his collaborators envisioned.[42]

As I suggested with some of the photographs in *Camera Lucida,* there is a retrospective, deeply temporal element in black modernism. The suspension between past and present and the aesthetic and political representation of Harlem is memorably evoked in Wallace Thurman's contemporaneous parody *Infants of the Spring* and a 1969 exhibition at the Metropolitan Museum of Art, the subject of the following chapter. The exhibition registers a different version of "art vs. propaganda," once again complicated by the representation of time.

Harlem is still in the process of making. It is still new and mixed; so mixed that one may get many different views—which is all right so long as one view is not taken to be the whole picture.

James Weldon Johnson, *Black Manhattan*

Conclusion: Remembering Harlem

Wallace Thurman, Alain Locke, and the Metropolitan Museum of Art's "Harlem" Exhibition

LIKE NO other period in African American culture, the Harlem Renaissance invites romanticization. Continually remembered, discussed, debated, the period is perhaps one of the few moments in twentieth-century African American history that does not suffer from a willing forgetting. Inevitably, because of this always animate history, the efforts to resituate and reconstruct the moment result in inventing, rather than recording, the period. Daylanne English notes that it is only a certain Harlem Renaissance that gets remembered, that attains canonical-like status in the cultural memories of black America. Through a "contemporary academic selection process . . . the Harlem Renaissance often emerges as the most compelling moment in the history of African American culture, one that (not coincidentally) lends itself particularly well to generalization as well as periodization."[1] Her comments on *The Norton Anthology of African American Literature* reveal Harlem's status as a symbolic community, actively fashioned and refashioned throughout the twentieth century. Anthologies like the *Norton* and collected essays of the Harlem Renaissance inevitably reflect the presence of the editor or collector of such texts, the scholar of black literary studies. Whether a scholar perceives the period as a success or a failure is never a disinterested choice, and determining how best to present the Renaissance inevitably leads to an attempt to answer this question, resulting in an embattled process of inclusion and exclusion of certain writers, events, and moments.

English's essay demonstrates how scholarly or reflective work about the Harlem Renaissance requires a delicate balance between choice and remembrance, implicit elements of James Weldon Johnson's injunction for "less picturesque" aesthetic creations of blackness. Johnson's statement that literature and art are necessary in order for African Americans in the early twentieth century to gain national acceptance and respect also calls for active remembering of what would become a crucial period, for such art memorializes that period in objects of lasting importance and reshapes historically entrenched ideas about blackness.

I close this book by examining two examples of such memorialization, one contemporaneous with the Harlem Renaissance and its putative "end," the other developed and staged decades after the movement: Wallace Thurman's 1932 satire of the Harlem Renaissance, *Infants of the Spring,* and the controversial 1969 exhibition at the Metropolitan Museum of Art, "Harlem on My Mind: The Cultural Capital of Black America, 1900–1968."

This pairing of a novel and a museum exhibition, the last pairing in a book that includes a series of dualities, elucidates "image" and "text," a dynamic I have posited as crucial to black modernism, in unexpected ways. It may seem that literature resides definitively in one term of the pairing and visual art in the other. What we find, however, is that each retrospective on the Harlem Renaissance privileges and complicates the unexpected term. As both attempt to make concrete their representations not just of African Americans but of the Harlem Renaissance itself, the novel and the exhibition complicate ideas about the possibilities—and limitations—of the Renaissance.

Wallace Thurman's novel, a postmortem on the Harlem Renaissance, debates the goals of the Renaissance, how it should be remembered, and how it should be celebrated, if in fact at all. The novel ponders the creative anxiety caused by a too lenient appraisal of black writers. In the process it does not offer a satisfying combination of image and text. Rather, if the question of the success or failure of the Renaissance continually haunts the study of the period, *Infants* answers the question decidedly with the judgment of failure in its concluding visual image of the Renaissance's imminent demise. Previous interpretations of *Infants* have used it to corroborate the charge that the Harlem Renaissance did not succeed because of declining white interest.[2] *Infants,* however, shows a more compelling reason. Read in conjunction with Wallace Thurman's and Alain Locke's essays written near the conventionally recognized end of the period, *Infants of the Spring* suggests that the root of the dissatisfaction as the period came to an end was not the failure of black writers to cater to white audiences but the disappointment of black writers with the style and artistry of contemporaneous black writing.

Thurman and Locke thus provide two opportunities for challenging a romanticized Harlem. Writing at a moment when the giddy celebration of African American writers and artists had passed, the two men detail their own dissatisfaction with the Renaissance and offer sober, penetrating analyses of ways to capture the interest in African American themes so as to represent and extend black modernism more successfully. Whether it is the danger of artistic insignificance and nonpermanence expressed in Thurman's *Infants of the Spring* or Locke's call, in a series of review essays in *Opportunity* and *Crisis,* for a more concrete demarcation of the "indefiniteness" of the New Negro, both writers reflect the progressively experimental moment of the early 1930s and challenge earlier periodizations of the movement.

Infants of the Spring revolves around several young black writers living in a Harlem brownstone, affectionately nicknamed Niggeratti Manor, during the Harlem Renaissance. The Manor's residents, the Niggeratti, include Raymond, Paul, and Pelham Gaylord, all of whom desire to be New Negro artists. Raymond's earliest writing task in the novel is a book review, a task he takes on primarily so that he can express what he perceives to be the inadequacy of black writing and writers "who had nothing to say, and who only wrote because they were literate and felt they should apprise white humanity of the better classes among Negro humanity."[3] Raymond is particularly "disgusted with the way everyone sought to romanticize Harlem and Harlem Negroes" (368). Like Thurman's own sometimes caustic reviews, Raymond's appraisal both analyzes the texts he reviews and provides an outlet to express his dissatisfaction with the current crop of black writing in general. In the *New Republic* and the *Independent* in 1927, for example, Thurman sounded a necessary note of circumspection with regard to African American writers and challenged the encomiums piled on black literature.[4] To use Du Bois's phrase, Thurman took exception to the then current "criteria of Negro art," claiming that the "critical standards have been ignored and the measure of achievement has been racial rather than literary." Thurman indicts white readers for misguidedly lowering standards: "The Negro will not be benefitted by mediocre and ephemeral works, even if they are hailed by well-meaning, but for the moment, simple-minded, white critics as works of genius."[5] In language similar to George Schuyler's in "The Negro-Art Hokum," Thurman censures white publishers for the uncritical publication of black writers who provide representations of African Americans that are "constructive," a pejorative adjective as Thurman uses it in the review.[6]

Raymond's thoughts about the period and his peers are ambivalent. On the one hand, he is encouraged that publishing opportunities are becoming available for himself and his friends, and he is confident enough to think that he can take advantage of those opportunities, despite the obvious impediment his lackadaisical lifestyle poses. On the other hand, editors and publishers are rewarding people with little talent, especially, according to Ray, those who are harder-working than he and his friend Paul are. This is made evident in the novel's best-known passage, in which Raymond contemplates the present and future of the Harlem Renaissance:

> There had been throughout the nation an announcement of a Negro renaissance. The American Negro, it seemed, was entering a new phase in his development. . . .
> Word had been flashed through the nation about this new phenomenon. Novels, plays, and poems by and about Negroes were being deliriously acclaimed and patronized. . . . And yet the more discerning were becoming more and more aware that nothing, or at least very little, was being done to substantiate the current fad, to make it the foundation for something truly epochal. For the time being, the Negro was more in evidence in the high places than ever before in his American career, but unless, or so it seemed to Raymond, he, Paul and others of the group who had climbed aboard the bandwagon actually began to do something worth while, there would be little chance of their being permanently established. (61–62)

Embedded within this reflection is a desire for permanence in the midst of a fleeting moment, as well as an anxious recognition of the ineptitude of Raymond and his friends. For Raymond has lofty aesthetic goals but little discipline to realize them. He and his friends only talk of writing better novels; they accomplish little creatively within the time frame of the book. The dilemma raised by *Infants* is not only art versus propaganda but also talent versus persistence: How do you motivate a promising yet indolent younger generation?

Can a movement be made out of hard workers with no talent or talented people who do not want to work hard? The most prolific resident of Niggeratti Manor is also the one who is most ridiculed and the one considered to have the least amount of aesthetic promise: Pelham Gaylord, once known simply as George Jones.

Positioning the most productive member of the Niggeratti as the least talented has considerable consequences. First, it allows Thurman to satirize young black artists who dream of fame despite a lack of skill, and changes Pelham from a humorous to a humiliating figure. Pelham is what everyone who migrates to Harlem represents, including even Paul and Raymond: the New York transplant who dreams of becoming a famous artist. Originally from the South and equipped only with a servant's background, Pelham is enamored of the group of writers he meets at Niggeratti Manor, for Raymond and his friends "were often mentioned in magazine and newspaper articles. This was just the group he needed to know, just the people he should cultivate" (124). Paul, Ray, and the other residents make disparaging comments about Pelham's work, both behind his back and in front of his face, but Pelham's lack of talent eventually becomes too uncomfortable for them. When Pelham reads one of his poems about a young girl to the group, the reaction is sadness, for "it was impossible to ridicule when his voice was so tender, his eyes so bright, his smile so pleased and ingratiating" (126)—when, in short, Pelham believes so fervently in the possibility of his artistic success, just as fervently as Paul and Raymond believe in theirs. And this similarity transforms Pelham from laughable to depressing. How can Raymond be sure that he is not, in fact, just a slightly more sophisticated version of Pelham Gaylord? Only Pelham's work is received with the regard, albeit in a punitive context, that one expects of an "artist." Pelham is accused of raping a teenage girl who lives several floors above Raymond and his friends. The poem Pelham writes in the girl's honor becomes proof of his seduction of the girl. Entered into evidence, the poem is recited in open court and gives weight to the false charge of statutory rape. Pelham's words are taken seriously, at least by the law, more seriously than those of any of the other young writers. Moreover, unlike the other residents, Pelham ultimately derives a living from his "art." That the form of art is commercial and utilitarian—"calcimining and painting" because he has experience "redecorating [prison] cell walls" (266)—matters little to Pelham. He is the only one of the Niggeratti who, after being placed on probation, actually will use his skills and earn money from his "artistic" endeavors.

Creative or literary growth does not result from relationships or artistic events in the novel. By the end of *Infants,* Niggeratti Manor will be transformed "from a congenial home for Negro artists to a congenial dormitory for bachelor girls" (182). Celibacy and sobriety replace the once fertile but ultimately unfulfilled wasteland of Niggeratti Manor. The final act of the Niggeratti is not the self-generation of the New Negro but the decadent self-destruction of one of its star members: Paul commits suicide by slashing his wrists in a bathtub in an ill-fated attempt to garner "delightful publicity" before his novel is published (283). Though the act of one individual, Paul's death indicts not only the other members of the Niggeratti but also, and more significantly for Thurman, a period seduced by celebrity.

The destruction of Paul's final creative product serves as a concluding warning against transience and insubstantial aesthetic output. The bathwater in which Paul commits suicide erases his manuscript, written in pencil. The only art left is a drawing that illustrates his book: "[Paul] had drawn a distorted, inky black skyscraper, modeled after Niggeratti Manor, and on which were focused an array of blindingly white beams of light. The foundation of this building was composed of crumbling stone. At first glance it could be ascertained that the skyscraper would soon crumple and fall, leaving the dominating white lights in full possession of the sky" (284). The image of the diseased, decaying Manor is the only artistic object not destroyed by Paul's suicide and the one that resonates at the conclusion of *Infants.* If one of the goals of the Harlem Renaissance was to transfuse evanescent qualities of blackness into recognizable and respected forms of art, Paul's book and Ray's still incomplete novel do indeed fail to accomplish this goal.[7] Moreover, one cannot escape the impression that Raymond's unspoken attraction to Stephen, a white visitor to Harlem and Raymond's roommate for a brief period, contributes to his failure to complete his novel. The character who is most open about his sexuality, Paul, is the one character who actually finishes his various artistic projects. Thurman's own experimental risk in *Infants of the Spring* is in the matter-of-fact portrayal of Paul's sexuality, yet this is masked by Raymond's unexpressed homoerotic feelings for Stephen, a curious silence when one considers Thurman's other works such as *The Blacker the Berry* and "Cordelia the Crude," both of which contain characters who experience several sexual encounters and are unapologetic about their sexuality.[8]

And so a visual image is the lasting testament to the inhabitants of Niggeratti Manor, not the novels by two of its most talented inhabitants. Image memorializes the Harlem Renaissance and replaces the promise of what could be with the lost promise of unfulfilled hope. Although the novel opens with a description of the "astonishing" modernist drawings by Paul which fascinate Stephen, the final visual image of the Manor starkly suggests failure and fulfills Raymond's earlier prediction about the danger of promoting a movement without the aesthetic creations "to substantiate the current fad, to make it the foundation for something truly epochal." Niggeratti Manor itself represents the "contagious blastments" that threaten and finally bury the young New Negro writers, or as Thurman terms them and himself, the "infants of the spring."[9] Like Carl Van Vechten, who criticizes the direction of the Harlem Renaissance in *Nigger Heaven* by having the New Negro writer Byron drugged and arrested, Thurman also reproves his characters who, by the end of the novel, have not realized their full potential.

Although the fictional counterparts of Locke and Thurman appear to be on opposing sides of the aesthetic debates, in fact by the 1930s both men were voicing similar criticisms of the Harlem Renaissance. In *Infants,* Locke is caricatured as Dr. Parkes, whose "first and last salon" dramatizes a portion of the *Crisis* symposium as well as Thurman's conversations with friends regarding the representation of black art (160). The salon quickly descends into disorder and chaos, for example, when the attendees question the proper role of Africa in their writing and drawings, a role frequently emphasized by Locke.[10] Other disagreements involve Parkes's distaste for "post-Victorian license" and the younger artists' more decadent literary proclivities (234). Despite their differences, by the 1930s both Locke and Thurman were expressing dissatisfaction with the New Negro/Harlem Renaissance movement, and this shared discontent helps us to reevaluate the period's familiar timeline.

Alain Locke's retrospective reviews of African American literature provide a cogent way to measure the shift in style and subject matter of black writing during the concluding moments of the Renaissance and the movement's aftermath. A series of thirteen essays in *Opportunity* and one essay in *Crisis,* published from 1929 to 1942, the reviews enable Locke to pass judgment on the writing of both black and white authors and highlight emerging trends in the literary and scholarly fields. Offering a discussion of the previous year's work by or about the African American in "panoramic perspective" (271) over an expanse of several months, the reviews chart the progression of the final highlights of the Harlem Renaissance from tempered praise to later, targeted criticism. Throughout the yearly reviews, Locke notes the decreasing number of poetry volumes by African Americans and a corresponding increase in nonfiction writing, particularly sociology and works on the history and culture of Africa by writers of various ethnicities. Locke's last review in *Opportunity* covers the literature of 1941; significantly, Richard Wright's *12 Million Black Voices* dominates his evaluation of the year's output. Wright's photo-text, along with his *Native Son,* reviewed by Locke the preceding year, signals for Locke a decidedly new and welcome style in African American literature.[11]

The most significant discussions in the reviews are those in which Locke touches on, either briefly or in detail, the New Negro Movement and its afterlife. In 1929 Locke welcomes the fading interest in African American writing, noting that "the movement for the vital expression of Negro life can only truly begin as the fad breaks off." If in the 1920s black literature was in the midst of a "renaissance," Locke claims that it is, by 1933, in a "reformation"; and in 1934 he writes that "as the fad subsides, a sounder, more artistic expression of Negro life and character takes its place."[12] During the 1930s Locke repeatedly attempts to distinguish a more restrained period of black writing that was different from the earlier moments of the Harlem Renaissance. He continues to see this development, particularly in the review for 1938, "The Negro: 'New' or Newer." Calling the "New Negro" a "convenient but dangerous caption," Locke here somewhat heatedly responds to an *Opportunity* essay that characterized the Harlem Renaissance as a "philosophy [which] believed that racial prejudice soon would disappear before the altars of truth, art, and intellectual achievement."[13] Despite the fact that there was some truth to this description, Locke chided the author for not fully reading or understanding Locke's "Enter the New Negro" in *The New Negro* anthology. Locke extensively quotes from that earlier essay to revisit the goals of the Renaissance and to point out that he had urged artists to identify with the masses and to draw upon the folk for inspiration. He notably identifies some of the problems of the Renaissance, especially problems of generality:

> The primary source of confusion perhaps was due to a deliberate decision not to define the "New Negro" dogmatically, but only to characterize his general traits and attitudes. And so, partly because of this indefiniteness, the phrase became a slogan for cheap race demagogues who wouldn't know a "cultural movement" if they could see one, a handy megaphone for petty exhibitionists who were only posing as "racialists" when in fact they were the rankest kind of egotists, and a gilded fetish for race idolaters who at heart were still sentimentalists seeking consolation for inferiority.[14]

In contrast to such "indefiniteness," the literature of the 1930s, through an attention to documentation and realism, provides clearer outlines of the definition of "the Negro." By 1943, in the review of literature appropriately titled "Who and What Is Negro?" Locke answers his question by stating that no one type of African American portrayed in literature can adequately express all African Americans. Locke instead uses the year's literary and scholarly output to further delineate blackness.

When Locke's retrospective reviews of literature over the expanse of thirteen years are read consecutively, a sense of movement becomes apparent, from cautious concern about the decline of publishing opportunities to a welcoming "sobriety." Examining Thurman's and Locke's essays together encourages us not to look at the level of white interest in black life as the only or dominant contribution to the end of the Harlem Renaissance, but to consider as well African Americans' own demands for different and better forms of art. One of the larger questions writers such as Thurman, Locke, and to a certain extent Richard Wright in "Blueprint for Negro Writing" raise for us is how do writers become aware of the need for literary excellence without languishing under the weight of criticism, a question asked repeatedly in Thurman's *Infant of the Spring*.[15]

Just as the Harlem Renaissance made its transition into what Locke called a "sober inventory, analysis, and appraisal" and a period Thurman called "a state of near sanity"—a moment that has traditionally been perceived as the "end" of the Harlem Renaissance—Thurman and Locke voiced their disappointment with New Negro writing and offered direction for future possibilities.[16] One hope I have for my own book is to distinguish a gradual yet perceptible shift in the contemporaneous evaluation of black writing in the late 1920s and early 1930s and to acknowledge how this shift may have affected constructions of blackness later in the twentieth century. Perhaps the most significant lesson we can take from both Thurman's and Locke's writings is to read a more nuanced relationship between the Harlem Renaissance of the 1920s and the documentary strain symbolized by the writings of Richard Wright in the 1930s. Thus, instead of being "influenced perhaps by the commercial demand for what was in effect a generic Harlem novel," black writers were themselves more critical about the state of black writing, more concerned, that is, with raising aesthetic standards while not paying exclusive homage to the desire for black "respectability," and with separating the racial identity of the writer from the evaluation of his or her skills.[17]

The Metropolitan's Harlem

Thirty-seven years after the publication of *Infants of the Spring,* the front pages of major New York newspapers rearticulated the questions that infused the Renaissance and troubled Raymond. The art exhibition "Harlem on My Mind: The Cultural Capital of Black America, 1900–1968," at the Metropolitan Museum of Art from January 18 to April 6, 1969, reflects the late-twentieth-century contentiousness about how to (re)present and market the Harlem Renaissance. The exhibit itself functions as an artifact, an event that, in an effort to celebrate the city's past, could not be divorced from the aesthetic debates about black representation in the 1920s, or from the racial politics of the 1960s. Like the literary anthology, a museum exhibition requires deliberate choices; it confers value, or "cultural capital," on the artists included. An exhibition tells a story, and its location within a privileged institutional space such as a museum influences how the exhibition's arts and artifacts are perceived and remembered. Writing of the aesthetic and political purposes of the museum in Western culture, specifically the role of the Louvre in French culture, Carol Duncan notes how the museum space both reflects the power of the nation-state and fashions the nation's citizens: "Such public institutions made (and still make) the state look good: progressive, concerned about the spiritual life of its citizens, a preserver of past achievements and a provider for the common good." In 1969 the Metropolitan Museum of Art, which, according to Duncan, was "directly inspired by the Louvre," reflected Harlem's past in its historic and artistically significant galleries.[18] By devoting such space to Harlem, the Metropolitan, or at least the exhibition's decision makers, appeared to acknowledge the incontrovertible role that Harlem and its inhabitants played in one of the great cities in the United States.

Why would a display riddled with charges of racism, anti-Semitism, and paternalism; that had limited input from African American scholars and artists; that inspired an anonymous patron to deface one of the Metropolitan's paintings by Rembrandt; an exhibit that, even before it opened, offended numerous New Yorkers, including African Americans, Jewish Americans, Latinos, the mayor of New York City, and New York art patrons—why is such an exhibit instructive of the problematic remembering process and an example of an unsuccessful weaving of image and text?[19] "Harlem on My Mind" reproduced some of the most divisive issues of the Harlem Renaissance, for example, the questions of white patronage, the qualities that signified "art," and the best way

Figure 6.1. "Harlem on My Mind" exhibition (1969), Metropolitan Museum of Art. Courtesy of Allon Schoener, Metropolitan Museum of Art. © Donna Mussenden Van Der Zee. Image © Metropolitan Museum of Art.

to represent African Americans. The exhibit became a microcosm of the debates that defined black Harlem in the 1920s and the 1930s, and it mirrored the concerns that continue to influence Harlem's portrayal. The Metropolitan's "Harlem on My Mind" celebrated Harlem, yet it did so by focusing heavily on photography. The exhibition quite literally staged its narrative through a juxtaposition of image and text, a contest between pictures and words. In addition to photographs by such artists as Aaron Siskind and Gordon Parks, the exhibit consisted primarily of enlarged photographs by James Van Der Zee (figure 6.1) and reprints from New York–area newspapers.[20] And because the event took place after a highly charged moment of racial crisis in New York City's history,

it resurrected the too familiar binary of "art or propaganda." The exhibit's textual counterpart, a catalogue published by Random House, demonstrated in
particular the problems surrounding the textual commemoration of Harlem. I
am concerned not so much with the actual exhibit as I am with the controversies
and aesthetic discussions it engendered and the exhibition's reception by both
Harlemites and notable reviewers. The exhibit was noteworthy not only for
the controversy surrounding it but also for the skill it displayed in marketing
for popular consumption an *idea* of the Harlem Renaissance.

The exhibition's presentation of the period, as well as the battle over what
Harlem is and how it should be represented, instructs us about how this space
functions in American culture, who if anyone "owns" it, and the tension between the visual and the written, image and text, that continues to influence
contemporary portrayals of black culture. What is the "cultural capital" of
Harlem, and who gets to define it? What are the images Harlem and its Renaissance evoke and why? Examining the Metropolitan's attempt to refashion the
Renaissance offers a timeless lesson on the construction and appropriation of
Harlem's commodifiable history and about a place that continually reflects
an early and paradigmatic black modern moment.[21]

Politics and Art

Highly contentious national and local politics surrounded the organization,
promotion, and eventual opening of the Metropolitan exhibition. The idea of
celebrating Harlem's past originated in the late 1960s, a traumatic period inter-
nationally and in American culture. It was at this time that, nationally, the
country was dealing with the assassinations of two influential men, Martin
Luther King Jr. in April and Robert F. Kennedy in June 1968, and the political
and diplomatic fallout from the Tet Offensive in Vietnam. Locally there were
tensions as well, for reasons that had little to do with art. The exhibit followed
a racially turbulent period in New York City politics, months after mostly
white public school teachers in the Ocean Hill–Brownsville section of Brook-
lyn went on strike, affecting the schools and the communities of inner-city
African American and Latino students.[22]

It was within this charged environment that the Metropolitan Museum of
Art's exhibition was conceived. "Harlem on My Mind" was the idea of Allon
Schoener, the visual arts director of the New York State Council on the Arts.
Schoener's motivation for the display recalled that of Charles Johnson, Alain

Locke, and other leaders of the Harlem Renaissance of the 1920s: to increase the public's awareness of the artistic center located in Harlem and to promote Harlem's history and talent. Schoener had already presented a successful multimedia exhibit on Jewish American culture at the Jewish Museum in New York called "The Lower East Side: Portal to American Life." He wanted to create a similar exhibit on Harlem and draw more diverse groups to the Metropolitan. His ideas were welcomed by Thomas P. F. Hoving, one of the youngest men to be named director of the Met. Hoving brought a level of exuberance that, according to one historian of the institution, caused some "trepidation" among museum trustees.[23] The conservative museum had, and continues to have, a privileged status even in relation to other New York museums. Mieke Bal, for example, argues that there is a geographical, and implicitly an ideological, significance to the Met's location on the *right* side of Central Park (as seen from downtown), "as if to propose an aesthetic base for the strictures of domination that reign in this society."[24] Hoving was interested in "popularizing" the museum, making it more accessible to the average New Yorker and a place where young people could meet and "makes dates, pick up girls, [and] pick up boys."[25] As an example of Hoving's acknowledgment of popular culture, one of his innovations was to place advertisements for the Met's shows in newspapers and New York–area magazines. Hoving's previous job was as the parks commissioner. Initially his transition from the parks to the museum seemed to subdue his more extravagant tendencies, a shift the *New York Times* appeared to approve: "The art world has noticed a change in Mr. Hoving since he joined the museum. The word is that he has displayed more 'dignity' and 'restraint.'"[26]

Part of the exhibition's problems resulted from the fact that both Schoener and Hoving admittedly had little knowledge of Harlem's quite diverse and expansive history, particularly Harlem's role in the polemical issue surrounding African Americans and artistic representation. These two men of the 1960s and the exhibition they organized fell into the aesthetic quagmire previously experienced by Harlem Renaissance artists and scholars: Can art be used for purposes other than aesthetic ones? Can art by African Americans help eradicate racism? That is, in James Weldon Johnson's words, can black art "alter the [white] national mental attitude" toward African Americans?[27] To some extent "Harlem on My Mind" repeated and reaffirmed W. E. B. Du Bois's pronouncement that "all art is propaganda."[28] Announcements of the exhibition referred to the local and national racial conflicts and drew attention to the possible healing effects the display could provide: "The role of the Museum has always been to make people see with their eyes. Today we must ask people to look searchingly at things that have to be looked into—such as our communities and our environment. . . . And hopefully it will generate a continuing situation in which white and black people can confront each other with more respect for each other's roles in American life."[29] Schoener and Hoving hoped that making others aware of black artists would help to soothe the tensions between blacks and whites, Jewish Americans and African Americans, in New York City. Remarkably, then, decades after Du Bois's and Johnson's calls for the artistic depiction of a "New Negro" to help challenge racism, Schoener and Hoving perceived a similar function in art created by African Americans, as demonstrated in Hoving's official statements about the exhibition. Sounding a note like that of Arthur A. Schomburg's essay "The Negro Digs Up His Past," the "Director's Note" in the Metropolitan's publication the *Bulletin* acknowledged that Harlem has a vibrant history that all New Yorkers should experience: "We must begin to look to the great Negro past for our understanding of the American experience, and look to it as well for whatever common hope we have for the future."[30] Hoving's note echoed Johnson's, Du Bois's, and Schomburg's humanistic appeals to art to challenge the negative social conditions and perceptions of African Americans.

The dilemma of the proper image and the image proper also returned as the "Harlem on My Mind" exhibition raised the contentious question of the "proper" way to display art. Schoener's conceptual ideas for the exhibit were, to say the least, unconventional, and thus contributed to the strident opposition voiced in prominent New York newspapers. As Carol Duncan argues, "museum space is carefully marked off and culturally designated as special, reserved for a particular kind of contemplation and learning experience and demanding a special quality of attention."[31] But Schoener wanted to fracture the conventional bounds of interiority constructed by gazing upon art. He intended to create a "new exhibition aesthetic," one in which "information, not art, dominated." He later recalled: "I wanted to demonstrate new ideas about how museums could become information environments that inundated people with images and sounds rather than artifacts. The era of museums as places for silent contemplation of works of art had ended. . . . I conceived the *Harlem on My Mind* exhibition as an environment that would parallel the sensations we experience in our own lives—a deluge of information stimuli."[32] Schoener's attempt to create an experience of sensory overload, one that replicated the sensations of living in populous and crowded New York, was innovative. The deliberate removal of traditional boundaries and the use of different technologies to contribute to the museum experience pioneered museum practices that are now considered standard. Schoener succeeded in creating a "deluge of stimuli"; but, as I discuss shortly, this effect was routinely criticized by reviewers of various artistic and political leanings.

As the first "nonart" exhibition in the Metropolitan's history, "Harlem on my Mind" challenged traditional categories of art and aesthetics and took risks in using the museum's space. Filling eighteen thousand square feet, the display consisted of "700 photographic enlargements, 500 project images, and a five-minute video."[33] The floor plan and content were designed so that the patron could take in the exhibit within sixty minutes.[34] There were no sculptures or paintings on display; instead Schoener mounted newspaper images and written text on the walls.[35] "Harlem on My Mind" was an experiment in both space and method. The exhibit opened with large-scale representations of Harlem apartments, "from floor to ceiling," as well as a fifty-two-by-fourteen-foot mural depicting Adam Clayton Powell Jr. with a class of Sunday school students.[36] According to one reviewer, this use of the museum's physical space suggested the crowded conditions of Harlem: "One penetrates [a succession of galleries] as in almost a maze. . . . In one, depicting the Thirties, the display structures are so close together that one maneuvers about in an atmosphere seemingly tense and constrained."[37] Schoener would later call "Harlem on My Mind" the "first audiovisual environment ever created in a major art museum."[38] Experimentation ruptured the traditional contemplation of visual art to depict African American history. In the museum's *Bulletin* Hoving conceded that "Harlem on My Mind" was "an exhibition that has nothing to do with art in the narrow sense—but everything to do with this Museum." The exhibition "doesn't interpret or explain. It sticks to the facts."[39] Such a fact-based exhibit precluded a consideration of the aesthetic sensibilities of Harlem artists.

According to some critics, Schoener's and Hoving's innovations created the perception that they were eroding the museum's prestige. The "Harlem on My Mind" exhibit occurred one year before the Metropolitan's one hundredth anniversary. The *New York Times*' art critic Hilton Kramer used the exhibit, and others like it that were organized around the work of African American artists, to censure what he called the "politicization" of art. Kramer chided Hoving, arguing that the exhibit was "lamentable in so many fundamental ways—in its conception, in its execution, and in its general ideological assumptions." Hoving's worst offense was not just bad artistic taste; it was violating the museum's august reputation: "Mr. Hoving has for the first time politicized the Metropolitan, and has thereby cast doubt on its future integrity as an institution consecrated above all to the task of preserving our artistic heritage from the fickle encroachment of history."[40] Tradition and innovation, then, appeared to be publicly at odds at the Metropolitan Museum of Art in the planning and eventual launching of the exhibit.

"Harlem on My Mind" also replicated the Renaissance concerns about white presence in and influence on black art. There was the question not only of who would represent Harlem but also of who and what would be included as representatives of African American art. Who could "speak" of and for African American art? What should be the role of white philanthropy and organizers? The exhibition's creators were neither African American nor specialists in African American art or culture, and of the seven people who formed the "core exhibition staff," three were African American, but only one, A'lelia Nelson, was from New York; Donald Harper was from Chicago and Reginald McGhee, a photojournalist, was from Milwaukee.[41] The absence of black decision makers from Harlem became an issue that, along with the exhibit itself, was criticized by reviewers.[42]

Because so much of the exhibition was mediated by the written word, it is perhaps fitting that the most significant controversy concerned its textual souvenir, the 255-page exhibition catalogue, designed by Herb Lubalin and Ernie Smith. The contributors to the volume often failed to move beyond the typecasting of the ethnic groups the exhibit was supposed to celebrate. The preface by Hoving, for example, situated the exhibit from the perspective of one with limited knowledge of African American culture. Discussing his interaction with African Americans during his childhood, Hoving noted that "Negroes were people. But they were happy, foot-twitching, smiling and sunny. They were not to be (and when they were, it was a problem) sour, moody, bitter, silent and mad like Frank, the chauffeur. 'Why can't he be like Bessie the maid? Always friendly, always gay and warm?'"[43] Looking back on his tenure at the Metropolitan in 1993, Hoving confessed that he had "embellished" and fictionalized this account in the hope that "Harlem on My Mind" would initiate a discussion between black and white people and remove some of these misconceptions.[44]

But the dialogue Hoving had wished for turned into confrontations and accusations. The final, most-noted controversy was caused by the introduction to the exhibition's catalogue, written by an African American high school student, Candice Van Ellison. The essay, which, according to Schoener, was an attempt to give a broad overview of Harlem's history by one of the city's young residents, managed to disparage nearly all ethnicities. Racial stereotypes were used to characterize the living conditions of diverse groups in Harlem ("Project apartments number from one to three bedrooms. What happens to the Puerto Rican family of twelve?"). The passage that caused the most unease attempted to explain the relations between African Americans and Jewish Americans in New York:

> Another major area of contact involves the Jewish landlord and the Black tenant. A large portion of Harlem's Black women serve as domestics in middle-class Jewish homes. Perhaps this would explain the higher rate of anti-Semitism among Black women than men. . . . One other important factor worth noting is that psychologically, Blacks may find that anti-Jewish sentiments place them, for once, within a majority. Thus, our contempt for the Jew makes us feel more completely American in sharing a national prejudice.[45]

Ironically, in writing this introduction Van Ellison used unattributed quotations from Daniel Patrick Moynihan, who, with Nathan Glazer, wrote *Beyond the Melting Pot* (1963), a sociological look at different ethnic groups in New York, which prefigured Moynihan's infamous 1965 report on the black family.[46] Schoener had advised the young student to remove the quotation marks and citations which initially appeared in her essay. Newspapers covered extensively the problems incited by the catalogue, particularly when Hoving's friend, the mayor of New York, John V. Lindsay, publicly called the catalogue racist and stated that it should be withdrawn. Eventually, after numerous protests, the Metropolitan did decide to recall the catalogue from circulation, although copies were still available in bookstores.

The catalogue functions as an instance of one of the exhibition's touristic "markers." It omits much of what was included in the exhibit other than the photographs, thereby offering a more "traditional" version of the museum experience, without music or other audiovisual effects to complicate the act of textual reading. Paradoxically, as one *Village Voice* reviewer pointed out, the catalogue succeeded where the exhibition did not precisely because of this absence: "Once the pictures are stripped of Allon Schoener's distracting gimmickry, once all the multi-screen projections, closed-circuit interviews, and other trappings are removed, the pictures have an opportunity to speak for themselves, and do."[47]

While the exhibit took some experimental risks, the catalogue itself is formal. Despite the striking cover in bright red and yellow, the pages within are starkly black and white. Each section is divided into a decade, beginning with

1900 and ending with 1968, and each begins with the headlines of newspaper clippings in white letters on a black background. While the clippings give an adequate historical summation of events in the city and detail the city's shift from a predominantly white locale to a black metropolis, they do not suggest the creativity that impelled and inspired the output during the 1920s and 1930s. The starkness is more pronounced as the catalogue covers the latter half of the twentieth century; only in the section on the 1940s does the austerity of the reporting seem fitting to the mood conveyed by the photographs. A series of images from riots in 1944, 1951, and 1964, though taken in different time periods, appear remarkably similar. Notably, it is the catalogue version of the exhibition that endures. Although "Harlem on My Mind" was designed so that it could be transported and shown in other areas of the country, because of the controversy, it was not.[48] Paradoxically, one of the early victims of the exhibition, the catalogue, has had the longest life: It has had four reprint editions; and the last, published in 2007, contains a foreword by U.S. Representative Charles Rangel of New York that celebrates the diversity of Harlem (though Rangel never refers to the exhibition).[49]

"Harlem on My Mind" received mixed reviews, and some of them were prescient. According to the reviewers, there was something that the exhibition was not able to capture despite the huge scale of the display. Commentators noted that the exhibit presented a purchasable Harlem. There was a sense that the exhibit, created in honor of Harlem and its inhabitants, actually was designed for those who only rarely had Harlem on their minds. Art critics applied the terms and images that had suffused the period of the Renaissance. The *New York Times'* senior art critic, John Canaday, offered a critique of "Harlem on My Mind" that notably recalled the "picturesque" terminology and imagery that James Weldon Johnson had tried hard to erase, the anachronistic picture of the black artist in front of the cabin, playing the banjo and shuffling for white spectators:

> Harlem is largely unexplored not only as an area of a city but as a sociological structure—unexplored, at any rate, by the public for whom "Harlem on My Mind" is planned. We know Harlem only as a surface that we have become familiar with by proxy over the years. It has supplied picturesque material for photographers, sensational events for journalistic reportage, and a background for novels about Negro suffering, occasionally observed by a white man (does anybody here remember Carl Van Vechten's "Nigger Heaven" of 1926?).[50]

Canaday criticizes the memories of Harlem which consist of the city's various sensational representations, capped with a hazy recall of *Nigger Heaven*. His review suggests that, despite the passage of time, Harlem continued to be received as myth by white nonresidents: "In retrospect I see that in spite of all the talk about a renaissance of the arts in Harlem, we thought of the place in terms of de ole plantation modernized and transplanted. All those entertainers we were admiring (along with their expatriate sister, Josephine Baker) were really just the happy cullud folk a-singin' and a-dancin' in their happy, talented way. The saxophone had replaced de banjo, and yeah man had taken over from yassuh massah, but we were enjoying a translation of a picture that had been false in the first place."[51] Grace Glueck, also of the *Times,* concurred with Canaday, stating that the exhibit "panders to our penchant for instant history, packaged culture, the kind of photojournalistic 'experience' that puts us at a distance from the experience itself."[52] Both Canaday's and Glueck's reviews suggest an inauthenticity not only of the exhibit but also of the frequently anthologized Harlem that we have come to know, a charge repeated in the stereotypical language so heavily criticized by the black architects of the Harlem Renaissance.[53]

Despite its "failures," there are some lessons to be learned from this late-twentieth-century attempt to remember and (re)present the Negro mecca.[54] The Metropolitan's exhibition did succeed in bringing diverse members of the New York public into the museum. Despite the controversy, thirty years after the exhibit opened Schoener would claim that "for the first time, blacks came to the Met as gallerygoers, not janitors."[55] On the first day of the exhibit, nearly ten thousand patrons attended the Met, which, according to museum officials, was twice the average for an opening, and 15 percent of them were African American, approximately six times the average.[56]

More significantly, the exhibition revealed how, nearly thirty years after the putative end of the Harlem Renaissance, the period was remembered and still romanticized. As Canaday's review suggests, this romanticized Harlem may end precisely at the moment when the celebration ceased and African American literature became more experimental, the gradual endpoint, after the heyday of cabarets and salons, when the work of representing blackness in art engaged a multitude of visual and literary dilemmas. In this book I have tried to complicate and expand the ineluctable bond of image and text in black cultural production, in order to reflect critically on how visual culture permeates African American literary and cultural traditions, to make us think differently about the visual imperatives of one of the most romanticized moments in black cultural history, and to understand the strategies used to depict a crucial moment in black history that was itself concerned with black representation. I have also sought to expand our sense of who and what constitutes this period. As James Weldon Johnson remarks in the epigraph to this chapter, having different perspectives—of Harlem, of a "renaissance," of African Americans—is "all right so long as one view is not taken to be the whole picture." Posing and understanding the questions of black representation can open up the dialogue to include other overlooked black modernist writers who experimented with broadening the definitions of blackness, such as Melvin Tolson and Ralph Ellison. If nothing else, the Metropolitan Museum of Art's exhibition demonstrates the problem of repeating history, repeating the demands for the "right" representation of blackness. Indeed it demonstrates the need to eschew "correct" or proper representation—as the writers and figures of this study did as well.

Abbreviations

CVV–NYPL   Carl Van Vechten Papers, Manuscripts and Archives Division, New York
Public Library

CVV–Y   Carl Van Vechten Correspondence, Yale Collection of American Literature,
Beinecke Rare Book and Manuscript Library, Yale University

HLM   H. L. Mencken Papers, Manuscripts and Archives Division, New York
Public Library

JWJ   James Weldon Johnson and Grace Nail Johnson Papers, James Weldon
Johnson Collection, Yale Collection of American Literature, Beinecke Rare
Book and Manuscript Library, Yale University

LH   Langston Hughes Collection, Yale Collection of American Literature,
Beinecke Rare Book and Manuscript Library, Yale University

Notes

Introduction

1. George Hutchinson, *The Harlem Renaissance in Black and White* (Cambridge: Harvard University Press, 1995), 166.

2. *Crisis,* February 1926, 165. For clarity and simplicity I give here the full bibliographic information for all of the months (February–June and August–November 1926) in which the symposium's questions and answers were printed: March, 219–20; April, 278–80; May, 35–36; June, 71–73; August, 193–94; September, 238–39; "Criteria of Negro Art," October, 290–97; November, 28–29. Subsequent citations are given parenthetically in the text by the month and page number. Although no responses were printed in the July issue, there was an anonymous article (134) about the emerging African American theater movement and the support it received from the New York Public Library in Harlem. The article, "Krigwa Players Little Negro Theatre: The Story of a Little Theatre Movement," described the efforts to create and sustain an African American dramatic community. Rather than viewing the *Crisis* symposium as one that was limited only to the issues in which the questions and responses were printed, I propose viewing the symposium as beginning with Du Bois's review of *The New Negro* in January, continuing with the publication of his "Criteria of Negro Art" in October, and concluding with his review of Van Vechten's *Nigger Heaven* in December, a trajectory that makes 1926 a crucial year in which African American representational tactics were debated and discussed. In both the essay and the reviews, Du Bois elaborates upon his idea of "proper" Negro literature and art, even criticizing Alain Locke

in the review of *The New Negro*. Though he praised the collection, Du Bois presaged the topics that would consume the period. Noting that "Mr. Locke has newly been seized with the idea that Beauty rather than Propaganda should be the object of Negro literature and art," Du Bois chides the other scholar, warning, "If Mr. Locke's thesis is insisted on too much it is going to turn the Negro renaissance into decadence." In the same review Du Bois also dismissed "the young Negro [who] tries to do pretty things." W. E. B. Du Bois, review of *The New Negro, Crisis,* January 1926, 140–41.

3. Dubey delineates both the attractions and the limitations of literal representation in postmodern African American fiction. Examining Toni Morrison's *Song of Solomon* and Gloria Naylor's *Mama Day,* Dubey persuasively shows how evocations of the South and concepts of magic and conjuring help writers contend with the ambivalence of postmodern urban literary representation. In contrast to the technology-inflected space of the urban setting, the South functions on the level of magic: "Magical modes of reading, which affirm literal connections between language and referent, story and place, author and community, serve to establish stable grounds for the writer's claim to racial representation. The push toward literal meanings posits a closed circuit of community, characterized by sameness, cultural coherence, and a transparency of communication, and it allows the author a directly reflective relation to this community." Dubey argues that Morrison's and Naylor's use of the literal betrays some anxiety with regard to print culture and the book as commodity; similarly, the urge for literal representation by some proponents of the New Negro Movement displayed a willful desire for "a closed circuit of community, characterized by sameness, cultural coherence, and a transparency of communication." The difference, of course, is that Morrison and Naylor privilege a romanticized Southern folk community, while the New Negro artists deliberately attempted to fashion an urban, cosmopolitan Northern elite. The *Crisis* questions aim to limit the images of blackness that will be able to circulate as "authentic." Madhu Dubey, *Signs of Cities: Black Literary Postmodernism* (Chicago: University of Chicago Press, 2003), 179.

4. Gerald Early, in his introduction to *My Soul's High Song: The Collected Writings of Countee Cullen* (New York: Anchor Books, 1991), draws an active distinction between the New Negro Movement and the Harlem Renaissance, arguing that the former took place between 1908 and 1938 and that the latter was "only a phase, a kind of peak moment" of the New Negro Movement (24).

5. Nathan Huggins, *Harlem Renaissance* (New York: Oxford University Press, 1971), 306, 303. David Levering Lewis, in *When Harlem Was in Vogue* (New York: Penguin, 1981), claims that the "failure" of the Harlem Renaissance was "inevitable," not only because of the Great Depression but also because of the strategy of "the maximizing of the exceptional" (305). Both historians suggest that the temporal end of the Renaissance can be marked by the 1935 riot in Harlem. Huggins, *Harlem Renaissance,* 303; Lewis, *When Harlem Was in Vogue,* 306.

6. Houston A. Baker Jr., *Modernism and the Harlem Renaissance* (Chicago: University of Chicago Press, 1987), 12, 6.

7. George Hutchinson, *The Harlem Renaissance in Black and White* (Cambridge: Harvard University Press, 1995); Michael North, *The Dialect of Modernism: Race, Language, and Twentieth-Century Literature* (New York: Oxford University Press, 1994); Brent Hayes Edwards, *The Practice of Diaspora: Literature, Translation, and the Rise of Black Internationalism* (Cambridge: Harvard University Press, 2003). Cheryl Wall, *Women of the Harlem Renaissance* (Bloomington: Indiana University Press, 1995), is nota-

ble for focusing on the female writers of this time, who are usually overlooked in these other studies.

8. Since the early 2000s scholarship has appeared that recognizes the significance of the visual in the discussion of the Harlem Renaissance; these works focus primarily on the graphic illustrations and book covers of some of the period's most notable fictional and poetical publications, which is not the main subject of my book. These recent books include Anne Carroll, *Word, Image, and the New Negro: Representation and Identity in the Harlem Renaissance* (Bloomington: Indiana University Press, 2005); Daylanne English, *Unnatural Selections: Eugenics in American Modernism and the Harlem Renaissance* (Chapel Hill: University of North Carolina Press, 2004); Cherene Sherrard-Johnson, *Portraits of the New Negro Woman: Visual and Literary Culture in the Harlem Renaissance* (New Brunswick: Rutgers University Press, 2007); Martha Jane Nadell, *Enter the New Negroes: Images of Race in American Culture* (Cambridge: Harvard University Press, 2004); and Caroline Goeser, *Picturing the New Negro: Harlem Renaissance Print Culture and Modern Black Modernity* (Lawrence: University of Kansas Press, 2007).

9. See, for example, J. Martin Favor, *Authentic Blackness: The Folk in the New Negro Renaissance* (Durham: Duke University Press, 1999). Favor critiques geography in addition to race, class, and gender, and argues that the South emerges during the early twentieth century as another category denoting black "authenticity." He demonstrates, for example, how the Northern-born, Harvard-educated Du Bois "feels the necessity to travel south to create a more complete notion of his own racial identity" (11).

10. I am, of course, alluding to Martin Jay's monumental *Downcast Eyes: The Denigration of Vision in Twentieth-Century French Thought* (Berkeley: University of California Press, 1993), which examines "antivisual discourse" in well-known French thinkers. For a detailed history of early visual science, see Jonathan Crary, *Techniques of the Observer: On Vision and Modernity in the Nineteenth Century* (Cambridge: MIT Press, 1990). For analyses of the cognitive process of seeing, see Donald D. Hoffman, *Visual Intelligence: How We Create What We See* (New York: W. W. Norton, 1998); and Richard L. Gregory, *Eye and Brain: The Psychology of Seeing* (1966), 5th ed. (Princeton: Princeton University Press, 1997).

11. Shawn Michelle Smith, *Photography on the Color Line: W. E. B. Du Bois, Race, and Visual Culture* (Durham: Duke University Press, 2004); English, *Unnatural Selections;* and Karen Jacobs, *The Eye's Mind: Literary Modernism and Visual Culture* (Ithaca: Cornell University Press, 2001), 4.

12. Jonathan Crary, *Techniques of the Observer: On Vision and Modernity in the Nineteenth Century* (Cambridge: MIT Press, 1990), 16.

13. The subjective qualities of perception were familiar to persons whose nonwhite appearance made them subject to others' power. Although one could turn to any of the African American slave narratives that appeared during the nineteenth century to find the forced susceptibility of the black body to a white one, one of the more interesting accounts of this hierarchy of vision, body, and power appears in Olaudah Equiano's narrative, published in 1789. Equiano's story details how categories of the body, defined by the visual perception of the differences in skin color, ratify the possession of one body by another. See Olaudah Equiano, *The Interesting Narrative and Other Writings,* ed. Vincent Caretta (New York: Penguin, 2003). See also Hortense Spillers's discussion of the narrative in her essay "Mama's Baby, Papa's Maybe: An American Grammar Book," in *Black, White, and in Color: Essays on American Literature and Culture* (Chicago: University of Chicago Press, 2003), 203–29.

14. Lindon Barrett, "Handwriting: Legibility and the White Body in *Running a Thousand Miles for Freedom*," *American Literature* 69, no. 2 (1997): 318, 315, 325.

15. Robyn Wiegman, *American Anatomies: Theorizing Race and Gender* (Durham: Duke University Press, 1995); and Karen Sánchez-Eppler, *Touching Liberty: Abolition, Feminism, and the Politics of the Body* (Berkeley: University of California Press, 1993).

16. Wiegman, *American Anatomies*, 63. One recent book that refutes high modernism's rejection of mass culture is Sara Danius, *The Senses of Modernism: Technology, Perception, and Aesthetics* (Ithaca: Cornell University Press, 2003). Danius highlights the relation between aesthetics and the technology of mass culture, perhaps one of the more familiar versions of the abstract versus the concrete that has reappeared in modernist studies. She rereads European modernism with a focus on such forms of technology as the x-ray machine and the telephone to demonstrate how technology was "a fundamental, even constitutive, part of modernist culture" (40). Alexander Weheliye's explication of sound recording and black modernity in *Phonographies: Grooves in Sonic Afro-Modernity* (Durham: Duke University Press, 2005) supports Danius's argument regarding the significance of the technological, even to the elite high modernists. Weheliye discusses the materiality and ephemerality of sound in order to delineate the "interface" between "the technological and social histories of sound recording and reproduction as they cut across twentieth-century black cultural production" (3). This crossing plays a pivotal role in the construction of what he calls a "sonic Afro-modernity." While Weheliye concentrates on the sonic and its constitutive role in the formation of black modernity, an equally pressing case can be made for the significance of the visual to the black modern.

17. One version of this division is revealed by Walter Benn Michaels's conception of "internal difference." Discussing the doubleness of symbols such as the corporation and money, he notes that, like writing, the symbols can function as both "material and ideal" representations, both physical "manifestations" of a company or currency and the subjective representation of a collective idea or monetary value. In terms of writing, this doubleness reveals itself in that "for writing to be writing, it can neither transcend the marks it is made of nor be reduced to those marks." For Michaels, the "internal difference of writing" means that the textual image can only inadequately approximate the object described. Textual description, like paper money, can never actually be what it represents; there is always some distance, some gap between sign and referent. But as I suggest throughout these pages, when writing concerns the black image, such gaps or internal differences are denied. That is, blackness as represented by "Negro" dialect—with visual deformities that did not reflect normative language—was indeed "reduced to those marks." Walter Benn Michaels, *The Gold Standard and the Logic of Naturalism: American Literature at the Turn of the Century* (Berkeley: University of California Press, 1987), 21.

18. Spillers, "Mama's Baby, Papa's Maybe," 205.

19. Huggins, *Harlem Renaissance*, 237.

20. Dubey, *Signs of Cities*, 179.

21. W. J. T. Mitchell, *Iconology: Image, Text, Ideology* (Chicago: University of Chicago Press, 1986), 43.

22. Ibid., 19, 28.

23. Mitchell explicitly refers to race and gender in one brief section of *Iconology*, mainly to note how Edmund Burke's contradictory reading of power and otherness, invoked in an anecdote about a formerly blind boy reacting with "horror" at the sight of a black woman, influences Burke's discussion of the French Revolution. Horror for Burke is associated

with the masculine attributes of power and the sublime (ibid., 129–31). On reading Mitchell's explication of Burke, one thinks immediately of Stephen Crane's 1898 short story "The Monster," in which the sight of a badly burned African American man frightens the citizens of a small town. For a compelling examination of Crane's story in light of a "cultural logic" of lynching, see Jacqueline Goldsby, *A Spectacular Secret: Lynching in American Life and Literature* (Chicago: University of Chicago Press, 2006), 105–63.

24. Henry Louis Gates Jr., "The Trope of a New Negro and the Reconstruction of the Image of the Black," *Representations* 24 (1998): 143, 133, 135. Gates demonstrates that the term "New Negro" was in circulation in America as early as 1895 and had a more violent, aggressive connotation than its suggestion of the urbane African American in the 1920s.

25. James Weldon Johnson, *The Book of American Negro Poetry* (New York: Harcourt, Brace, 1922), vii.

26. Mitchell, *Iconology*, 43.

27. For a more recent though brief look at the symposium in the history of the *Crisis*, see Amy Kirschke, *Art in "Crisis": W. E. B. Du Bois and the Struggle for African American Identity* (Bloomington: Indiana University Press, 2007).

28. Toni Morrison, *Playing in the Dark: Whiteness and the Literary Imagination* (Cambridge: Harvard University Press, 1992), xi.

29. David Levering Lewis, *W. E. B. Du Bois: The Fight for Equality and the American Century, 1919–1963* (New York: Henry Holt, 2000), 176.

30. Hughes's essay has functioned as a type of manifesto for both the younger writers of the Harlem Renaissance and black young writers in later periods. Trey Ellis echoed Hughes's sense of a mission in his 1989 essay "The New Black Aesthetic," *Callaloo* 12, no. 1 (Winter 1989): 233–43. See chapter 3 for a more detailed reading of "The Negro Artist and the Racial Mountain" and the essay with which it is frequently paired, "The Negro-Art Hokum" by George Schuyler.

31. Ironically, author Charles Chesnutt issued the final response to the seven questions in the November 1926 issue (28–29). I call this ironic because, although Chesnutt was the author of several books and short stories in the late nineteenth and early twentieth centuries, he was unable to capture or take advantage of the literary interest in African American subject matter prevalent in the 1920s. See his essay "Post-Bellum, Pre-Harlem," in *Chesnutt: Stories, Novels, and Essays* (New York: Modern Library of America, 2002), 906–12.

32. According to the *Chicago Defender*, Du Bois's "brilliant oration" received "an ovation of the sort rarely yielded by a Chicago audience." The report continued, "Dr. Du Bois was at his best and his speech, a ringing challenge to members of the Race to make the most of the present renaissance of Race art and culture, evoked repeated rounds of applause." J. Blaine Poindexter, "Crowd Mass Meetings of N.A.A.C.P.," *Chicago Defender*, July 3, 1926, sec. 1, 1.

33. English, *Unnatural Selections*, 64. English further identifies the eugenicist tendencies in black and white modernism. In contrast to the skepticism of other moderns about the veracity of vision, the pictures accompanying Du Bois's speech in the *Crisis* reveal a belief that the gaze could be reappropriated and reframed. English's analysis elucidates the work of Shawn Michelle Smith, who cogently examines Du Bois's photography exhibition of the "Georgia Negro" at the 1900 Paris Exposition in *Photography on the Color Line: W. E. B. Du Bois, Race, and Visual Culture* (Durham: Duke University Press, 2004).

34. Du Bois, "Books," *Crisis*, December 1926, 82.

35. The *Crisis* symposium may have led to another symposium in an African American periodical. In December 1926 *The Messenger* published responses to its eight-question symposium regarding, among other items, the compatibility of "Negro racial consciousness" with "the ideal of Americanism." See "Plan Symposium on Race's Future," *New York Amsterdam News,* November 24, 1926, 15.

36. For a discussion of Toomer and his exchange with his publishers regarding his racial background, see Nellie Y. McKay, *Jean Toomer, Artist: A Study of His Literary Life and Work, 1894–1936* (Chapel Hill: University of North Carolina Press, 1984), 180–82.

37. Researching the genesis of the questions, one finds that Van Vechten may have influenced the questions but that the idea of the symposium originated with Du Bois. Van Vechten wrote a letter to "the editor of *Crisis,*" complaining about Emmett J. Scott's review of *The Wooings of Jezebel Pettyfer* by the white author Haldane MacFall. Dated October 29, 1925, the letter included arguments and statements about African Americans' sensitivity to negative literary representations that would later appear in Van Vechten's *Vanity Fair* article "Moanin' Wid a Sword in My Hand." Du Bois writes to Van Vechten on November 5, asking if he can quote from the letter. On November 9 Du Bois writes again to Van Vechten, informing him of his idea of "a symposium on freedom in Negro art. I am going to use your letters and also get, if possible contributions from Heyward DuBose [*sic*], Rudolph Fisher, Winold Reiss and others. I think we can get some interesting reactions." W. E. B. Du Bois to Carl Van Vechten, November 5, 1925, and November 9, 1925, Du Bois Correspondence, James Weldon Johnson Collection, Beinecke Library, Yale University (hereafter JWJ).

38. Michael North distinguishes the years 1922 to 1927 as the period in which "two different modernisms, tightly linked by their different stakes in the same language, emerge[d]." Michael North, *The Dialect of Modernism: Race, Language, and Twentieth-Century Literature* (New York: Oxford University Press, 1994), 11. North's argument that prominent modernists such as T. S. Eliot and Ezra Pound used black dialect in innovative ways in their poetry and in personal correspondence is discussed briefly in chapter 1. There is a hint of the period's "failure" also in North's account of white and black literary activity in the 1920s, but the discussion of shortcomings is more weighted toward those Anglo-American modernists who used the conventions of Negro dialect without expanding them. See in particular North's discussion of several poetry magazines of the time in chap. 6 of *Dialect of Modernism* (127–46).

39. Chidi Ikonné, *From Du Bois to Van Vechten: The Early New Negro Literature, 1903–1926* (Westport, Conn.: Greenwood Press, 1981), xii. I disagree with Ikonné, who maintains that the years prior to 1926, before the publication of *Nigger Heaven,* were the most fruitful of the Harlem Renaissance. See also Hutchinson, *Harlem Renaissance,* 435.

40. Wallace Thurman, "A Thrush at Eve with an Atavistic Wound: Review of *Flight* by Walter White," in *The Collected Writings of Wallace Thurman: A Harlem Renaissance Reader,* ed. Amritjit Singh and Daniel M. Scott III (New Brunswick: Rutgers University Press, 2003), 183.

41. Alain Locke, "Art or Propaganda?" in *The Critical Temper of Alain Locke: A Selection of His Essays on Art and Culture,* ed. Jeffrey C. Stewart (New York: Garland Publishing, 1983), 27–28.

42. Romare Bearden, "The Negro Artist and Modern Art," *Opportunity,* December 1934, 372.

43. Thurman, *Collected Writings,* 166.

44. It is interesting to note here a book review in the *Chicago Defender* with the large, disarming headline "Books by Race Authors Prove Disappointing as 1932 List Is Scanned" (January 7, 1933, 10). The author, Dewey R. Jones, counted among the "disappointing" books a biography of Abraham Lincoln, Countee Cullen's *One Way to Heaven,* and Thurman's *Infants of the Spring.* Among the better-written books, according to Jones, are Fisher's novel *The Conjure Man Dies* and *The Chinaberry Tree* by Jessie Fauset. Jones does not mention Brown's *Southern Road.* Although Jones dismisses Thurman as "the black sheep of the Race authors," both Jones and Thurman ask a similar question of the celebrated New Negro writer. In Jones's words, "Where is that great American Race novel for which we have waited for so long a time?" *Chicago Defender,* January 7, 1933, 10.

45. Although Tolson is well known for his 1965 poetry collection *Harlem Gallery,* his first collection, *Rendezvous with America* (New York: Dodd, Mead), appeared in 1944.

46. This book differs from Martha Jane Nadell's *Enter the New Negroes: Images of Race in American Culture* (2004), Anne Carroll's *Word, Image, and the New Negro: Representation and Identity in the Harlem Renaissance* (2005), and Caroline Goeser's *Picturing the New Negro: Harlem Renaissance Print Culture and Modern Black Identity* (2007), which focus on illustrations in black periodicals, anthologies, and graphic texts. These studies show how illustrations work in support of or in opposition to the periodicals' textual arguments and provide useful accounts of the publishing and editorial histories of major Harlem Renaissance works. By exploring the collaboration between writers and visual artists, Nadell and Carroll disclose the economic and aesthetic considerations that determined some of the most significant black literary collections of the 1920s. I am interested, however, in the various literary and visual works that question the epistemological power of the gaze and that challenge the hypervisibility and devaluation of blackness. The figures in this study offered some of the most experimental attempts to rupture or at least to question the assumed relationship between body and blackness and to reconfigure the image of blackness as a textual deformity. In its attention to the cultural significance of the visual in black literary studies, my project has fewer similarities to Carroll's and Nadell's work than to Robyn Wiegman's *American Anatomies* (1995), Laura Doyle's *Bordering on the Body: The Racial Matrix of Modern Fiction and Culture* (1994), and Karen Jacobs's study *The Eye's Mind* (2001). Like these three works, mine attends to the theoretical implications of the gaze and investigates how images circulate and shape the production of (racial) knowledge.

47. Johnson, *Book of American Negro Poetry,* xli.

48. Gavin Jones, *Strange Talk: The Politics of Dialect in Gilded Age America* (Berkeley: University of California Press, 1999), 188; North, *The Dialect of Modernism,* 79.

49. Nella Larsen, *"Quicksand" and "Passing,"* ed. Deborah McDowell (New Brunswick: Rutgers University Press, 1987), 235.

50. Lauren Berlant, "National Brands/National Body: *Imitation of Life,*" in *Comparative American Identities: Race, Sex, and Nationality in the Modern Text,* ed. Hortense Spillers (New York: Routledge, 1991), 112.

51. Brown frequently voiced his dislike for Van Vechten. See Sterling Brown, "The New Negro in Literature (1925–1955)," in *New Negro Thirty Years Afterward: Papers Contributed to the Sixteenth Annual Spring Conference* (Washington, D.C.: Howard University Graduate School, Division of the Social Sciences, 1955), 59.

52. Genevieve Ekaete, "Sterling Brown: A Living Legend," *New Directions: The Howard University Magazine* 1 (Winter 1974): 9.

53. Jonathan Culler, *The Pursuit of Signs: Semiotics, Literature, Deconstruction* (Ithaca: Cornell University Press, 1981), 156.

54. Joseph Allen Boone, *Libidinal Currents: Sexuality and the Shaping of Modernism* (Chicago: University of Chicago Press, 1998), 24–25.

55. Ibid., 24.

56. Michele Wallace, "Modernism, Postmodernism, and the Problem of the Visual in Afro-American Culture," in *Dark Designs and Visual Culture* (Durham: Duke University Press, 2004), 366.

57. Nick Chiles, "Their Eyes Were Reading Smut," *New York Times,* January 4, 2006, A15.

58. Tracy Brown, *Dime Piece* (New York: Triple Crown Publications, 2004).

1. Tone Pictures

1. William Foster to James Weldon Johnson, August 1929, Correspondence, JWJ. William Foster owned Foster Photo Play Company, an early black movie company. Film historian Thomas Cripps in *Slow Fade to Black: The Negro in American Film, 1900–1942* (New York: Oxford University Press, 1977) notes that Foster may have directed the first African American film, *The Railroad Porter,* in 1912. He died in Los Angeles in 1940 (79–80). The sentiment about black and white voices was echoed by Wallace Thurman, as indicated in a 1929 letter he wrote to Langston Hughes: "There are countless senegambians in Hollywood who sing and talk for the white stars, remaining hidden behind a screen while the movie morons move their lips. But it took James Cruze to put on the final touch. Needing voices for a chorus scene in his new picture *The Great Gabbo* he tried out hundreds of whites. All voices were flat. In desperation he hired a colored chorus, white washed them, placed them in the background and gave the sign for them to sing." *The Collected Writings of Wallace Thurman: A Harlem Renaissance Reader,* ed. Amritjit Singh and Daniel M. Scott III (New Brunswick: Rutgers University Press, 2003), 124. James Cruze was an actor and director of the 1920s. *The Great Gabbo* was a 1929 musical about a ventriloquist.

2. Johnson to William Foster, August 15, 1929, Correspondence, JWJ. Johnson corresponded with Foster in order to obtain information about the blackface entertainers Bert Williams and George Walker and the varieties of the cakewalk they performed for a section on black entertainment in Johnson's 1930 history of Harlem, *Black Manhattan.* According to Henry Sampson, Foster was the publicity agent for Williams and Walker's stage shows *In Dahomey* and *Abyssinia.* Henry T. Sampson, *Blacks in Black and White: A Source Book on Black Films* (Metuchen, N.J.: Scarecrow Press, 1977), 68–69. For more about Foster, see Jacqueline Stewart, *Migrating to the Movies: Cinema and Black Urban Modernity* (Berkeley: University of California Press, 2005).

3. Michael North, *The Dialect of Modernism: Race, Language, and Twentieth-Century Literature* (New York: Oxford University Press, 1994), 7.

4. Gavin Jones, *Strange Talk: The Politics of Dialect Literature in Gilded Age America* (Berkeley: University of California Press, 1999).

5. This reading has some resonances with issues of copyright and black representation. See Stephen Best, *The Fugitive's Properties: Law and the Poetics of Possession* (Chicago: University of Chicago Press, 2003); and Katherine Biers, "Syncope Fever: James Weldon Johnson and the Black Phonographic Voice," *Representations* 96 (Fall 2006): 99–125. Biers argues that "black cultural practices are phonographic because, in reproducing themselves

without writing, they emphasize the materiality of sound and therefore resist reduction to either side of the [oral/written] binary" (99).

6. Thomas Wentworth Higginson, "Negro Spirituals," *Atlantic Monthly*, June 1867, 685–94. The lyrics are also reprinted in Higginson's *Army Life in a Black Regiment* (1870; repr., New York: W. W. Norton, 1984).

7. Higginson, "Negro Spirituals," 685.

8. Nathaniel Mackey, "Sight-Specific, Sound-Specific . . . ," in *Paracritical Hinge: Essays, Talks, Notes, Interviews* (Madison: University of Wisconsin Press, 2005), 230–31.

9. Ibid., 231; Walter J. Ong, *Orality and Literacy: The Technologizing of the Word* (New York: Routledge, 1982), 120, 134.

10. Dena J. Epstein, *Sinful Tunes and Spirituals: Black Folk Music to the Civil War* (Urbana: University of Illinois Press, 1977), 280.

11. Charlotte Forten, "Life on the Sea Islands," *Atlantic Monthly*, May 1864, 593–94, quoted ibid., 280.

12. Ronald Radano, "Denoting Difference: The Writing of the Slave Spirituals," *Critical Inquiry* 22, no. 3 (Spring 1996): 525. Radano's argument raises several questions: What are the implications of singling out a difference constructed by whites as fundamentally black? What of Hurston's belief that such spirituals are not in fact "black"? And how can that which cannot be expressed be "contained" within musical script, a question we will also ask of James Weldon Johnson?

13. Zora Neale Hurston, "Spirituals and Neo-Spirituals," in *Negro: An Anthology*, ed. Nancy Cunard (London: Wishart and Co., 1934), 360.

14. Nathaniel Dett, "Religious Folk-Songs of the Negro as Sung at Hampton Institute," in *Cabin and Plantation Songs as Sung by the Hampton Students*, ed. Thomas Fenner (1874; Hampton, Va.: Hampton Institute, 1927), xviii.

15. Sterling Brown identifies Richard Wallaschek, *Primitive Music: An Inquiry into the Origin and Development of Music, Songs, Instruments, Dances, and Pantomimes of Savage Races* (1893; repr., New York: Da Capo Press, 1970), as an early instance in which African American spirituals were said to be derived from white hymns. See Sterling Brown, "Folk Literature," in *A Son's Return: Selected Essays of Sterling A. Brown*, ed. Mark A. Sanders (Boston: Northeastern University Press, 1996), 209.

16. See William Francis Allen, Charles Pickard Ware, and Lucy McKim Garrison, eds. *Slave Songs of the United States* (1867; repr., New York: Dover, 1995); H. E. Krehbiel, *Afro-American Folksongs: A Study in Racial and National Music* (1914; repr., Portland, Me.: Longwood Press, 1976); Nathaniel Dett, *Religious Folk-Songs of the Negro* (Hampton, Va.: Hampton Institute Press, 1927).

17. See, for example, Thurman's "Tribute" to Johnson and Alain Locke, in which he distinguishes the two men from other "Negro[es] of prominence": "It is from these two alone that [the younger African American writers] have to any extent received the sympathy, the encouragement, and sane criticism, which they most certainly need if they are to mature and survive." Wallace Thurman, "Tribute," in *Collected Writings*, 251, 252.

18. Some notable exceptions are Brent Hayes Edwards, "The Seemingly Eclipsed Window of Form: James Weldon Johnson's Prefaces," in *The Jazz Cadence of American Culture*, ed. Robert G. O'Meally (New York: Columbia University Press, 1998), 580–601; Biers, "Syncope Fever"; and Jacqueline Goldsby, *A Spectacular Secret: Lynching in American Life and Literature* (Chicago: University of Chicago Press, 2006).

19. Sterling Brown, *Negro in American Fiction* (1937; repr., Port Washington, N.Y.: Kennikat Press, 1968), 3.

20. North, *The Dialect of Modernism*, 90; "A Questionnaire," *Crisis*, February 1926, 165.

21. James Weldon Johnson, *Along This Way: The Autobiography of James Weldon Johnson* (1933; New York: Viking Press, 1968), 159; Thomas Nelson Page, *In Ole Virginia* (New York: Scribner's Sons, 1887); Thomas Dixon, *The Clansman* (New York: Doubleday, Page, and Co., 1905). For an examination of Thomas Dixon, whose book was the basis for D. W. Griffith's film *The Birth of a Nation,* see Anthony Slide, *American Racist: The Life and Films of Thomas Dixon* (Lexington: University Press of Kentucky, 2004).

22. James Weldon Johnson, *The Book of American Negro Poetry, Chosen and Edited with an Essay on the Negro's Creative Genius* (New York: Harcourt, Brace, and Co., 1922), vii. Subsequent citations are given parenthetically in the text with the abbreviation *NP*.

23. Moreover, in his analysis of black dialect in American literature, Arthur Huff Fauset in "American Negro Folk Literature," in *The New Negro,* ed. Alain Locke (1925; repr., New York: Simon and Schuster, 1997), acknowledged the rich product Harris made of black folktales but notes: "It is doubtful whether Negroes generally ever used the language employed in the works of Joel Chandler Harris. Rather, in these works, we observe the consciously devised, artistically wrought, patiently carved out expressions of a story writer who knew his art and employed it well" (239). Curiously, Fauset also invokes the image of the phonograph: "As in the case of all true folk tales, the story teller himself was inconsequential; he did not figure at all—a talking machine might serve the purpose just as well" (240).

24. Robert Stepto, *From Behind the Veil: A Study of Afro-American Narrative* (1979; repr., Urbana: University of Illinois Press, 1991), 67.

25. Carrie Tirado Bramen, "The Urban Picturesque," *American Quarterly* 52, no. 3 (September 2000): 450, 448. The essay is part of a larger study, *The Uses of American Variety: Modern Americanism and the Quest for National Distinctiveness* (Cambridge: Harvard University Press, 2000). Bramen follows a similar argument made briefly by Alan Trachtenberg in *Reading American Photographs: Images as History, Matthew Brady to Walker Evans* (New York: Hill and Wang, 1989), 183–90.

26. See Kevin Mumford, *Interzones: Black/White Sex Districts in Chicago and New York in the Early Twentieth Century* (New York: Columbia University Press, 1997).

27. Bramen, "The Urban Picturesque," 452.

28. James Weldon Johnson, *The Autobiography of an Ex-Colored Man,* in *Three Negro Classics,* ed. John Hope Franklin (1912; repr., New York: Avon Books, 1965), 498.

29. This is in significant contrast to the young narrator of Johnson's novel, who, when faced with a word he didn't recognize while reading a story, came up with his own words—based on the picture accompanying the text. His teacher later tells him that he "would substitute whole sentences and even paragraphs from what meaning I thought the illustrations conveyed." Johnson, *The Autobiography of an Ex-Colored Man,* 397–98.

30. Henry Louis Gates Jr. also makes use of this term in order to refer to the stagnancy of dialect: "Dialect was an oral remnant of slavery." Henry Louis Gates Jr., "Dis and Dat: Dialect and the Descent," in *Figures in Black: Words, Signs, and the "Racial" Self* (New York: Oxford University Press, 1987), 182.

31. Johnson, *Book of American Negro Poetry,* xli; James Weldon Johnson and J. Rosamond Johnson, *The Book of American Negro Spirituals* (New York: Viking Press, 1925), 44. Subsequent citations are given parenthetically in the text with the abbreviation *NS*.

32. For more discussion on the difficulty of transcribing the sounds of black dialect, see Eric J. Sundquist's discussion on dialect and the writings of Charles Chesnutt in *To Wake the Nations: Race in the Making of American Literature* (Cambridge: Harvard University Press, 1993), 301–13.

33. As Cheryl Wall observes in *Worrying the Line: Black Women Writers, Lineage, and Literary Tradition* (Chapel Hill: University of North Carolina Press, 2005), "worrying the line" is a musical technique in which the main rhythm or phrase of a song is repeated and altered "for purposes of emphasis, clarification, or subversion" (8). See also Stephen Henderson, *Understanding the New Black Poetry* (New York: William Morrow, 1972), 41; and Sherley Anne Williams, "Blues Roots of Contemporary Afro-American Poetry," in *Afro-American Literature: The Reconstruction of Instruction,* ed. Dexter Fisher and Robert Stepto (New York: Modern Language Association, 1978), 77.

34. Edwards, "The Seemingly Eclipsed Window of Form," 580.

35. Ibid., 585.

36. As I discuss in chapter 5, Roland Barthes affects a type of "realization" when he refuses to reproduce the famous Winter Garden Photograph of his mother in *Camera Lucida.*

37. Johnson, *Along This Way,* 158–59.

38. James Weldon Johnson, "Negro with a Big 'N,'" in *Writings,* ed. William Andrews (New York: Library of America, 2004), 637.

39. Sterling Brown to Johnson, February 17, 1932, Correspondence, JWJ.

40. Gates, "Dis and Dat," 187.

41. James Weldon Johnson, introduction to *Southern Road* by Sterling Brown (1932; repr., Boston: Beacon Press, 1974), xxxv–xxxvii.

42. Sterling Brown, "Luck Is a Fortune," in *A Son's Return,* 291–92. Brown's review of Hurston's novel is, for the most part, positive. He does, however, refute the claim, made in the foreword to the novel's first edition, that *Their Eyes* is "*the* Negro American novel." According to Brown, such a novel does not exist.

43. In his well-known reading of the novel, Henry Louis Gates Jr. argues that *Their Eyes* is a "speakerly text" which negotiates between dialect, standard English, and free indirect discourse. See Henry Louis Gates Jr., *The Signifying Monkey: A Theory of Afro-American Literary Criticism* (New York: Oxford University Press, 1988), 170–238.

44. Zora Neale Hurston, "Characteristics of Negro Expression," in Cunard, *Negro: An Anthology,* 39–46. Subsequent citations are given parenthetically in the text with the abbreviation CNE. The book was a hodgepodge collection of essays, short stories, photographs, and poems. For competing interpretations of Cunard's anthology, see North, *The Dialect of Modernism,* 189–94, which criticizes the disjunctive nature of the volume; and Brent Hayes Edwards, *The Practice of Diaspora: Literature, Translation, and the Rise of Black Internationalism* (Cambridge: Harvard University Press, 2003), 309–18. Edwards views the collection as innovative. Hurston's essay is reprinted in a smaller, more widely available edition of the anthology abridged by Hugh Ford (New York: F. Ungar Publishing, 1970), 24–31.

45. Lindon Barrett, "Hand-writing: Legibility and the White Body in *Running a Thousand Miles for Freedom,*" *American Literature* 69, no. 2 (1997): 315.

46. Karen Jacobs, *The Eye's Mind: Literary Modernism and Visual Culture* (Ithaca: Cornell University Press, 2001), 121.

47. Ezra Pound, "A Stray Document," in *Make It New: Essays by Pound* (London: Faber and Faber, 1934), 337, 336. Sections of "A Stray Document" were written in 1912 and

1913. It is intriguing to note here Pound's criticism of Langston Hughes's poetry in a letter to the younger poet. According to Pound, certain poems in Hughes's second book of poetry, *Fine Clothes to the Jew* (1927), were not "firm" enough: "A poem, especially in vers libre, but ANY poem ought to be like a steel spring with the ends held firm so that the whole thing is kept tense. Every word that don't [*sic*] work ought to be put out. 'Sinister' does no good in 'Ruby Brown.' Poem on next page much better done." The letter was part of Pound's unsuccessful quest to encourage a black university such as Howard, Hampton, or Tuskegee to translate the German anthropologist Froebenius into English. Pound to Langston Hughes, July 8, 1932, Langston Hughes Collection, Yale Collection of American Literature, Beinecke Rare Book and Manuscript Library, Yale University (hereafter LH).

48. Eric J. Sundquist, *The Hammers of Creation: Folk Culture in Modern African-American Fiction* (Athens: University of Georgia Press, 1992), 33.

49. Ibid., 26.

50. One also sees this reluctance, for example, in Johnson's characterization of the ex-colored man. The narrator's blackness registers most visually and physically to him when he examines himself in the mirror after being called by a racial epithet in school, but the narrator's body remains conspicuously absent throughout the rest of novel; instead, other characters' bodily appearance registers more fully in his narrative: Shiny's oily face, Red's red hair, the fragile bodies of his sister and his eventual wife. Watching an African American being burned also evokes the narrator's blackness, but only as a form of displacement: the horrific scene compels him to let "people take him for what [they] would" and passively pass as white. Johnson, *Autobiography of an Ex-Colored Man,* 499.

51. At least in Johnson's prefaces, if not in Johnson's novel. See note 29.

52. Karen Jacobs in *The Eye's Mind* has noted the presence of the body in Hurston's essays as well as the visual metaphors that resonate throughout Hurston's works. Exploring Hurston's ambivalence toward anthropology's participant-observer method, which distances the observer from his or her subject, Jacobs reads *Their Eyes Were Watching God* in relation to Emerson's "Nature" in order to demonstrate how Hurston moves from "objective" anthropological science to the body, from the "spyglass" to the "horizon." The advantage of this admittedly unusual juxtaposition is that it foregrounds the scopic character of Hurston's work as well as makes evident the implicit assumption of "universality" of Emerson's quite privileged male body (111–44). What attracts me to Jacobs's reading is her analyses of the "visual metaphors of cultural hierarchy" in *Their Eyes* and Hurston's other works. Although she makes no reference to James Weldon Johnson, Jacobs does unintentionally uncover a significant point of difference between Hurston and Johnson. Discussing how Hurston translated oral expression into written text, she notes that *Mules and Men* shows how Hurston collected music, placed her findings into narrative, and demonstrated "the attractions that embodiment held for her over that of pure textualization" (119, 120). Jacobs concentrates on *Their Eyes* in order to delineate how Hurston wrestled with the contradictory demands of recording the customs of various communities of which she necessarily saw herself as a member. Participation trumps observation, as Jacobs argues it does for Hurston's own ethnographic work.

53. James Weldon Johnson, *God's Trombones: Seven Negro Sermons in Verse* (1927; repr., New York: Penguin, 1990), 8. Subsequent citations are given parenthetically in the text with the abbreviation *GT.*

54. W. J. T. Mitchell, *Iconology: Image, Text, Ideology* (Chicago: University of Chicago, 1986), 19.

55. In addition to altering the representation of black speech on the space of the page, *God's Trombones* was published with illustrations created by the African American artist Aaron Douglas and lettering created by C. B. Falls. While Douglas's and Falls's artistry adds to the effect of Johnson's poetical work, I am concerned not with the way "Douglas's illustrations provide a visual counterpoint to Johnson's poems," as Anne Carroll ably demonstrates in "Art, Literature, and the Harlem Renaissance: The Messages of *God's Trombones*," *College Literature* 29, no. 3 (2002): 68, but rather with the visual imagery conjured by Johnson's poetical constructions.

56. Perhaps a better-known instance of Johnson's uncertainty about his titles is *The Autobiography of an Ex-Colored Man*. Johnson considered calling his novel "The Chameleon." See Johnson, *Along This Way*, 238–39. For help with the title of *God's Trombones*, Johnson also sought the opinion of Du Bois, Countee Cullen, Arthur Spingarn, and William Stanley Braithwaite.

57. Working titles for *God's Trombones*, box 60, folder 218, JWJ.

58. Johnson to Joel E. Spingarn, December 30, 1926, Correspondence, JWJ.

59. Johnson to Joel E. Spingarn, February 3, 1927, Correspondence, JWJ.

60. Johnson, *Along This Way*, 378.

61. Zora Neale Hurston, *Jonah's Gourd Vine* (Philadelphia: J. B. Lippincott, 1934).

62. Zora Neale Hurston to Johnson, May 8, 1934, Correspondence, JWJ.

63. Booker T. Washington, *The Papers of Booker T. Washington*, vol. 2, *1860–1889,* ed. Louis R. Harlan (Urbana: University of Illinois Press, 1972), 449.

64. The black preacher was also a subject that captured the imagination of visual artists. In their survey of African American musical images from the 1770s to the 1920s, Eileen Southern and Josephine Wright note that over one-third of the 168 images in their study were of African American preachers. Eileen Southern and Josephine Wright, *Images: Iconography of Music in African-American Culture, 1770s–1920s* (New York: Garland Publishing, 2000), 122.

65. Johnson, *Autobiography of an Ex-Colored Man,* 490. This is not the well-known abolitionist John Brown.

66. Ong, *Orality and Literacy,* 74.

67. *God's Trombones,* box 60 folder 217, JWJ.

68. There is, however, a brief rhymed couplet of "hell"/"well" in "Listen, Lord—A Prayer."

69. Johnson, *Along This Way,* 377.

70. Ibid., 80, 81.

71. Braithwaite was a Boston-based African American poet and editor of several anthologies of American poetry in the early twentieth century. His evaluations of Harlem Renaissance writers such as Richard Bruce Nugent and Wallace Thurman were often conservative. For more about Braithwaite, see Phillip Butcher, *The William Stanley Braithwaite Reader* (Ann Arbor: University of Michigan Press, 1972).

72. William Stanley Braithwaite to Johnson, January 19, 1919, *God's Trombones,* box 59, folder 204, JWJ. Braithwaite's comments continue on a draft of a poem that refers to God as "Jehovah God": "This is by far the most spontaneous part. . . . I think also 'Jehovah God' takes a little [from?] doubling the greatness of the figure, from the immensity of it. Is this so much stronger than 'This Great God Like a mammy bending over her baby'?"

73. Goldsby, *A Spectacular Secret,* 165.

74. It is difficult to read this letter writer's signature. It appears to be Aaron S. Bernard or Berund, and the writer is from Macon, Georgia. Letter of May 17, 1927, in "Echoes From God's Trombones," *God's Trombones,* box 63, folder 240, JWJ. Another intriguing letter comes from the writer Marita Bonner, who, upon reading "Go Down, Death" and later hearing Johnson recite the poem, immediately thought of her own mother who had passed away. She wrote to Johnson: "You wrote 'Go Down, Death' for my mother. It does not matter whether the name was different or the city to which Death rode was Savannah— you wrote it for my mother. . . . I could not talk about it Saturday night. You must never, I find, talk of things that let your blood drip inside. You must appear to skim—so I appear to skim. But I do not skim. That is, the real I. For I know that Death does go down—and that Death did go down." There is no date typed on Bonner's letter.

75. Helen Keller to Edna Porter, "Copy made by E.P. for J.W.J.," Correspondence, n.d., JWJ.

76. *Narrative of a Life of Frederick Douglass, an American Slave, Written by Himself,* in *Autobiographies,* ed. Henry Louis Gates Jr. (New York: Library of America, 1994), 24.

77. Jean Wagner, *Black Poets of the United States, from Paul Laurence Dunbar to Langston Hughes,* trans. Kenneth Douglas (1962; repr., Urbana: University of Illinois Press, 1973), 384. In general, Wagner is somewhat harsh on Johnson. While Johnson did display a degree of reserve, I believe if Johnson was really "excessively concerned with respectability and conformity," as Wagner states, he would not have been so willing to defend Carl Van Vechten and *Nigger Heaven* (351). Johnson's personal letters to friends also reveal that he could depart from the cool reticence he sometimes adopted in his public writings.

78. Sundquist, *Hammers of Creation,* 56. Sundquist is comparing *God's Trombones* as a sermon and Hurston's version of Rev. C. C. Lovelace's sermon published in "Spirituals and Neo-Spirituals" and *Jonah's Gourd Vine.*

79. Conversely, Wallace Thurman predicted in 1927, erroneously as it would turn out, that "*God's Trombones* will be remembered long after the *Autobiography [of an Ex-Colored Man]* has been forgotten, even by sentimental white folk and Jeremiah-like Negroes." Thurman, "Nephews of Uncle Remus," in *Collected Writings,* 204.

80. Alice Dunbar-Nelson to Johnson, June 20, 1917, Correspondence, JWJ. See Alice Dunbar-Nelson, *The Dunbar Speaker and Entertainer, Containing the Best Prose and Poetic Selections by and about the Negro Race, with Programs Arranged for Special Entertainments* (Naperville, Ill.: J. L. Nichols and Co., 1920). Dunbar Nelson was herself a skilled elocutionist, and her book includes a model program for "arranging an evening's or a morning's entertainment" (278). Requests for permission to use Johnson's poems were made by authors of similar textbooks, such as Severina E. Nelson and C. H. Woolbert, authors of *The Art of Interpretative Speech: Principles and Practices of Effective Reading* (New York: Crofts, 1927).

81. A musical adaptation of *God's Trombones* lends additional credence to this failing of the poems and any variations on them. *Trumpets of the Lord* was a musical adaptation of *God's Trombones* by Melvin Tolson, the author of *Harlem Gallery* (1965). The musical ran for five months in 1964 off Broadway. In 1968 a televised production was aired, and according to one reviewer from the *New York Times,* the "intimacy of television" offered a better format for the sermon-poems than "the larger confines of the stage": "Essentially a collection of dramatized sermons connected by traditional spirituals and gospel songs, [*Trumpets*] would seem to require the intense introspection provided by the close-up to maximize

its limited dramatic content." George Gent, "Off Broadway Musical Is Revived by N.E.T.," *New York Times,* May 11, 1968, 70.

2. Reading the Body

1. Roland Barthes, "On *The Fashion System," The Language of Fashion* (New York: Berg, 2006), 99.

2. Jonathan Culler, *Structuralist Poetics: Structuralism, Linguistics, and the Study of Literature* (New York: Cornell University Press, 1975), 33.

3. Pierre Bourdieu, *Distinction: A Social Critique of the Judgement of Taste,* trans. Richard Nice (Cambridge: Harvard University Press, 1984), 57.

4. Throughout this essay I am speaking of the specific issue of white-black miscegenation in the United States. The contemporary terms "mixed" and "mixed race" have many meanings; in the context of *Passing* they imply the mixture of black and white in North America. In addition, I use the phrase "ambiguously raced" to describe the female characters in the novel; and the phrase is meant to describe people of color who may or may not be mixed with white (it is assumed, for instance, that both of Irene's parents are African American) and who appear more physically white than black or any other race. The difficulty of assigning definitive racial categories is, I argue, one of Larsen's central points in both *Passing* and *Quicksand.*

5. In newspaper accounts of the trial Alice and the Jones family members were referred to as "Negro" or "colored." Alice's lawyer, when it was necessary to refer to her race, used the term "colored." George Jones, Alice's brown-skinned English father, was at various times called "West Indian," "Negro," and "colored"; his immigration papers listed him as "colored." See "Rhinelander Annulment Suit," *New York Amsterdam News,* November 11, 1925, 3.

6. Nella Larsen, *"Quicksand" and "Passing,"* ed. Deborah McDowell (New Brunswick: Rutgers University Press, 1986), 228. All subsequent citations are from this edition and are given parenthetically in the text. Citations from *Quicksand* are identified with the abbreviation *Q;* citations from *Passing* are identified with the abbreviation *P. Quicksand* was originally published in 1928, *Passing* in 1929.

7. "Honorable Marriage Creates Furore," *Chicago Defender,* November 22, 1924, 11. The trial passed into obscurity until the recent publication of a historical account of the events and people involved in the case, Earl Lewis and Heidi Ardizzone, *Love on Trial: An American Scandal in Black and White* (New York: W. W. Norton, 2001). In the 1986 Rutgers University Press edition of *Quicksand* and *Passing,* Deborah McDowell offers a brief explanation of the case (245 n. 8). Mark J. Madigan offers a short reading of the trial in relation to *Passing* in "Miscegenation and 'The Dicta of Race': The Rhinelander Case and Nella Larsen's *Passing," Modern Fiction Studies* 36 (Winter 1990): 523–29. See also Sarah E. Chinn, *Technology and the Logic of Racism* (London: Continuum, 2000). Chinn looks at *Passing* through the lens of the Rhinelander case but for different purposes from mine. She argues that the novel and the case demonstrate the distinguishable reading practices of both black and white spectators (67) and that "cultural texts show us how vision is segregated by race, by gender, by class" (59). Her interpretations of the trial focus on reading the skin as evidence, the belief that dark skin operates as "epidermal obviousness" (70) for blackness, and on how the black spectator is usually more skillful in such reading practices

than the white spectator. I focus less on how courtroom participants and spectators viewed Alice than on the assumption that the black female body can be easily read by any spectator, and the role of etiquette or manners as a type of racial performance. As I do, she suggests that certain white spectators are less inclined to question the knowledge assumed or obtained from looking (64, 65). Other writings on the Rhinelanders and the infamous trial include Angela Onwuachi-Willig, "A Beautiful Lie: *Rhinelander v. Rhinelander* as a Formative Lesson on Race, Identity, Marriage, and Family," *California Law Review* 95 (2007): 2393; and Elizabeth M. Smith-Pryor, *Property Rites: The Rhinelander Trial, Passing, and the Protection of Whiteness* (Chapel Hill: University of North Carolina Press, 2009).

8. Michel Foucault, "Nietzsche, Genealogy, History," in *Language, Counter-Memory, Practice: Selected Essays and Interviews,* ed. Sherry Simon and Donald F. Bouchard, trans. Donald F. Bouchard (Ithaca: Cornell University Press, 1977), 148; Judith Butler, "Foucault and the Paradox of Bodily Inscriptions." *Journal of Philosophy* 86, no. 11 (1989): 605.

9. Butler, "Foucault and the Paradox of Bodily Inscriptions," 601.

10. Hortense Spillers, "Mama's Baby, Papa's Maybe: An American Grammar Book," in *Black, White, and In Color: Essays on American Literature and Culture* (Chicago: University of Chicago Press, 2003), 209.

11. Ibid., 211.

12. Leslie W. Rabine, "A Woman's Two Bodies: Fashion Magazines, Consumerism, and Feminism," in *On Fashion,* ed. Shari Benstock and Suzanne Ferriss (New Brunswick: Rutgers University Press, 1994), 60.

13. Toby Fischer-Mirkin, *Dress Code: Understanding the Hidden Meanings of Women's Clothes* (New York: Clarkson Potter, 1995), 12.

14. Meredith Goldsmith, "Shopping to Pass, Passing to Shop: Bodily Self-Fashioning in the Fiction of Nella Larsen," in *Recovering the Black Female Body: Self-Representations by African American Women,* ed. Michael Bennett and Vanessa D. Dickerson (New Brunswick: Rutgers University Press, 2001), 98.

15. Judith Butler, *Gender Trouble: Feminism and the Subversion of Identity* (New York: Routledge, 1990), 140.

16. Amy Robinson, "It Takes One to Know One: Passing and Communities of Common Interest," *Critical Inquiry* 20, no. 4 (1994): 716. Reading Robinson's account of the passing performance, one is struck by how it resembles Barthes's account of perceiving distinction and taste. Barthes writes that "distinction takes the signaling aspect of clothes down a semi-clandestine path: for, on the one hand, the group that reads its signs are a limited one, on the other the signs necessary for this reading are rare and, without a particular knowledge of the new vestimentary language, perceptible only with difficulty." See Roland Barthes, "Dandyism and Fashion," in *The Language of Fashion* (New York: Berg, 2006), 66.

17. Thadious Davis, *Nella Larsen, Novelist of the Harlem Renaissance: A Woman's Life Unveiled* (Baton Rouge: Louisiana State University Press, 1994), 447.

18. Rabine, "A Woman's Two Bodies," 69–70.

19. Diana Fuss, "Fashion and the Homospectatorial Look," in *Identities,* ed. Kwame Anthony Appiah and Henry Louis Gates Jr. (Chicago: University of Chicago Press, 1995), 99, 113.

20. Ibid., 107.

21. Ibid., 90–91.

22. Deborah McDowell, foreword to Larsen, *"Quicksand" and "Passing,"* xxiii.

23. Marjorie Ellis Ferguson McCrady and Blanche Wheeler, *Manners for Moderns* (New York: E. P. Dutton and Co., 1942), v–vi.

24. Edward S. Green, *National Capital Code of Etiquette* (Washington, D.C.: Austin Jenkins Company, 1920), 14.

25. The equality offered by etiquette would seem to be particularly significant for the class-conscious Larsen, who lacked the family, sorority, and church connections that provided the foundation for the black middle and upper classes in the early twentieth century. Larsen did, however, obtain a higher level of social status when she married Elmer Imes, a doctor who worked at Fisk University. See Davis, *Nella Larsen,* 128; and George Hutchinson, *In Search of Nella Larsen: A Biography of the Color Line* (Cambridge: Belknap Press, 2006), 123. Despite her characters' and her own ambivalence about the "strenuous rigidity of conduct" that the black middle class required (*Q,* 1), Larsen maintained an appearance of grace and elegance, particularly during the years of the Renaissance. Those who knew the writer have commented on her extremely poised social manners. As Bruce Nugent noted to her biographer, "her 'air' exuded social status"; Davis, *Nella Larsen,* 142.

26. Goldsmith, "Shopping to Pass," 113.

27. Lauren Berlant, "National Brands/National Body: Imitation of Life," in *Comparative American Identities: Race, Sex, and Nationality in the Modern Text,* ed. Hortense Spillers (New York: Routledge, 1991), 110.

28. Fuss, "Fashion and the Homospectatorial Look," 95.

29. J. C. Flügel, *The Psychology of Clothes* (1930; repr., New York: International Universities Press, 1966), 34.

30. Judith Butler, *Bodies That Matter: On the Discursive Limits of "Sex"* (New York: Routledge, 1993), 170–71.

31. Irene exemplifies Bourdieu's statement that members of an elite class determine what is tasteful "by the refusal of other tastes," that is, that "all determination is negation." Bourdieu, *Distinction,* 56.

32. Fuss, "Fashion and the Homospectatorial Look," 215.

33. McDowell, foreword, xxvi.

34. Jennifer DeVere Brody makes a similar argument that the cup Irene drops at her party "foreshadows Clare's own broken body at the end of the novel" (1992, 1062). Jennifer DeVere Brody, "Clare Kendry's 'True' Colors: Race and Class Conflict in Nella Larsen's *Passing,*" *Callaloo* 15, no. 4 (1992): 1062.

35. Mary Ann Doane, *Femmes Fatales: Feminism, Film Theory, and Psychoanalysis* (New York: Routledge, 1991), 106.

36. Ibid., 105, 106.

37. Madigan, "Miscegenation and 'The Dicta of Race,'" 528.

38. "To Drop Mrs. Rhinelander," *New York Times,* March 16, 1925, 19.

39. "Kip Placed On 'Rack,'" *Pittsburgh Courier,* November 14, 1925, 2.

40. "Calls Rhinelander Dupe of Girl He Wed," *New York Times,* November 10, 1925, 8.

41. "Rhinelander Suit Suddenly Halted," *New York Times,* November 20, 1925, 9.

42. "Calls Rhinelander Dupe of Girl He Wed," 1.

43. "Rhinelander Faces Thorough Quizzing," *New York Times,* November 15, 1925, 14.

44. "Kip's 'Soul Message'; Notes Read," *Chicago Defender,* November 28, 1925, 4.

45. "Young Kip Stammers as He Tells of Pursuing Alice during Three Years' Wooing," *Chicago Defender,* November 21, 1925, 12.

46. Ibid.

47. "Rhinelander's Wife Cries under Ordeal," *New York Times,* November 24, 1925, 3.

48. "Rhinelander Wilts; Gets Adjournment," *New York Times,* November 19, 1925, 6.

49. Roland Barthes, *The Fashion System* (New York: Hill and Wang, 1983), 243.

50. The threat of soiling feminine ears was not that great for some female spectators. The *Times* noted that "several women left, but others who had been standing took their places." "Rhinelander's Wife Cries under Ordeal," 3.

51. "Text of Rhinelander's 'Scarlet Letters' as Read to the Jury," *Pittsburgh Courier,* November 28, 1925, 9.

52. Jolson's appearance was another sensational aspect of the trial. As expected, the entertainer lightened the tension in the courtroom, "smiling broadly" as he entered the witness stand. In response to Alice's claim that Jolson was a big flirt, the singer responded, "You have to be a flirt in the theatrical business." Discussing how his connection to the case affected him, he noted: "Every time I start for the dressing room the orchestra plays 'Alice where art thou going?' This is no joke." "Rhinelander Says He Pursued Girl," *New York Times,* November 18, 1925, 4.

53. "Loved Rhinelander, Wife's Letters Say," *New York Times,* November 13, 1925, 1.

54. Ibid., 3, 1. Ironically, the words that seemed to verify her race were actually from a song in a play, and the reporter appears to have overlooked the paradox of accusing Alice of plagiarizing "truly negro" yet inauthentic lines. The *Times* identified some of the lyrics as those sung by Alice Delysia, a stage actress, in the show *Afgar.* The music was by Charles Cuvillier and the lyrics by Douglas Furher. "Rhinelander Verses Familiar to Stage," *New York Times,* November 19, 1925, 6.

55. In addition Phillip Brian Harper points out how Alice's lawyer determined her racial heritage from her writing. Davis read to Leonard one letter in which Alice referred to a "strutting party" and "roll[ed]" the term "out in the best negro dialect." Davis then asked Leonard, "Didn't you recognize that as being a typically negro expression?" "Rhinelander Says He Pursued Girl," 4. As Harper notes, through this particular exchange Davis "imputed to [Alice] patterns of diction and intonation that clinched her negro identification." Phillip Brian Harper, *Are We Not Men? Masculine Anxiety and the Problem of African-American Identity* (New York: Oxford University Press, 1996), 135.

56. "Rhinelander Jury Warned," *New York Times,* December 2, 1925, 3.

57. Alice's exposure in the jury room is only briefly mentioned in the *New York Times*. Referring to the strip incident as "the other sensation of the day," the paper focused more on Leonard's "smut[ty]" letters. "Rhinelander's Wife Cries under Ordeal," 3. The *Amsterdam News* presented only an editorial on the trial. See "Rhinelander Trial Reaches Editorial Page," *New York Amsterdam News,* November 25, 1925, 16. The *Pittsburgh Courier* covered the trial in its "theatrical section" on November 28, noting that Alice shrank "like a frightened animal." "Alice Tears Her Pride to Shreds to Hold Her Man," *Pittsburgh Courier,* November 28, 1925, 9.

58. "Kip's 'Soul Message'; Notes Read," *Chicago Defender,* November 28, 1925, 4.

59. Doane, *Femmes Fatales,* 106.

60. Discussing Davis's decision in the context of past incidences of black women being objectified, Lewis and Ardizzone wonder if the lawyer thought that the jury "would take pity on the unfortunate girl on display before them? . . . Or was he hoping that precisely that image of a sexually available, exotic woman would itself reinforce the blackness he was trying to emphasize?" (*Love on Trial,* 157–58). Lewis and Ardizzone link the scene to the

exhibition of Sarah Baartmann, the "Hottentot Venus," the breast-baring of Sojourner Truth, and images of enslaved black women on the auction block, as Chinn does as well (*Technology and the Logic of Racism,* 76). Truth's scene of disrobing has proved to be so useful that it functions as the "paradigmatic body" in discussions concerning black women and the body. See Deborah McDowell, "Afterword: Recovery Missions: Imaging the Body Ideals," in Bennett and Dickerson, *Recovering the Black Female Body,* 308.

61. Susan Bordo, *Unbearable Weight: Feminism, Western Culture, and the Body* (Berkeley: University of California Press, 1993), 11.

62. "Rhinelander Loses; No Fraud Is Found; Wife Will Sue Now," *New York Times,* December 6, 1925, 27. The Rhinelanders were legally divorced in 1930. Alice agreed not to use the Rhinelander name and dropped an alienation of affection suit against Leonard's father and a separation suit against Leonard. See Lewis and Ardizzone, *Love on Trial,* 246.

63. Brian Carr argues that scholars' analyses of the novel tend to "supplement" Irene's paranoid readings of events. Carr, "Paranoid Interpretation, Desire's Nonobject, and Nella Larsen's *Passing,*" *PMLA* 119, no. 2 (2004): 287.

64. Ann duCille, *The Coupling Convention: Sex, Text, and Tradition in Black Women's Fiction* (New York: Oxford University Press, 1993), 108.

65. Ibid., 107.

66. Lewis and Ardizzone, *Love on Trial,* 254.

3. Surface Effects

1. James Weldon Johnson to Mr. Moe, Guggenheim Foundation, December 2, 1933, Correspondence, JWJ. Neither writer received an award.

2. W. E. B. Du Bois, "The Browsing Reader," review of *Black No More* by George Schuyler, *Crisis,* March 1931, 100. Curiously, however, Du Bois was more critical of Schuyler in a confidential letter to Joel E. Spingarn just two years later: "Schuyler has many good points and ideas, but I feel strongly that he is not the type of man that we ought permanently to tie to for the N.A.A.C.P. I think that all arrangements with him should be temporary and strictly limited. He has, in my opinion, neither the education nor the character that we need." Du Bois to Joel E. Spingarn, January 27, 1933, W. E. B. Du Bois Collection, Yale Collection of American Literature, Beinecke Rare Book and Manuscript Library, Yale University.

3. Although Schuyler was at one point a member of the Socialist Party of America and a writer and editorialist at the *Messenger,* A. Philip Randolph's socialist-influenced paper for the Brotherhood of Sleeping Car Porters, Schuyler was quite critical of socialism and communism by the time *Black No More* was published. Schuyler joined the Socialist Party in 1921, later explaining his membership by saying that he had little intellectual companionship in Syracuse, New York; the party was "just the type of stimulation [he] had been hungering for," as he states in his autobiography *Black and Conservative: The Autobiography of George S. Schuyler* (New York: Arlington House Publishers, 1966), 113. In June 1923 Schuyler debated communism with a communist: "I took the position that the Negro had difficulties enough being black without becoming Red" (146). By 1924 Schuyler expressed dissatisfaction and cynicism about communism and socialism: "This did not come to me suddenly like a bolt out of the blue. . . . It took some time to sense the proportions of what seemed to me to be a conspiracy to plant collectivism in America and nourish it to the final harvest" (150). A close reading of Schuyler's autobiography and his essays reveals a writer

who was concerned not only with parodying common assumptions about everyday American life but also with the writer's craft, like the satirical writer he so admired, H. L. Mencken. Schuyler's keen reading of and commentary on the news of the day creates a remarkably prescient text that reads surprisingly well even today.

4. George Schuyler, *Black No More: Being an Account of the Strange and Wonderful Workings of Science in the Land of the Free, A.D. 1933–1940* (1931), intro. by Ishmael Reed (New York: Modern Library, 1999), 11. Subsequent citations are from this edition and are given parenthetically in the text with the abbreviation *BNM*.

5. Langston Hughes, "The Negro Artist and the Racial Mountain," *Nation,* June 23, 1926, 694; and George Schuyler, "The Negro-Art Hokum," *Nation,* June 16, 1926, 662. Subsequent citations are given parenthetically in the text with the abbreviation NAH. According to Schuyler, it was not a planned "debate," but unfortunately the two articles have been interpreted as such. In an unpublished 1960 interview and in his autobiography *Black and Conservative,* Schuyler states that the *Nation's* editors held on to his essay for nearly a year while soliciting responses from other African American writers. See Schuyler, "Reminiscences of George Samuel Schuyler," interview by William T. Ingersoll, New York, 1960, transcript, Columbia University Oral History Research Office; and Schuyler, *Black and Conservative,* 157.

6. For a discussion of Schuyler's and Hughes's essays, see Nathan Huggins, *Harlem Renaissance* (New York: Oxford University Press, 1971), 203–5; George Hutchinson, *The Harlem Renaissance in Black and White* (Cambridge: Harvard University Press, 1995), 219–23; J. Martin Favor, *Authentic Blackness: The Folk in the New Negro Renaissance* (Durham: Duke University Press, 1999), 120–26; Jeffrey Ferguson, *The Sage of Sugar Hill: George S. Schuyler and the Harlem Renaissance* (New Haven: Yale University Press, 2005), 183–98; and Gene Jarrett, *Deans and Truants: Race and Realism in African American Literature* (Philadelphia: University of Pennsylvania Press, 2007), 101–7. In "The Negro Artist and the Racial Mountain," Hughes argued for the uniqueness of black art. Hughes's essay is a celebration of black difference, the creativity that originates in lower-class black life; and it has been read as an affirmation of the ambition of the younger participants in the Harlem Renaissance. The exchange illustrates the difficulties of constructing and defining the New Negro: How does culture constitute identity? What are the identifiable elements that construct blackness and black art? The two essays were reprinted side by side in the *New York Amsterdam News,* June 23, 1926, 16.

7. One such recent look at this issue is Jarrett, *Deans and Truants.*

8. For a discussion of Mencken's relationship with other African American writers, particularly during the Harlem Renaissance, see Charles Scruggs, *The Sage in Harlem: H. L. Mencken and the Black Writers of the 1920s* (Baltimore: Johns Hopkins University Press, 1984); Scruggs, "H. L. Mencken and James Weldon Johnson: Two Men Who Helped Shape a Renaissance," in *Critical Essays on H. L. Mencken,* ed. Douglas C. Stenerson (Boston: G. K. Hall, 1987), 186–203; and Hutchinson, *Harlem Renaissance in Black and White,* 326–41. Scruggs provides an interesting account of the friendship and reciprocal literary influences of Mencken and Johnson. Scruggs credits Mencken with Johnson's well-known reference to Irish writer John Synge in Johnson's preface to *The Book of American Negro Poetry* ("Two Men," 198). Hutchinson provides a detailed analysis of race-related articles in the *American Mercury.* In addition to the *Atlantic Monthly, American Mercury* was one of the few national magazines that regularly published African American writers during the Harlem Renaissance. Fenwick Anderson reviews the *American Mercury* articles either by

or about African Americans during the period in which Mencken was the editor in "Black Perspectives in Mencken's Mercury," *Menckeniana: A Quarterly Review,* no. 70 (Summer 1979): 2–65. Mencken declined Schuyler's request that he write a preface for *Black No More,* indicating that such a move might be interpreted as "patronizing." See Schuyler to Mencken, August 30, 1930, and Schuyler to Mencken, September 18, 1930, H. L. Mencken Papers. Manuscripts and Archives Division, New York Public Library (hereafter HLM).

9. Mencken to Schuyler, August 25, 1927, JWJ.

10. Mencken, response to symposium, *Crisis,* March 1926, 220.

11. Schuyler to Mencken, September 10, 1927, HLM.

12. "The Sahara of the Bozart" was originally published in the *New York Evening Mail* on November 13, 1917. A longer version of the essay was published in Mencken's *Prejudices: Second Series* (New York: Alfred A. Knopf, 1920), 136–54. According to Fred Hobson, it was this version that created a furor in the South in the summer of 1921. Fred C. Hobson, *Serpent in Eden: H. L. Mencken and the South* (Chapel Hill: University of North Carolina Press, 1974), 27.

13. Mencken, "Sahara," *Prejudices,* 136, 143, 150, 149.

14. Scruggs, "Two Men," 179–80.

15. Hobson, *Serpent in Eden,* 28.

16. H. L. Mencken, preface to *The American Language: A Preliminary Inquiry into the Development of English in the United States,* 1st ed. (New York: Alfred A. Knopf, 1919), vii.

17. The phrase appears in Mencken's "On Being an American," in *Prejudices: Third Series* (New York: Alfred A. Knopf, 1922), 16. Mencken's writings on eugenics include "Note for Eugenicists," *Baltimore Evening Sun* April 16, 1928, 17; and "Utopia by Sterilization," *American Mercury* 41 (August 1937): 399–408.

18. In reference to this discussion of neologisms, it is interesting to consider Mencken's views on the various terms used to describe African Americans, the decision of the *New York Times* to capitalize "Negro," and the attention that decision garnered in the African American press. Mencken's views on this topic were undoubtedly influenced by Schuyler, whom he quotes frequently during this discussion. See H. L. Mencken, *Supplement I* to *The American Language* (New York: Alfred Knopf, 1945), 618–39.

19. Ferguson, *The Sage of Sugar Hill,* 180.

20. James Branch Cabell, *Let Me Lie: Being in the Main an Ethnological Account of the Remarkable Commonwealth of Virginia and the Making of Its History* (New York: Farrar, Straus, and Co., 1947), 208; also quoted in Hobson, *Serpent in Eden,* 28.

21. In a discussion of African American satire and definitions of the genre, Darryl Dickson-Carr notes that "Schuyler's unremitting iconoclasm precludes taking him at his word." Darryl Dickson-Carr, *African American Satire: The Sacredly Profane Novel* (Columbia: University of Missouri Press, 2001), 15.

22. Rudolph Fisher, "A Novel That Makes Faces," review of *Black No More* by George Schuyler, *New York Herald Tribune,* February 1, 1931, sec. 11, 5.

23. Schuyler, "Our Greatest Gift to America," in *Ebony and Topaz,* ed. Charles Johnson (New York: National Urban League, 1927), 123.

24. Hughes, "Negro Artist and the Racial Mountain," 694.

25. Several scholars have interrogated the relationship among narrative, bodies, and the concept of "America," constructing a type of literary genealogy of race and nation in nineteenth-century America. Russ Castronovo, for example, in *Fathering the Nation: American Genealogies of Race and Freedom* (Berkeley: University of California Press, 1995),

analyzes the stories of America's "founding fathers" such as George Washington and Thomas Jefferson, and finds that "America" is a narrative that achieves coherence by repressing dissonant voices and experiences.

26. Schuyler, "Our Greatest Gift to America," 124.

27. Karen Sánchez-Eppler suggests that to be a citizen of this country, to be a subject who both counts and is counted, one must disassociate oneself from the body, a detachment that reaches its ultimate version in the form of white masculinity, the most "representative" form of the American subject. Karen Sanchez-Eppler, *Touching Liberty: Abolition, Feminism, and the Politics of the Body* (Berkeley: University of California Press, 1993), 5–6. In contrast, the "overmarked particularity" of certain groups, primarily women and people of color, has functioned as a barrier prohibiting them from participating in the ideal of American citizenship. See Robyn Wiegman, *American Anatomies: Theorizing Race and Gender* (Durham: Duke University Press, 1995), 49.

28. In the novel, Schuyler refers to the whitened Max as Matthew, a distinction I follow as well. I call the character Max when I refer to episodes before the character experiences the "Black No More" process.

29. Lauren Berlant, *The Anatomy of National Fantasy: Hawthorne, Utopia, and Everyday Life* (Chicago: University of Chicago Press, 1991), 11.

30. Hortense Spillers, "Mama's Baby, Papa's Maybe: An American Grammar Book," in *Black, White, and In Color: Essays on American Literature and Culture* (Chicago: University of Chicago Press, 2003), 205.

31. Laura Doyle, *Bordering on the Body: The Racial Matrix of Modern Fiction and Culture* (New York: Oxford University Press, 1994), 175.

32. Ibid., 191–97.

33. Ralph Ellison, "Out of the Hospital and Under the Bar," in *Soon One Morning: New Writing by American Negroes, 1940–1962,* ed. Herbert Hill (New York: Knopf, 1963), 242–90.

34. Doyle, Bordering on the Body, 193.

35. Ralph Ellison, *Invisible Man* (1952; New York: Vintage Books, 1995) 258.

36. Time is also important in the use of the seasons to mark the progression of the plot. Often Schuyler selects times that resonate with rebirth and renewal, when the past can become distant, forgettable memories. The novel opens on New Year's Eve, and the Easter holiday functions as a significant marker. Three days after Good Friday ("the Monday after Easter" [*Black No More,* 44]), Matthew lectures to the Knights of Nordica congregation. Matthew and Rev. Givens's daughter Helen are married on Easter Sunday a year later.

37. Ellison, *Invisible Man,* 6.

38. This reading of the family as a racial group with national implications necessarily invokes Walter Benn Michaels's discussion about nativism and American modernism: "What's at stake in the desire to keep someone in the family is thus the sense that what is outside the family is also outside the race. . . . Insofar as the family becomes the site of national identity, nationality becomes an effect of racial identity." And yet, as Daylanne English points out, "because the family is never solely a racial site, neither, then, is the modern nation. Race . . . is itself only one (though arguably the most powerful and pernicious one) among multiple categories of collective modern subjectivity." See Walter Benn Michaels, *Our America: Nativism, Modernism, and Pluralism* (Durham: Duke University Press, 1995), 7–8; and Daylanne English, *Unnatural Selections: Eugenics in American Modernism and the Harlem Renaissance* (Chapel Hill: University of North Carolina Press, 2004), 14.

39. There is a significant parallel between this statement made by Rev. Givens and a comment made by a white Southern man that Schuyler heard during a trip to the South. In an unpublished interview Schuyler refers to the historically unequal positions of whites and blacks in the segregated South, an imbalance rendered moot by the difficult economic conditions in the area. The white individual uses the same words as Givens: "We're all niggers now." Both statements suggest a parity between whites and blacks that is recognized only during moments of crisis. See Schuyler, "Reminiscences," interview by Ingersoll, transcript, 235.

40. It is intriguing to note here that Schuyler also uses the term "race patriot" in reference to his own mother. In a letter to NAACP secretary Walter White, Schuyler talks about his upbringing. While describing his childhood, he discusses how he came to be aware of racial issues: "My mother, who was quite a race patriot, told me about Sojourner Truth, Frederick Douglass, Booker T. Washington . . . and the past glories of Egypt and Ethiopia." Although the term has a positive valence in this memory of his mother, Schuyler uses it pejoratively later in the same letter, though not with specific reference to his mother: "With time, study and thought I have grown much more tolerant and understanding and am able to see white folks just as human beings. . . . I also see the Negro, I believe, more as he is and not as Negro race patriots had me thinking he was." Schuyler to Walter White, October 4, 1929, Walter Francis White and Poppy Cannon Papers, Yale Collection of American Literature, Beinecke Rare Book and Manuscript Library, Yale University. Jeffrey Ferguson also makes an intriguing connection between Madeline Scranton and Schuyler's own mother. In a footnote Ferguson observes that Schuyler may have named the characters of *Black No More* after members of his own family: "Bunny Brown has the same last name as Schuyler's stepfather, Joseph Eugene Brown, whom he describes in his autobiography as a good but somewhat ridiculous man. This may associate the minor character Madeline Scranton, the wise and race-proud 'sweet Georgia brown' who becomes Bunny's girlfriend at the end of the satire, with Schuyler's mother" (*Sage of Sugar Hill*, 286 n. 27).

41. Howard J. Faulkner, "A Vanishing Race," *CLA Journal* 37 (1994): 281, 286. Even Mencken seemed to dislike the conclusion. In his brief review of the novel he writes that Schuyler "depends upon the devices of rough farce, and now and then, especially when he lampoons the current leaders of Black America, his satire is uncomfortably savage. However, there are some excellent scenes in the story, notably in the first half." H. L. Mencken, review of *Black No More* by George S. Schuyler, *American Mercury* 22 (April 1931): xxxvi.

42. Amy Robinson, "It Takes One to Know One: Passing and Communities of Common Interest," *Critical Inquiry* 20, no. 4 (1994): 715–36.

43. Ralph Ellison pondered the motivation for the fantasy of a blackless America and the reason for its pathological, oddly repetitive appearance in "What America Would Be Like without Blacks," in *The Collected Essays of Ralph Ellison,* ed. John F. Callahan (New York: Modern Library, 1995), 581–88.

44. Langston Hughes, *The Big Sea* (New York: Hill and Wang, 1940), 268.

45. Ralph Ellison, "Change the Joke and Slip the Yoke," in *Collected Essays,* 53.

46. Hughes, *The Big Sea,* 268.

4. Collectin' Van Vechten

1. The debate over Van Vechten's title foreshadows, of course, late-twentieth- and early-twenty-first-century debates over the use of the epithet and its banal euphemism, "the

n-word." Does not saying it increase its power? Who is authorized to speak it? When is the word emptied of its power? In 2001 Randall Kennedy published *Nigger: A Strange Career of a Troubling Word* and was criticized by commentators and scholars of African American culture. The black economist and writer Julianne Malveaux noted that Kennedy "giv[es] a whole bunch of racists who love to use the word permission to use it even more, like, 'I am not really using it, I am just talking about a book!'" Houston Baker Jr. said of Kennedy's book: "I see no reason whatsoever to do this, except to make money. It is a crude marketing technique unworthy of someone with the kind of penetrating intelligence that Professor Kennedy has." David D. Kirkpatrick, "A Black Author Hurls That Word as a Challenge," *New York Times,* December 1, 2001, A15. Van Vechten's decision to use the term and the resulting controversy must be included in any account of the historicity of the word. Van Vechten's book was not the first of the period to use the racial epithet in a title. This distinction belongs to Clement Woods, *Nigger* (New York: E. P. Dutton, 1922), followed by Ronald Firbank, *Prancing Nigger* (New York: Bretano's, 1924).

2. Carl Van Vechten, *Nigger Heaven* (1926), intro. by Kathleen Pfeiffer (Urbana: University of Illinois Press, 2000), 149. Subsequent references are given parenthetically in the text.

3. Charles Scruggs, "Crab Antics and Jacob's Ladder: Aaron Douglas's Two Views of *Nigger Heaven,*" in *The Harlem Renaissance Re-examined,* ed. Victor A. Kramer, (New York: AMS Press, 1987), 165. Notably, it is the second plate, the drawing that appeared more widely in African American periodicals, that graces the 2000 reprint of the novel by the University of Illinois Press.

4. Genevieve Ekaete, "Sterling Brown: A Living Legend," *New Directions: The Howard University Magazine* 1 (Winter 1974): 9.

5. James Weldon Johnson, "Double Audience Makes Road Hard for Negro Authors," in *The Selected Writings of James Weldon Johnson,* ed. Sondra Kathryn Wilson (New York: Oxford University Press, 1995), 409.

6. Peter Flora, "Carl Van Vechten, Blanche Knopf, and the Harlem Renaissance," *Library Chronicle of the University of Texas at Austin* 22, no. 4 (1992): 77–78, 82.

7. Van Vechten quite confidently calls it "my Negro novel" in a letter to Gertrude Stein dated June 30, 1925. See *The Letters of Gertrude Stein and Carl Van Vechten, 1913–1946,* vol. 1, ed. Edward Burns (New York: Columbia University Press, 1986), 116.

8. James Clifford, *The Predicament of Culture: Twentieth-Century Ethnography, Literature, and Art* (Cambridge: Harvard University Press, 1988), 12.

9. Jonathan Weinberg, "'Boy Crazy': Carl Van Vechten's Queer Collection," *Yale Journal of Criticism* 7, no. 2 (1994): 25–49. Weinberg examines the large number of scrapbooks created by Van Vechten and now held at Yale University. The collection of montages is notable for the explicit presentation of the male nude figure. It consists of "twenty-odd scrapbooks of photographs and newspapers clippings" which "are essentially homemade sexbooks" (28). The scrapbooks give some indications of Van Vechten's method of creation and reflect his skill in reading and decoding popular culture: "Van Vechten appears to have been scanning the newspapers looking not only for the public naming of homosexuality, but for the way in which same-sex love can only be deduced by reading between the lines" (31). He also used the scrapbooks to state explicitly what may appear ambiguous within the larger culture: "He found homosexuality where homosexuality had been suppressed—the crime reports—and he found homosexuality where it was not supposed to be—the tennis court or the wrestling mat. If it were not implicit in a photograph he provided a caption that made it clear" (31).

10. *Remember Me to Harlem: The Letters of Langston Hughes and Carl Van Vechten,* ed. Emily Bernard (New York: Alfred A. Knopf, 2001), 7, 13, 11.

11. Jessie Fauset was the first person to publish Hughes, printing "The Negro Speaks of Rivers" in 1921 in *Crisis*. Van Vechten would also claim credit for "discovering" Ethel Waters, though even before the singer met Van Vechten, she was well known throughout the Theatre Owners' Booking Association circuit, a network of owners who booked black talent. Countee Cullen's dislike of Van Vechten is suggested in a letter from Cullen to Harold Jackman, October 7, 1925, JWJ.

12. Significantly, one of the early images invoked with some contempt by Du Bois in his essay "Criteria of Negro Art" is that of the American tourist. Du Bois was visiting the setting of Sir Walter Scott's "Lady of the Lake" when his contemplation of the beautiful scene was interrupted by a group of noisy Americans. The "excursionists," implicitly white, "struck a note not evil but wrong. They carried, perhaps, a sense of strength and accomplishment, but their hearts had no conception of the beauty which pervaded [the] holy place." Here Du Bois subtly alludes to white authors interested in black subject matter, authors who, like the tourists, have no appreciation for their surroundings. W. E. B. Du Bois, "Criteria of Negro Art," *Crisis,* October 1926, 290.

13. Jonathan Culler, "The Semiotics of Tourism," in *Framing the Sign: Criticism and Its Institutions* (Norman: Oklahoma University Press, 1988), 155.

14. Susan Stewart, *On Longing: Narratives of the Miniature, the Gigantic, the Souvenir, the Collection* (Baltimore: Johns Hopkins University Press, 1984), 135, 136. Stewart also writes, "Each element within the collection is representative and works in combination toward the creation of a new whole that is the context of the collection itself" (152–53).

15. Mieke Bal speaks of museums' practice of "abstracting the artifacts from their social and historical environments." Mieke Bal, "Telling, Showing, Showing Off," *Critical Inquiry* 18, no. 3 (1992): 559.

16. Stewart, *On Longing,* 152.

17. Ibid., 159.

18. Ibid., 157–69.

19. Mieke Bal, "Telling Objects: A Narrative Perspective on Collection," in *The Cultures of Collecting,* ed. John Elsner and Roger Cardinal (Cambridge: Harvard University Press, 1994), 100.

20. George H. Douglas, *The Smart Magazines: 50 Years of Literary Revelry and High Jinks at Vanity Fair, the New Yorker, Life, Esquire, and the Smart Set* (Hamden, Conn.: Archon Books, 1991), 98.

21. Quoted ibid., 99, 96.

22. "Countee Cullen: A Note by Carl Van Vechten," *Vanity Fair,* June 1925, 62.

23. Carl Van Vechten, "Langston Hughes: A Biographical Note," *Vanity Fair,* September 1925, 62. Van Vechten's appraisal of Hughes reappears, with the same primitive imagery, in his introduction to Hughes's book *The Weary Blues*: "Herein may be discerned that nostalgia for color and warmth and beauty which explains this boy's nomadic instincts." Van Vechten, "Introducing Langston Hughes to the Reader," in Hughes, *The Weary Blues* (New York: Alfred A. Knopf, 1926), 12.

24. Siobhan Somerville, *Queering the Colorline: Race and the Invention of Homosexuality in American Culture* (Durham: Duke University Press, 2000), 126; and John Young, *Black Writers, White Publishers: Marketplace Politics in Twentieth-Century African American Literature* (Jackson: University Press of Mississippi, 2006), 13.

25. Bernard, *Remember Me,* 11.

26. Ibid., 24–25.

27. Carl Van Vechten, "'Moanin' Wid a Sword in Ma Han': A Discussion of the Negro's Reluctance to Develop and Exploit His Racial Gifts," *Vanity Fair,* February 1926, 102.

28. Ibid., 100, 102.

29. Ibid., 100.

30. Carl Van Vechten, "Prescription for the Negro Theatre: Being a Few Reasons Why the Great Colored Show Has Not Yet Been Achieved," *Vanity Fair,* October 1925, 46, 92, 98.

31. Ibid., 46, 92.

32. Ibid., 96, 98. Notably, the producer for Baker's 1925 revue, Carolyn Dudley Reagan, visited Van Vechten at this time, according to Van Vechten's "daybooks," or diaries. See the entries for August 26 and September 9, 1925, in Carl Van Vechten, *The Splendid Drunken Twenties: Selections from the Daybooks, 1922–1930,* ed. Bruce Kellner (Urbana: University of Illinois Press, 2003), 94, 95.

33. James Weldon Johnson, *Book of American Negro Poetry* (New York: Harcourt, Brace, and Co., 1922), vii.

34. Van Vechten, "Moanin'," 100, 100, 102.

35. Ibid., 61.

36. Clifford, *Predicament of Culture,* 221.

37. Douglas, *Smart Magazines,* 99.

38. Charles R. Larson, "Three Harlem Novels of the Jazz Age," *Critique* 11, no. 3 (1969): 72.

39. Jean Baudrillard, "The System of Collecting," in *The Cultures of Collecting,* ed. John Elsner and Roger Cardinal (Cambridge: Harvard University Press, 1994), 12.

40. There is much about Mary Love and Lasca Sartoris that foreshadows Larsen's heroines in her two novels *Quicksand* and *Passing.* Like Helga Crane, Mary Love continually wonders what distinguishes her from other African Americans and why she cannot simply fit in with the crowd. Moreover, Mary's inexplicable attraction to Lasca Sartoris and her feelings of both desire and envy mirror the relationship between Irene and Clare in *Passing.* Larsen dedicated *Passing* to Van Vechten and his wife, Fania. See Cheryl Wall, *Women of the Harlem Renaissance* (Bloomington: Indiana University Press, 1995), 129; and Kathleen Pfeiffer, *Race Passing and American Individualism* (Amherst: University of Massachusetts Press, 2003), 128–46, for a more detailed discussion about the similarities between Van Vechten's and Larsen's novels.

41. Lewis Erenberg, *Steppin' Out: New York Nightlife and the Transformation of American Culture, 1890–1930* (Westport, Conn.: Greenwood Press, 1981), 84, 85.

42. Susan Bordo, *The Male Body: A New Look at Men in Public and Private* (New York: Farrar, Straus, and Giroux, 1999). Bordo specifically notes that African American men are able to alter signs traditionally perceived as feminine. In the chapter "Beauty (Re) Discovers the Male Body" (168–225), she examines African American male style and focuses on Michael Jordan as *GQ*'s Man of Style for 1995. She claims that "among many young African-American men, appearing in high style, 'cleaned up' and festooned with sparkling jewelry, is not a sign of effeminacy, but potency and social standing" (206). Despite her awareness of the presence of black style in (white) American consumer and popular culture, at times Bordo displays a disconcerting blindness about how black styles end up so popular. She notes, for instance, that "African-American styles have done a great

deal to add color . . . and in general *permission* to be slightly dramatic, flirtatious, and ironic with one's clothes" (212; emphasis added). The wide presence of "African American styles" in mainstream white media may be seen as "permission" for experimentation or, as I believe, yet another instance of a dominant culture appropriating elements of a group whose physical appearance has historically been disparaged and denigrated.

43. The idea of Harlem as a space for sexual freedom is also presented in Blair Niles's 1931 novel *Strange Brother* (New York: Horace Liveright, 1931). The novel picks up the discussion of markings, writings, and interpretation first raised with Larsen's *Passing*. Larsen asks us, "How do you tell a person's race?" Niles asks us, "How do you tell a person's sexuality?" *Strange Brother* frames this critique within the world of Harlem, within a discourse about the law in a sexualized space. For more on the novel, see Anthony Slade, *Lost Gay Novels: A Reference Guide to Fifty Works from the First Half of the Twentieth Century* (New York: Harrington Park Press, 2003), 137–40. As with *Nigger Heaven,* the most interesting aspects of *Strange Brother* reside not in the novel's putative center but elsewhere, with the story's minor figures, such as Seth. Both novels explore the intersections of black and white life in New York, the intersections of race and gender in the city's gay subculture. For a more detailed look at the "queer" space of Harlem, see Joseph Allen Boone, *Libidinal Currents: Sexuality and the Shaping of Modernism* (Chicago: University of Chicago Press, 1998); and Eric Garber, "A Spectacle in Color: The Lesbian and Gay Subculture of Jazz Age Harlem," in *Hidden from History: Reclaiming the Gay and Lesbian Past,* ed. Martin Bauml, Martha Vicinus, and George Chauncey Jr. (New York: New American Library, 1989), 318–31.

44. James Weldon Johnson, *Black Manhattan* (1930; repr., Salem, N.H.: Ayer Company, 1988), 163.

45. Van Vechten, in this initial view of Harlem, presents the scene through subtle phallic undertones. As Anatole Longfellow fails to get a woman to return his glance, he bumps into another man, significantly older, with a gray beard and a limp, recalling Freud's ideas on blindness and castration. As he thinks of his good fortune and roams Harlem looking for a fresh "piece," his chest expands, dangerously stretching his watch chain. Van Vechten, *Nigger Heaven,* 9.

46. Kevin Mumford, in *Interzones: Black/White Sex Districts in Chicago and New York in the Early Twentieth-Century* (New York: Columbia University Press, 1997), indicates how spaces become politicized and sexualized: "Simultaneously marginal and central, interzones were located in African-American neighborhoods, unique because their (often transient) inhabitants were black and white, heterosexual and homosexual, prostitute and customer" (20). The Creeper and Lasca reflect these categories.

47. Wallace Thurman, "Fire Burns: A Department of Comment," *Fire!!* November 1926, 48.

48. Peter Flora also notes that the novel concludes on a depressing and questionable note: "Given Van Vechten's lifelong efforts to encourage and promote African American artists, Byron's frustrations are puzzling, particularly because in Van Vechten's earlier novel, *Peter Whiffle,* the white writer Whiffle succeeds under circumstances quite similar to those faced by Byron in *Nigger Heaven.*" Flora, "Carl Van Vechten, Blanche Knopf, and the Harlem Renaissance," 75.

49. In this respect it foreshadows the ending of Wallace Thurman's satire on the Renaissance, *Infants of the Spring* (1932).

50. Scruggs, "Crab Antics and Jacob's Ladder," 157.

51. Emily Bernard, "Unlike Many Others: Exceptional White Characters in Harlem Renaissance Fiction," *Modernism/modernity* 12, no. 3 (2005): 409, 408.

52. Ibid., 408. Bernard's article raises the equally, if not more, compelling question of the absence of sympathetic white *female* characters in black-authored novels.

53. Wallace Thurman, *The Blacker the Berry* (1929; repr., New York: Scribner, 1996), 186; Thurman, "Fire Burns," 47.

54. Countee Cullen, *One Way to Heaven* (New York: Harper and Bros., 1932), 105, 99, 173. When Van Vechten informed Cullen of the title for *Nigger Heaven,* Cullen "turn[ed] white with hurt." Van Vechten, *Splendid Drunken Twenties,* 101.

55. Baudrillard, "The System of Collecting," 24.

56. When we turn to *Nigger Heaven*'s glossary to discover the meaning of certain Harlem phrases, some of the definitions are meaningless and have no referent or equivalent. For "boody," we are advised to "see hootchie-pap." Turning to "hootchie-pap," we are instructed to return to "boody." Van Vechten, *Nigger Heaven,* 285, 286.

57. James Weldon Johnson, "Romance and Tragedy in Harlem—A Review," *Opportunity* October 1926, 316; Charles Chesnutt to Carl Van Vechten, September 7, 1926, Carl Van Vechten Correspondence, Yale Collection of American Literature, Beinecke Rare Book and Manuscript Library, Yale University (hereafter CVV–Y).

58. Eric Walrond to Van Vechten, telegram, August 8, 1926; Nella Larsen to Van Vechten, "Wednesday the 11th"; and Charles Johnson to Van Vechten, August 10, 1926, all in Carl Van Vechten Collection, New York Public Library (hereafter CVV–NYPL).

59. Alain Locke, "Beauty Instead of Ashes," *Nation,* April 14, 1928, 433; Aaron Douglass to Van Vechten, August 5, 1926, CVV–NYPL.

60. George Schuyler, "*Phylon* Profile XXII: Carl Van Vechten," *Phylon* 11, no. 4 (1950): 362–68; Schuyler, introduction to Carl Van Vechten, *Nigger Heaven* (New York: Avon, 1951), ii.

61. This point also helps to explain Jessie Fauset's reputed negative reaction to being caricatured as Hester Albright in *Nigger Heaven.* The seventh question of the *Crisis* symposium asked if there is a "danger" in having young Negro writers present black characters of the "underworld," to which Fauset answered: "Emphatically. This is a grave danger making for a literary insincerity both insidious and abominable." *Crisis,* June 1926, 72. Despite calling Van Vechten "dull" in a letter to Langston Hughes, Fauset later wrote to Van Vechten for assistance in publishing *Plum Bun.* See Jessie Fauset to Langston Hughes, June 15, 1925, LH; and Fauset to Van Vechten, October 21, 1925, CVV–Y.

62. Carl Van Vechten, "Portraits of the Artists," *Esquire,* December 1962, 174. See also editor's introduction to Van Vechten, *Splendid Drunken Twenties,* xvi.

63. Three examinations of Van Vechten's photography are Rudolph P. Byrd, ed., *Generations in Black and White: Photographs of Carl Van Vechten from the James Weldon Johnson Memorial Collection* (Athens: University of Georgia Press, 1993); Nancy Kuhl, ed., *Extravagant Crowd: Carl Van Vechten's Portraits of Women* (New Haven: Beinecke Rare Book and Manuscript Library, Yale University, 2003); and James Smalls, *The Homoerotic Photography of Carl Van Vechten: Public Face, Private Thoughts* (Philadelphia: Temple University Press, 2006). The Beinecke Library has digitized and placed online several examples of Van Vechten's color photography. These are striking because of the background colors and imagery, often presenting familiar images of Harlem Renaissance personalities in new ways.

64. Kuhl, *Extravagant Crowd,* 9.

65. Van Vechten's image of Hurston laughing was the basis for the Zora Neale Hurston stamp issued by the United States Postal Service in 2003 as part of the "Black Heritage" series.

66. Roland Barthes, *Camera Lucida: Reflections on Photography,* trans. Richard Howard (New York: Hill and Wang, 1981), 27.

67. It is reasonable to assume that Van Vechten was familiar with Man Ray's images of Kiki; Man Ray was a friend of Van Vechten's. For more on Kiki, see *Kiki's Memoirs,* ed. Billy Klüver and Julie Martin (New Jersey: Ecco Press, 1996). Discussing one photographic session with Man Ray, Kiki writes: "What drives Man Ray to despair is that I have a nigger's tastes: I'm too fond of flashy colors! And yet, he loves the black race" (150). See also Whitney Chadwick, "Fetishizing Fashion/Fetishizing Culture: Man Ray's 'Noire et blanche,'" *Oxford Art Journal* 18, no. 2 (1995): 3–17.

68. The mask appears frequently in other Van Vechten photographs, including one with Alan "Juanite" Meadows, a dark-skinned man.

69. Recounting his experience of photographing Holiday in *Esquire,* a session that took one night but felt like "a complete career," Van Vechten wrote that Holiday arrived at his apartment "in a plain grey suit and facial expression equally depressing." This helps explain the overwhelming sense of melancholy apparent in some of the photographs until Van Vechten showed Holiday "one of [his] greatest photographs," that of Bessie Smith "in the mood of the blues." As the photographer notes, "from that moment on, she was putty in my hands." Carl Van Vetechen, "Portraits of the Artists," *Esquire,* December 1962, 256. Bessie Smith was a friend of Holiday's mother and the source of Holiday's inspiration. The change in facial expressions from the earlier to the later photos in the session is indeed remarkable. The sight of Smith's photograph encouraged Holiday to divulge her life story, bringing Van Vechten and his wife to tears.

70. Barthes, *Camera Lucida,* 43.

71. As Rudolph P. Byrd has recognized, the pose is a vital component of the Van Vechten photograph. Slight differences in a subject's pose can create altogether different photographs, as in the two images of Hurston. Byrd, *Generations in Black and White,* xxv.

72. Bal, "Telling Objects," 101.

73. Flora, "Carl Van Vechten, Blanche Knopf, and the Harlem Renaissance," 83. The book Van Vechten refers to is Walter White, *The Fire in the Flint* (New York: Knopf, 1924), one of the first books by an African American published in the 1920s. Jessie Fauset's *There Is Confusion* (New York: Boni and Liveright) was published the same year.

74. Clifford, *Predicament of Culture,* 218.

75. Weinberg, "'Boy Crazy,'" 47.

5. A Photographic Language

1. Roland Barthes, *Camera Lucida: Reflections on Photography* (New York: Hill and Wang, 1981), 5, 76. Subsequent citations are given parethentically in the text. *Camera Lucida* was originally published in French as *La Chambre Claire: Note sur la photographie* (Paris: Gallimard Seuil, 1980).

2. Alan Trachtenberg, *Reading American Photographs: Images as History, Mathew Brady to Walker Evans* (New York: Hill and Wang, 1989), 53–60.

3. Allan Sekula finds in this polarity the power of photographic language. Closely reading accounts from the early and mid-twentieth century of the developments and uses

of photography, Sekula demonstrates that photography, from its beginnings, "vacillated" between "truths" and "pleasures," and argues that in fact it is from such figurative movement or "traffic" that photographs derive their power. He examines what could be yet another rendition of the abstract-concrete divide, the two qualities of aestheticism and scientism, in order to understand the power that photographs have for capitalist societies and the state. Sekula's article is important for understanding how the polarity works historically (in the history of the photograph) and politically. Allan Sekula, "The Traffic in Photographs," *Art Journal* 41, no. 1 (Spring 1981): 15–25.

4. Trachtenberg, *Reading American Photographs,* 53–60; Barthes, *Camera Lucida,* 5; Frantz Fanon, "The Fact of Blackness," in *Black Skin, White Masks* (New York: Grove Press, 1967), 109.

5. Trachtenberg, *Reading American Photographs;* and Michael North, *Camera Works: Photography and the Twentieth-Century Word* (New York: Oxford University Press, 2005).

6. Martin Jay, *Downcast Eyes: The Denigration of Vision in Twentieth-Century French Thought* (Berkeley: University of California Press, 1993), 445. I quote the phrase as it appears, though Jay may have meant to say "denotative" rather than "connotative."

7. Nancy Shawcross concentrates an entire book on *Camera Lucida,* its construction and its antecedents. Despite her detailed and technically "correct" reading of Barthes's volume, there is something missing. This is not a fault of the book; rather it seems to be the effect of any writing about *Camera Lucida,* including my own. Perhaps, then, the only way to write about *Camera Lucida* is to write *around* it, not directly but obliquely. See Nancy Shawcross, *Roland Barthes on Photography: The Critical Tradition in Perspective* (Gainesville: University Press of Florida, 1997).

8. Brent Hayes Edwards, "The Seemingly Eclipsed Window of Form: James Weldon Johnson's Prefaces," in *The Jazz Cadence of American Culture,* ed. Robert G. O'Meally (New York: Columbia University Press, 1998), 591.

9. Noting "the difference between the son's inability to reproduce the photograph of his dead mother and the mother's insistence on the reproduction of the photograph of her dead son," Moten reads sound, specifically moaning, into the photograph. Fred Moten, *In the Break: The Aesthetics of the Black Radical Tradition* (Minneapolis: University of Minnesota Press, 2003), 206. Muñoz makes a larger argument about "disidentificatory pleasure," that is, the pleasure discovered through looking at images initially designed to "exploit and deny [one's] identity." José Muñoz, "Photographies of Mourning: Melancholia and Ambivalence in Van Der Zee, Mapplethorpe, and *Looking for Langston,*" in *Race and the Subjects of Masculinities,* ed. Harry Stecopoulos and Michael Uebel (Durham: Duke University Press, 1997), 337–58. See also Muñoz, *Disidentifications: Queers of Color and the Performance of Politics* (Minneapolis: University of Minnesota Press, 1999).

10. Avedon's photograph of A. Phillip Randolph appeared in the October 21, 1976, issue of *Rolling Stone* "to chronicle the 1976 bicentennial presidential election in the United States." Titled "The Family," Avedon's portfolio consisted of sixty-nine images of politicians and personalities.

11. Roland Barthes, *Roland Barthes,* trans. Richard Howard (New York: Hill and Wang, 1977), 41.

12. Jacqueline Goldsby, *A Spectacular Secret: Lynching in American Life and Literature* (Chicago: University of Chicago Press, 2006), 280.

13. Goldsby uses the term "unspeakable" (ibid., 280) in reference to lynching photographs, but the term also registers here, of course, with Toni Morrison's use of the word in her novel *Beloved* (New York: Knopf, 1987).

14. Some qualifications are necessary here in the discussion of the Winter Garden Photograph and the image of slavery Barthes saw as a young boy. Barthes *refuses* to reproduce the Winter Garden Photograph; in contrast, he is *unable* to reproduce the magazine image of slavery because it is lost. In addition, Barthes is personally invested and emotionally attached to the subject of the Winter Garden Photograph, his mother. No similar sense of investment or attachment is revealed in his discussion of the slavery image. In fact, because of the passage of time, Barthes would not have known the subjects in the magazine image. But—and yet— this temporal and emotional distance marks and distinguishes the image of slavery. A supposedly "neutral" picture evokes "horror and fascination" from Barthes. An image that should spark the *studium* instead compels the *punctum.* There was something quite wounding in the lost image of slavery.

15. "Whatever pertinence there happens to be comes only in the margins, the interpolations, the parentheses, aslant." Barthes, *Roland Barthes,* 73.

16. Goldsby, *A Spectacular Secret,* 280.

17. Van Der Zee was born in 1886 and grew up in Lenox, Massachusetts. After working for a period as a photographer's assistant, he opened a studio in Harlem in 1915. Van Der Zee's negatives were fortuitously discovered only days before he was to be evicted from his studio-home, enabling his photographs to become arguably the "star" of the "Harlem On My Mind" exhibition. Van Der Zee ran a mail-order business in his latter years, printing nostalgic calendars with his earlier images. Before his death in 1983 he photographed several well-known personalities such as Bill Cosby. Van Der Zee died shortly after receiving an honorary degree from Howard University. Perhaps the best work that details the history of early black photographers is Deborah Willis-Thomas, *Black Photographers, 1840–1940: An Illustrated Bio-Bibliography* (New York: Garland, 1985).

18. *The World of James Van Der Zee: A Visual Record of Black Americans* (New York: Grove Press, 1969), iv.

19. Ibid., 106.

20. Liliane De Cock and Reginald McGhee, eds., *Van Der Zee,* intro. by Regina A. Perry (Dobbs Ferry, N.Y.: Morgan and Morgan Publishers, 1973), 10–11.

21. Writing of the class dynamics of the portrait photograph, John Tagg, in *The Burden of Representation: Essays on Photographies and Histories* (London: Macmillan Education, 1988), notes that "the portrait is . . . a sign whose purpose is both the description of an individual and the inscription of social identity. But at the same time, it is also a commodity, a luxury, and an adornment, ownership of which confers status" (37).

22. De Cock and McGhee, *Van Der Zee,* 37.

23. Barthes capitalizes the term "Spectator," along with the other member involved in the photographic process, the "Operator" (*Camera Lucida,* 9). I have capitalized this term as well when it is used in this chapter to discuss Barthes's conceptions.

24. Van Der Zee's portraits of ordinary African Americans present a Harlem different from Van Vechten's. Indeed Van Vechten, his interracial parties, and his ironic photographs do not register with Van Der Zee at all. This is revealed in an interview reprinted in the 1969 *World of James Van Der Zee,* in which Van Der Zee claims that he "hadn't even heard of" Van Vechten. When informed that Van Vechten worked "during the Twenties primarily," Van Der Zee asks, "In New York?" Van Der Zee was interviewed by Candice

Van Ellison, who also wrote the introduction to the Random House catalogue for "Harlem on My Mind," which I discuss in the next chapter.

25. The woman who is standing appears transparent, particularly her face. Although this is not one of his famous "death" pictures, in which the departed magically appear with the living, the transparency of the woman's face reminds us that superimposing images was one of Van Der Zee's signature techniques. See James Van Der Zee, *The Harlem Book of the Dead* (New York: Morgan and Morgan, 1978). One such image inspired Toni Morrison's novel about Harlem, *Jazz* (New York: Knopf, 1992).

26. In fact, according to a 1969 *New York Times* article written as city officials began the process of evicting Van Der Zee from his studio brownstone, the photographer and the reporter came across a rolled-up American flag among the debris: "Mr. Van Der Zee picked up the flag. 'Do what you want to this old gray head,' he said, 'but spare your country's flag.' He chuckled." *New York Times* April 8, 1969, 32.

27. Ben Lifson, "James Van Der Zee, Photographer," *Portfolio,* March–April 1982, 104.

28. Even Van Der Zee's nude images conform to conventional standards of beauty. The women's long hair demurely suggests that the black female body, appropriately posed, can meet traditional standards of propriety. See *The World of James Van Der Zee,* 94–95.

29. As Jane Gallop notes in a discussion about Barthes and photography, "Barthes dared to theorize photography from the quite personal place of his subjectivity. He dared to presume that his subjective experience might count as knowledge for others." Jane Gallop, *Living with His Camera* (Durham: Duke University Press, 2003), 27. These "darings" serve as examples of writing about and around the referent. Barthes writes around the referent but not always successfully. What is surprising about his reading of the Van Der Zee photograph is that it doesn't measure up to his other readings of black images. His "darings," for example, work to his advantage in his discussion of a *Paris Match* article about a young couple traveling to Africa with their two-year-old son to paint. In the essay, "Bichon and the Blacks," Barthes carefully and humorously destroys the stereotype—both the image of blackness as cannibalistic and the image of a white masculinity that saves the black savage. A third type is also destroyed: the altruistic, class-inflected image of the child Bichon's art-loving parents. Stereotypes, like myths, convey a message, one that is imposed on the reader or spectator, and Barthes's writing helps to relieve the burden of the imposition. His writing about a Van Der Zee image, an image that, superficially, does not conform to the stereotype of blackness, complicates the writing strategy of rupturing stereotypes. Roland Barthes, "Bichon and the Blacks," in *The Eiffel Tower and Other Mythologies,* trans. Richard Howard (New York; Hill and Wang, 1979), 35–38.

30. Alain Locke, "Harlem: Dark Weather-Vane" *Survey Graphic* 25, no. 8 (August 1936): 457.

31. Aaron Siskind was born in New York in December 1903 to Russian Jewish parents. Interestingly, Siskind attended DeWitt Clinton High School, the same school the Harlem Renaissance poet Countee Cullen attended and where he was a teacher. Siskind went to DeWitt Clinton between 1915 and 1919–20, while Cullen was there between 1918 and 1921. Cullen, like Siskind, was born in 1903. DeWitt Clinton is the name given the Cullen-like character in Wallace Thurman's satire of the Harlem Renaissance, *Infants of the Spring.* There have been several recent studies of Siskind's photography which align the photographer with the larger social concerns of the time. John Raeburn places Siskind historically among other photographers practicing in the 1930s, such as Berenice Abbot and Margaret Bourke-White; Sara Blair includes him in considering the post–Harlem Renaissance

photographic image and its relation to black literary production, such as Ralph Ellison's *Invisible Man;* and Joseph Entin argues that Siskind, along with other contemporaneous photographers and writers such as Weegee, William Carlos Williams, and Richard Wright, practiced what Entin calls a "sensational modernism" that shocked the white American public into recognizing the unequal living conditions among Americans. My focus on Siskind is different and more specific in order to isolate those moments in which a process of the black modern may be discovered. John Raeburn, *A Staggering Revolution: A Cultural History of Thirties Photography* (Urbana: University of Illinois Press, 2006); Sara Blair, *Harlem Crossroads: Black Writers and the Photograph in the Twentieth Century* (Princeton: Princeton University Press, 2007); and Joseph Entin, *Sensational Modernism: Experimental Fiction and Photography in Thirties America* (Chapel Hill: University of North Carolina Press, 2007).

32. Siskind was a member of what Michael Denning termed the "cultural front," the "new generation of plebian artists and intellectuals who had grown up in the immigrant and black working-class neighborhoods of the modernist metropolis." Michael Denning, *The Cultural Front: The Laboring of American Culture in the Twentieth Century* (London: Verso, 1996), xv. For more information on Siskind and his work with the Photo League, see Carl Chiarenza, *Aaron Siskind: Pleasures and Terrors* (Boston: Little Brown, 1982). The Photo League was formed in 1936 from the splintering of the Film and Photo League.

33. Joseph Entin propels a reevaluation of Siskind's later images as not a complete opposition to his documentary photographs but rather a progression of them. Entin continually foregrounds the possible reaction of the white viewer of these photographs. But one can also consider the black viewer for whom the view may be "invasive" as well as intimate: the Sunday church service that goes on for too long, the picture of a girl sitting on her mother's or aunt's lap. In other words, there is a similarity in the larger outlines of the photos to the snapshots one has in the family photo album. In fact it is only the knowledge that the photographs were taken in the 1930s that prevents one from claiming a familial, and a familiar, relationship to them. Joseph Entin, "Modernist Documentary: Aaron Siskind's *Harlem Document*," *Yale Journal of Criticism* 12, no. 2 (1999): 357–82.

34. Aaron Siskind, "In 1943 and 1944 a Great Change Took Place," in *Photography: Essays and Images—Illustrated Readings in the History of Photography,* ed. Beaumont Newhall (New York: Museum of Modern Art, 1980), 306.

35. Ibid., 305–6.

36. Note, for instance, the way Siskind describes how he quite lovingly prepares to take a picture: "Producing a photographic document involves preparation in excess. There is first the examination of the idea of the project. Then the visits to the scene, the casual conversations, and more formal interviews—talking, and listening, and looking, looking. You read what's been written, and dig out facts and figures for your own writing. Follow the discussions to arrive at a point of view and its crystallization into a statement of aim. And finally, the pictures themselves, each one planned, talked, taken, and examined in terms of the whole. I worked pretty much this way in making 'Harlem Document.'" See Aaron Siskind, "The Drama of Objects," in *Photographers on Photography: A Critical Anthology,* ed. Nathan Lyons (Englewood Cliffs, N.J.: Prentice-Hall, 1966), 96.

37. Perhaps one of the more interesting personalities to emerge from the interviews reprinted in the written text of *Harlem Document* is Clyde "Kingfish" Smith, an African American seller of fish, meat, and eggs who creates his own impromptu songs to attract children and buyers to his wagon. In his interview Smith recounts how he used language

and rhythm to attract a crowd to his wares and, in the process, made creative decisions based on the racial distinctions among his potential customers: "In white and Jewish neighborhoods I feature the words but in the colored neighborhood I feature the tune. In the Jewish neighborhood they appreciate the rhyming and the words more, while in the colored neighborhood they appreciate the swinging and the tune, as well as the words." Aaron Siskind, *Harlem Document: Photographs 1932–1940* (Providence, R.I.: Matrix Publications, 1981), 12. By contrasting sounds against words, Smith's strategy recalls James Weldon Johnson's observation in *The Book of American Negro Spirituals* (New York: Viking Press, 1925) that Jewish Americans are the most likely among white Americans to "get" African American rhythm (28). One wonders, however, why and how Smith makes these racial distinctions when he discusses certain songs: "I wouldn't sing this one in a Jewish neighborhood. They don't know the tune and they couldn't appreciate that song. Only in a colored neighborhood." Smith was interviewed by Marion Hatch and Herbert Halpert in 1939.

38. See, for example, David Levering Lewis, *When Harlem Was in Vogue* (New York: Penguin, 1981), 306.

39. Entin emphasizes the fact that white spectators were the assumed audience of the pictures and that the photographs thus invoke "the politics of white looking." Entin, "Modernist Documentary," 373. It should be noted that the photographs were also exhibited in Harlem, and residents were invited to respond to the images. See the Photo League's journal *Photo Notes,* April 1939, 1.

40. Siskind, "A Great Change," 306.

41. In the published collection of *Harlem Document,* this photograph is cropped—the woman on the far right does not appear. The cropped image creates a further sense of intimacy between mother and daughter. Siskind, *Harlem Document,* 63.

42. Raeburn writes that "had its archive remained intact the Harlem Document almost certainly would have ranked among the most distinguished achievements of thirties photography." Raeburn, *A Staggering Revolution,* 230. Raeburn's discussion of *Look*'s feature including *Harlem Document* photographs reveals a unique example of the word/image dichotomy and the concern with the literality of images, particularly in documentary form. Although the *Harlem Document* group used documentary images, they also wanted to move beyond "uninspired literalness" and "transparent facticity" (230).

Conclusion. Remembering Harlem

1. Daylanne English, "Selecting the Harlem Renaissance," *Critical Inquiry* 25 (1999): 808. English's article was a response to an essay in which Henry Louis Gates Jr. posited four "renaissances" in the past century. English argues that "to suggest that four renaissances have occurred in ninety-three years is perhaps to drain the term of explanatory power" (807). See Henry Louis Gates Jr., "Harlem on Our Minds," *Critical Inquiry* 24 (1997): 1–12.

2. According to Robert Bone, "*Infants of the Spring* is a neurotic novel, in which Thurman broods introspectively on the 'failure' of the Negro Renaissance." Robert Bone, *The Negro Novel in America* (New Haven: Yale University Press, 1958), 93.

3. Wallace Thurman, *Infants of the Spring* (1932), foreword by Amritjit Singh (Boston: Northeastern University Press, 1992), 91. Subsequent citations are from this edition and are given parenthetically in the text.

4. The essay published in the *New Republic* was "Negro Artists and the Negro"; the essay published in the *Independent* was "Nephews of Uncle Remus." Both are reprinted in *The Collected Writings of Wallace Thurman: A Harlem Renaissance Reader*, ed. Amritjit Singh and Daniel M. Scott III (New Brunswick: Rutgers University Press, 2003), 195–205.

5. Ibid., 201.

6. In regard to the similarities between Thurman's argument in "Nephews of Uncle Remus" and Schuyler's in "The Negro-Art Hokum," note Thurman's charge that "the American Negro has absorbed all of the American white man's culture and cultural appurtenances. He uses the same language, attends the same schools, reads the same newspapers and books, [and] lives in the same kinds of houses" (ibid., 202). And compare it also to Schuyler's statement that "when [the Aframerican] responds to the same political, social, moral, and economic stimuli in precisely the same manner as his white neighbor, it is sheer nonsense to talk about 'racial differences' as between the American black man and the American white man." George Schuyler, "The Negro-Art Hokum," *Nation*, June 16, 1926, 662–63.

7. Even James Weldon Johnson acknowledged the problem of persistence among the younger black writers. In his foreword to the *Challenge*, a short-lived journal edited by Dorothy West, Johnson stated that "the greatest lack of our younger writers is not talent or ability but persistent and intelligent industry. That, I think, explains why, the work of so many of them was but a flash in the pan." James Weldon Johnson, foreword to *Challenge* 1, no.1 (1934): 2.

8. David Blackmore explains the pattern of silence and disavowal that marks the text and Ray and Stephen's relationship: "Ray allows other characters' racial complexes to function as a cover for the stigmatized same-sex desire that has given him a gender-identity complex." David Blackmore, "'Something . . . Too Preposterous and Complex to Be Recognized or Considered': Same-Sex Desire and Race in *Infants of the Spring*," *Soundings* 80, no. 4 (1997): 526.

9. The title *Infants of the Spring* comes from *Hamlet*, act 1, scene three, when Laertes warns his sister Ophelia against a relationship with the prince of Denmark.

10. The salon episode in *Infants of the Spring* is Thurman's second fictional enactment of the black aesthetic discussion, his first having appeared in *The Blacker the Berry* (1929; repr., New York: Scribner, 1996), 139–47.

11. The reviews are conveniently collected in Jeffrey Stewart's edition, *The Critical Temper of Alain Locke: A Selection of His Essays on Art and Culture* (New York: Garland, 1983), which also includes retrospective review essays that were published in *Phylon* from 1946 to 1953.

12. Alain Locke, "1928: A Retrospective Review," *Critical Temper*, 201; Locke, "Black Truth and Black Beauty: A Retrospective Review of the Literature of the Negro for 1932," *Critical Temper*, 215; Locke, "The Saving Grace of Realism: Retrospective Review of Negro Literature of 1933," *Critical Temper*, 221.

13. John A. Davis, "We Win the Right to Fight for Jobs," *Opportunity*, August 1938, 232.

14. Locke, "The Negro: 'New' or Newer: A Retrospective Review of the Literature of the Negro for 1938," *Critical Temper*, 272.

15. Although he does not state the Harlem Renaissance by name, Richard Wright, in his 1937 essay "Blueprint for Negro Writing," derides the period as "a liaison between inferiority-complexed Negro 'geniuses' and burnt-out white Bohemians with money."

Wright, "Blueprint for Negro Writing," *African American Literary Theory,* ed. Winston Napier (New York: New York University Press, 2000), 45.

16. Locke, "We Turn to Prose: A Retrospective Review of the Literature of the Negro for 1931," *Critical Temper,* 209; Thurman, "Negro Artists and the Negro," *Collected Writings of Wallace Thurman,* 200.

17. James De Jongh, *Vicious Modernism: Black Harlem and the Literary Imagination* (Cambridge: Cambridge University Press, 1990), 47.

18. Carol Duncan, "Art Museums and the Ritual of Citizenship," in *Exhibiting Cultures: The Poetics and Politics of Museum Display,* ed. Ivan Karp and Steven D. Lavine (Washington, D.C.: Smithsonian Institution Press, 1991), 93, 99, 102.

19. During the first day the exhibition was open to the public, someone defaced several artworks in the Metropolitan, the most famous being Rembrandt's *Christ with a Pilgrim's Staff.* The paintings were marked with a small "H," and even this act of defacement and anonymous assertion created ambiguous and contested meanings: commentators debated whether the "H" stood for "Harlem" or for "Hoving," the Metropolitan's director, Thomas Hoving. Murray Schumach, "Harlem Exhibition Opens to Crowds at Metropolitan Museum," *New York Times,* January 19, 1969, 61.

20. According to Aaron Siskind's biographer Carl Chiarenza, Reginald McGhee visited Siskind in Chicago and selected several images from the *Harlem Document* project for inclusion in the "Harlem on My Mind" exhibition. One review of the exhibition published a photograph of it. The photographs shows two *Harlem Document* images, "Mother and Son" and the image of a young black man asleep on his bed. See "Media Mix at the Met," *CA [Communication Arts] Magazine* 11, no. 1 (1969): 62–65.

21. Two contemporary analyses of the "Harlem on My Mind" exhibition are Sara Blair, *Harlem Crossroads: Black Writers and the Photograph in the Twentieth Century* (Princeton: Princeton University Press, 2007), 244–51; and Susan E. Cahan, "Performing Identity and Persuading a Public: The Harlem on My Mind Controversy," *Social Identities* 13, no. 4 (2007): 423–40. Blair considers the photograph as documentary and notes that one of the critics of the exhibition, the African American photographer Roy DeCarava, protested it because of "his fervent belief in the value as art—rather than mere 'documentary'—of photographic work" (*Harlem Crossroads,* 249). Cahan provides information about the genesis and impact of the exhibition in the context of museum studies.

22. A series of verbal accusations was made against and by various ethnic groups, and several synagogues and black churches in the area were vandalized. In his social history of the strike, Jerald Podair notes that "Ocean Hill–Brownsville did not itself create 'two New Yorks'—one black, one white, divided politically, socially, and culturally. It was, however, their most visible, palpable symbol." Jerald E. Podair, *The Strike That Changed New York* (New Haven: Yale University Press, 2002), 8.

23. Calvin Tomkins, *Merchants and Masterpieces: The Story of the Metropolitan Museum of Art* (New York: E. P. Dutton, 1970), 352.

24. Mieke Bal, "Telling, Showing, Showing Off," *Critical Inquiry* 18, no. 3 (1992): 556–57.

25. Thomas Hoving, "Reinventing the Museum," *New York,* April 6, 1998, 81.

26. Milton Esterow, "Hoving's Metropolitan to Offer Multimedia Look at Harlem History," *New York Times,* November 16, 1967, 56.

27. James Weldon Johnson, *The Book of American Negro Poetry* (New York: Harcourt, Brace, and Co., 1922), vii.

28. W. E. B. Du Bois, "Criteria of Negro Art," *Crisis,* October 1926, 296.

29. Allon Schoener, "Introduction to the New Edition," in *Harlem on My Mind: The Cultural Capital of Black America, 1900–1968,* ed. Allon Schoener (New York: Random House, 1995). This introduction is not paginated.

30. Thomas Hoving Jr., "Director's Note," in *The Metropolitan Museum of Art Bulletin,* January, 1969, 244; Arthur A. Schomburg, "The Negro Digs Up His Past," in *The New Negro,* ed. Alain Locke (1925; repr., New York: Simon and Schuster, 1992), 231–44.

31. Duncan, "Art Museums and the Ritual of Citizenship," 91.

32. Schoener, "Introduction to the New Edition." In his updated introduction Schoener explains his reasoning for using photographs: he hoped to create "a communications environment, without artifacts," a space "where cultural phenomena were interpreted through the use of communications technology." In short, he wanted "a documentary exhibition without original works of art." In order to achieve these then-unconventional objectives, Schoener relied on photographs.

33. Allon Schoener, "Madness at the Met," *George,* January 1999, 40.

34. According to one reviewer it took close to two hours to view the exhibition fully. See "Media Mix at the Met," 62.

35. Schoener and the Metropolitan's board justified this lack of artworks by noting: "There were some questions as to whether a nonart exhibition properly belonged in the Met. But it was pointed out that the charter of the Met stressed education, too. So there were no serious objections." Martin Arnold, "Metropolitan Yields on 'Racism' in Show Catalogue," *New York Times,* January 18, 1969, 32.

36. Jacob Deschin, "Harlem's History in Visual Survey," *New York Times,* January 19, 1969, D31. Powell was the pastor of the influential Abyssinian Baptist Church in New York from 1908 to 1937.

37. Ibid., D31.

38. Schoener, "Madness at the Met," 40.

39. Hoving, "Director's Note," 243.

40. Hilton Kramer, "Politicizing the Metropolitan Museum," *New York Times,* January 26, 1969, D31.

41. Schoener, "Introduction to the New Edition." There was also a Research Advisory Committee, made up of three African Americans: Regina Andrews, who lived in Harlem during the central years of the Renaissance; John Henrik Clark, who later resigned from the committee in protest over some of Schoener's decisions; and Jean Blackwell Hutson, who was the curator of the Schomburg Center for Black Research and Culture.

42. A writer for the *Village Voice* commented that "only a white man whose stick is Dixieland could have conceived such an extraordinarily dull exhibition." Charles Wright, "Harlem at the Met: For Lap Dogs Only," *Village Voice,* January 30, 1969, 17. Another reviewer for the same paper thought that the exhibit was "so predicable and perfect a statement of the white-liberal attitude as to be a grotesquely funny . . . self-parody." A. D. Coleman, "Christmas Gift," *Village Voice,* January 23, 1969, 16.

43. Thomas Hoving, preface to *Harlem on My Mind: Cultural Capital of Black America, 1900–1960* (New York: Random House, 1969). The preface is unpaginated.

44. Thomas Hoving, *Making the Mummies Dance: Inside the Metropolitan Museum of Art* (New York: Simon & Schuster, 1993), 168.

45. Candice Van Ellison, introduction to *Harlem on My Mind,* unpaginated.

46. Nathan Glazer and Daniel Patrick Moynihan, *Beyond the Melting Pot: The Negroes, Puerto Ricans, Jews, Italians, and Irish of New York City* (Cambridge: MIT Press and

Harvard University Press, 1963). At the time of the exhibit, Moynihan was the urban af-
fairs coordinator for President Richard Nixon. The complete passage in *Beyond the Melting Pot* reads: "Perhaps for many Negroes, subconsciously, a bit of anti-Jewish feeling helps
make them feel more completely American, a part of the majority group. There are probably other irrational bases for this anti-Jewish feeling—anti-Semitism is a complicated
thing—and yet the special tie-up of Jews with liberalism is certainly important" (77).

47. A. D. Coleman, "Latent Image," *Village Voice,* January 30, 1969, 16.

48. Cahan, "Performing Identity," 430.

49. Reprint editions of the catalogue were published by Dell in 1979 and the New Press
in 1995. The latter edition contained a new introduction by Schoener and a foreword by
Henry Louis Gates Jr. The fourth edition was published by W. W. Norton in 2007.

50. John Canaday, "Getting Harlem Off My Mind," *New York Times,* January 12, 1969,
D25.

51. Ibid.

52. Grace Glueck, "Art: 'Harlem on My Mind' in Slides, Tapes and Photos," *New York
Times,* January 17, 1969, 28.

53. One of the most insightful contemporaneous reviews of the exhibit was by the
freelance journalist Nora Sayre, who weighed the advantages and disadvantages of the
exhibition's technological innovations. Sayre was particularly keen about the mixture of
innovation and realism: "What can a photograph of Marcus Garvey tell us about his views?
Flashing slides that give figures of black unemployment pass too rapidly to make any point.
And how does a record label of 'Paradise Wobble-Stomp' instruct the spectator? The
trouble is mixed media can't think and that the sum of racial culture and racial agony is just
too serious for a twinkling discotheque style. . . . Of course, it's always sad when experimentation is a mistake. But a traditional show could have taught us much that's still unknown about Harlem." Nora Sayre Papers, New York Public Library, Box 35.

54. The exhibition's "failure" should be qualified because, as Schoener proudly states,
the controversy it engendered forced America's museums "to open their galleries to subjects and audiences they had excluded." Schoener, "Introduction to the New Edition."

55. Schoener, "Madness at the Met," 41.

56. Murray Schumach, "Harlem Exhibition Opens to Crowds at Metropolitan Museum," *New York Times,* January 19, 1969, 61.

Index

237